T0340361

Extremism

Extremism is one of the most charged and controversial issues of the twenty-first century. Despite myriad programmes of deradicalization and prevention around the world, it remains an intractable and poorly understood problem. Yet it is also sometimes regarded as a positive force – according to Martin Luther King Jr., 'the question is not whether we will be extremists, but what kind of extremists we will be'.

In this much-needed and lucid book, Quassim Cassam identifies three types of extremism – ideological; methods; and psychological extremism – and discusses the following fundamental topics and issues: What is extremism? What are the methods adopted by extremists? Is there an extremist 'mindset' and if so, what is it? What role do ideas of purity, victimhood and humiliation play in understanding extremism? How does extremism differ from fanaticism and fundamentalism? How does one become an extremist and how should we understand deradicalization?

Throughout the book, Quassim Cassam uses many compelling examples, ranging from the Khmer Rouge, the IRA, Al-Qaeda and Timothy McVeigh to Philip Roth's novel *American Pastoral* and counter-extremism programmes, including the UK's *Prevent* strategy.

Clear-headed and engaging, *Extremism: A Philosophical Analysis* is essential reading for anyone interested in this important topic, not only in Philosophy but related disciplines such as Politics and International Relations, Conflict and Terrorism Studies, Law, Education and Religion. It will also be of great interest to policy-makers and those engaged in understanding extremism at any level.

Quassim Cassam is Professor of Philosophy, University of Warwick, UK. He is the author of several books, most recently *Vices of the Mind: From the Intellectual to the Political* (2019) and *Conspiracy Theories* (2019).

Extremism

A Philosophical Analysis

Quassim Cassam

Routledge
Taylor & Francis Group

LONDON AND NEW YORK

First published 2022
by Routledge
2 Park Square, Milton Park, Abingdon, Oxon OX14 4RN

and by Routledge
605 Third Avenue, New York, NY 10158

Routledge is an imprint of the Taylor & Francis Group, an informa business

© 2022 Quassim Cassam

British Library Cataloguing-in-Publication Data
A catalogue record for this book is available from the British Library

Library of Congress Cataloging-in-Publication Data
Names: Cassam, Quassim, author.
Title: Extremism : a philosophical analysis / Quassim Cassam.
Description: 1 Edition. | New York City : Routledge, 2021. | Includes
bibliographical references and index.
Identifiers: LCCN 2021009083 (print) | LCCN 2021009084 (ebook) |
ISBN 9780367343880 (hardback) | ISBN 9780367343873 (paperback) |
ISBN 9780429325472 (ebook)
Subjects: LCSH: Radicalism—History.
Classification: LCC HN49.R33 C367 2021 (print) | LCC HN49.R33 (ebook) |
DDC 303.48/4—dc23
LC record available at https://lccn.loc.gov/2021009083
LC ebook record available at https://lccn.loc.gov/2021009084

ISBN: 978-0-367-34388-0 (hbk)
ISBN: 978-0-367-34387-3 (pbk)
ISBN: 978-0-429-32547-2 (ebk)

DOI: 10.4324/9780429325472

Typeset in Optima
by codeMantra

For Deborah

Contents

Preface

I hadn't planned to write a book on extremism, and would not have done so if the idea hadn't been suggested to me by Tony Bruce of Routledge. I was initially sceptical. What, I wondered, does philosophy have to say about extremism? More to the point, what did *I* have to say about it? When Tony approached me, I had already been working for some time on the epistemology of terrorism and counter-terrorism. In this context, I was familiar with the standard definition of radicalization as the process of becoming an extremist but I hadn't tackled the question: what is extremism?

When I gave the matter some serious thought, I quickly discovered that there are deep philosophical questions about extremism that had never been properly addressed. Robert Nozick wrote a useful short paper on the characteristic features of extremism, and many of the great, dead philosophers were interested in fanaticism. However, as far I could tell, philosophy had done no more than scratch the surface of the questions about extremism that interested me. So, I came up with a plan for this book and sent it to Tony. His readers were enthusiastic and I got to work in 2019. By the end of 2020, I had a complete draft. I was interested by what I read about extremism and extremists and, despite the subject matter, enjoyed writing this book more than any of my previous six books. What I take to be the main ideas of the book are summarized in the Introduction, and I hope that readers will find them worthwhile.

When I was a graduate student in Oxford in the mid 1980s, I listened to a set of lectures on scepticism by my supervisor, Sir Peter Strawson. The lectures were subsequently published (Strawson 2008b), and ended with a quotation from Gibbon: 'Philosophy alone can boast (and perhaps it is no more than the boast of philosophy) that her gentle hand is able to eradicate from the human mind the latent and deadly principle of fanaticism.' I must confess to being somewhat sceptical about the idea that philosophy can eradicate fanaticism from the human mind. I do believe, however, that it can contribute to an *understanding* of both fanaticism and extremism, and that there is no hope of developing an effective response to these things unless we know what we are talking about. If we are serious about preventing the rise of extremism, then we must do better than the UK government, with its bizarre definition of extremism as involving 'vocal or active opposition to fundamental British values'.

In writing this book I had the great good fortune to be able to share draft chapters as I wrote them with my dear friend and colleague Naomi Eilan. Her encouragement and feedback were invaluable. With my permission, she also shared my chapters with Avishai Margalit in Jerusalem. His reactions, conveyed to me by Naomi, were important to me, not least because my thinking has been influenced by his book *On Compromise and Rotten Compromises*. I thank Naomi and Avishai, and Deborah Ghate, whose trenchant comments led to some significant changes, including the addition of a substantial introduction. Thanks also to Tony Bruce and his three readers for their comments and encouragement.

I presented an early version of Chapter 4 to the Philosophy Department at the University of Tübingen and at a conference in Oxford organized by the Finnish Institute in London and the Academy of Finland. The book's central ideas also formed the basis of my keynote lecture for the 10th European Congress of Analytic Philosophy (ECAP) in 2020. I thank the audiences on these occasions for helpful comments and questions. I also thank Fabienne Peter, who was my Head of Department while this book was being written, for her wonderful support. I could not wish for a better working environment than the one I enjoy as a member of the Philosophy Department at Warwick.

Introduction

At the start of 2020, the year in which this book was written, *The Guardian* reported that British counter-terrorism police had identified Extinction Rebellion as an organization with an 'extremist' ideology.[1] Extinction Rebellion, which is committed to a strategy of non-violent civil disobedience in response to the climate emergency, responded with a furious press release. 'How dare they?', it asks.[2] Instead of trying to silence an organization that is trying to address the dire state of the planet, 'wouldn't it be nice if they focused on the real extremists, the fossil fuel companies and those that do their bidding?' In this and in countless other cases, there are arguments about who is and who isn't a real extremist because most people do not appreciate having this label applied to them. In America, anti-fascist and Black Lives Matter activists did not appreciate being labelled left-wing extremists by President Trump, whose more ardent supporters were seen by those same activists as right-wing extremists. Yet if pressed to define 'extremism', we struggle. This is one of those cases where we think we have an idea of what is meant but find the idea surprisingly difficult to articulate.

When faced with the challenge of defining pornography, a U.S. Supreme Court justice offered: 'I know it when I see it.' Is extremism like that? Do we know it when we see it? On 22 July 2011, Anders Behring Breivik murdered eight people in Oslo and a further 69 people attending a youth camp on an island near Oslo.[3] The killings were politically motivated and coincided with the release of Breivik's far-right political manifesto. Breivik is the archetypal extremist, and few people have any difficulty recognizing him as such even if they cannot define extremism. If Breivik is not an extremist, then heaven help us. Pointing to him and people like him is one way to explain the notion of an extremist and, by extension, the notion of extremism. However,

DOI: 10.4324/9780429325472

such explanations by example have their limitations. Since there are many things that are true of Breivik that are not true of all extremists, there is still the challenge of differentiating essential from non-essential elements of extremism.

For example, Breivik was a *violent* or *militant* extremist, but is all extremism like that? Can extremism be non-violent? Breivik was a political extremist but is all extremism political? Breivik was a right-wing extremist, but political extremists can also be on the extreme left. Are all political extremists either on the extreme left or the extreme right? Take the case of Khalid Sheikh Mohammed, who orchestrated the 9/11 attacks on America in 2001.[4] Mohammed, or KSM as he came to be known, can certainly be classified as an extremist but not necessarily as right-wing or left-wing. Like other Islamist extremists, KSM is hard to place on the left-right spectrum, though the case has been made that his views should be described as 'Islamofascist'.[5] To talk about a person's view in this sense is to talk about their ideology, their core political beliefs.[6] Should Breivik and KSM be classified as extremists on account of their *beliefs* or their *actions*? And where do extremist groups rather than individuals fit in?

However these questions are answered, one thing is clear: extremism can be, and often has been, lethal. It is not much of an exaggeration to say that the history of the twentieth century is essentially the history of extremism and its consequences. To get a sense of the scale of human misery for which extremism has been responsible, one only has to think of Hitler's Germany, Stalin's Russia, or Mao's China. Extremism has never gone away since the end of the Second World War, and is once again on the rise in the world today, as a result of rising levels of political polarization. That said, there are people who think that extremism is not necessarily a bad thing and is sometimes necessary in the fight against cruelty, oppression or, indeed, the dire state of the planet. It isn't actually true that *nobody* appreciates being called an extremist. Nineteenth-century abolitionist opponents of slavery called themselves fanatics, and fanaticism is closely related to extremism, if not identical with it. Can extremism be a good thing? A character in a Philip Roth novel says: 'Sometimes you have to fucking go to the extreme' (Roth 1997: 105). Isn't that what the abolitionists realized and what some climate activists realize today? If that's extremism, then bring it on, they might say.

While readers might not need much persuading that these are important issues, they might struggle with the notion that philosophy has anything worthwhile to say about them. It's worth noting that extremism is a subject that few philosophers have tackled, though a number of the great, dead philosophers had things to say about fanaticism.[7] Does their striking lack of engagement with extremism as such say more about the skewed priorities of philosophers today or about extremism's amenability to philosophical analysis? In my view, extremism *is* amenable to philosophical analysis, as reflected in the sub-title of this book. But what exactly is 'analysis' as philosophers understand it, and what would it even be to give a *philosophical* analysis of extremism? Is analysing extremism something that philosophy can do on its own or does it need help from other disciplines?

Describing what some (but not all) philosophers do as 'analysis' makes it sound more exotic than it is. As Timothy Williamson notes, 'Philosophy, like science, starts with ways of knowing and thinking all normal human beings have, and applies them a bit more carefully, a bit more systematically, a bit more critically, iterating that process over and over again' (2020: 4–5). To do these things is precisely to engage in 'philosophical analysis' as I understand it. One way to analyse a complex idea like extremism is to break it down into its constituent parts. Another is to link it to other, related concepts like fanaticism and fundamentalism.[8] Analysis on the first model will focus on the search for the core elements of extremism. For example, one might ask whether extremism requires extreme beliefs, extreme behaviour, or both. How are these elements themselves to be understood, and does extremism involve anything else? On the second model of analysis, one will be more concerned with questions such as: can a person be an extremist without being a fanatic, or vice versa? Is fundamentalism a variety of extremism, or is it something altogether different? On this 'connective' model of analysis, the idea of extremism is one of a network of ideas that can only be understood in relation to one another.

In asking how the idea of extremism relates to other ideas in the same neighbourhood, one should not make the mistake of thinking that analysing the *idea* of extremism is different from analysing or studying extremism itself. To analyse the idea of extremism is to *theorize* about extremism itself and related phenomena. It would be arrogant to assume that philosophy can do this without help from other disciplines like politics, history, psychology and sociology. Extremism cannot be understood without studying the forms that it takes in different places and at different times. The project of this book is to develop an understanding of extremism by means of philosophical analysis and by drawing on what is known about actual extremists and extremism.

Going back to Breivik and KSM, it is worth reflecting on the similarities and differences between them. They obviously have (or had) different beliefs and different ideologies. Their ideologies are not just different but diametrically opposed. Breivik is anti-Muslim, KSM is not. Yet their ideologies are both extreme. Breivik's is extreme in the sense that it is on the extreme right. If we think of ideologies as arranged on a spectrum running from extreme left to extreme right, then one way to be an extremist is to have political beliefs that are at either end of the spectrum. If KSM is not on the left-right spectrum, then all that goes to show is that this spectrum is not the only one, and that he must be at an extreme end of some other spectrum. Either way, both Breivik and KSM are *positional* extremists whose extremism is defined by their position on an ideological map. Groups and governments can also be extremists in this sense. Their extremism is *positional* or *ideological* extremism.

Another similarity between Breivik and KSM is that both were willing to use extreme methods to make a political point. Methods are methods for doing or achieving something, and political extremists use extreme methods for political ends. They are what might be called *methods* extremists and their extremism is *methods extremism*. The classic extreme method is terrorism, and this explains why many extremists resort to terrorism. However, terrorism is not the only extreme method, and there are extreme methods for achieving political ends that do not involve violence or harm to others.[9] This raises what sounds like a philosophical question: what makes a method 'extreme'? Another question is: when, if ever, is the use of extreme methods justified? Presumably, those who tried to assassinate Hitler with a bomb planted in a briefcase in 1944 were justified in doing so. Was this an extreme method, or does it make a difference whether the method is used in a just cause? Whatever the answers to these questions, it is clear that positional and methods extremism are closely related, since extremist ideologies tend to endorse the use of violence.

A third similarity between Breivik, KSM and many other extremists is psychological. It is often said that being an extremist is not just a matter of *what* one believes but of *how* one believes, that is, one's way of believing.[10] Extremists in the psychological sense are especially fervent and uncompromising in their beliefs, and this is part of what makes them extremists. This points to a distinction between positional and *psychological extremism*. Someone whose beliefs are in the middle of the left-right spectrum is a *centrist*. The opposite of a psychological extremist is a *moderate*. It seems that a centrist can be a psychological extremist and a positional extremist can be a psychological moderate. An extreme centrist would be someone whose centrist, middle-of-the-road views are uncompromisingly and fervently held, while a moderate positional extremist would be someone with extreme views that are weakly held.

Whether these are genuine possibilities is something that will need to be discussed but of greater immediate interest is the fact that, contrary to the impression given so far, being an extremist in the psychological sense is not just a matter of how one believes. Rather, extremism in the psychological sense means having an *extremist mindset*. The challenge for anyone trying to make sense of extremism is to analyse this mindset. The chapter on *mindset extremism* (Chapter 4) is in many ways the central chapter of this book. Neither the notion of a mindset nor that of an extremist mindset is new. What is new is my account of the different elements of this mindset and how they fit together to form a coherent whole. Recent accounts of the extremist mindset have focused on the *militant* extremist mindset and listed multiple ingredients of this mindset, based on studies of extremist groups, but failed to give a systematic analysis of these ingredients. My aim is to give just such an analysis, while leaving open the possibility of non-militant, non-violent extremism.

Among the novel features of my account is the notion that the extremist mindset is distinguished by, among other things, its *preoccupations*. Extremists who disagree on other matters nevertheless have shared preoccupations, and understanding these preoccupations is essential for an understanding of extremism. One common extremist preoccupation is with purity – religious, ideological or racial – and with anything that detracts from their supposed purity. Breivik was preoccupied with racial purity and KSM with purity of a religious nature. Another extremist preoccupation is with their victimhood and supposed humiliation by their enemies. Perhaps surprisingly, mindset extremists are also preoccupied with their own virtue, with the sense that they are only doing what is right to defend themselves and their fellows. The idea that people who massacre large numbers of innocents can think of themselves as morally virtuous is startling, but it explains the extremists' sense of absolute certainty and unwillingness to compromise.

Extremist preoccupations are only one element of the extremist mindset, and there are several others. Even without going into further details, it is worth emphasizing the extent to which *extremism is a state of mind*, and this state of mind is not confined to people who resort to terrorism or other forms of political violence. Having an extremist mindset is a matter of degree, and the prevalence of elements of this mindset in the advanced democracies is both striking and worrying. Extremist preoccupations, attitudes and ways of thinking both cause and are reinforced by polarization. However, our mindsets are not wholly separate from our beliefs. It is easier for psychological extremists to be positional extremists, and vice versa.

This book is organized around the distinction between the three forms of extremism – ideological, methods and psychological – and the chapters that follow are a philosophical exploration of these forms of extremism and the relationship between them. Since extremists are often described as fanatics and fundamentalists, it is also important to be clear about the relationship between extremism, fanaticism and fundamentalism. There is also the question whether there are circumstances in which extremism is defensible. Extremism is easily confused with other, more respectable approaches to politics. With relatively few exceptions, the abolitionists were neither extremists nor fanatics. They were *radicals*, and it is possible to be highly critical of extremism while endorsing their political radicalism. Critics of extremism, among whom I count myself, are taken to task for being prejudiced in favour of conservatism and moderation, and I have tried to be sensitive to this criticism. There are deep and difficult questions about how it is appropriate to respond *in extremis* to injustice and oppression if not with extremism. I have tried to address these questions in this book.

To the extent that extremism is a Bad Thing, one will want to know how and why people become extremists. The process of becoming an extremist has been called the *radicalization* process, and much official as well as scholarly time and attention has been devoted to making sense of this process. My own views about radicalization and counter-radicalization are set out in Chapters 7 and 8, which have clear policy implications. If there is one general lesson to be drawn from my discussion, it is that Western governments are in denial about the causes and nature of radicalization, and this goes some way to explaining the defects of their counter-radicalization policies. There are many myths about radicalization that need to be avoided, and one of the missions of this book is to tackle these myths and bring to the surface the wishful thinking on which they are based. Counter-radicalization is possible, but only if one is prepared to engage seriously with extremist narratives and develop counter-narratives that have some basis in reality.

Most of this book is about political extremism, and the examples I have given – Breivik and KSM – are examples of violent extremists. I've already conceded that extremism does not have to be violent. Does it even have to be political? Faced with this question, the first alternative many people think of is religious extremism. However, the distinction between politics and religion is deeply problematic. KSM acted on behalf of Al-Qaeda, whose members are often represented as religious extremists. However, their objectives were also political, and it is hard to differentiate between their religion and their politics. Are there better examples of apolitical or non-political extremism? If a methods extremist is someone who uses extreme methods to reach their objectives, then, at least in theory, methods extremism is not confined to the political realm. For example, fasting for a week at a time is an extreme method of losing weight. It is worth noting, however, people who adopt this or other extreme diets are not usually described as weight-loss or diet 'extremists'. People who are keen on extreme sports are not known as sports or fitness extremists. When someone is described as an extremist today, the extremism in question is almost always political.

There is a striking contrast between extremism and fanaticism. There aren't fitness extremists but there are fitness fanatics. There aren't football extremists but there are football fanatics, also known more colloquially as football fans. Fanaticism in these contexts connotes unusual dedication or excessive enthusiasm, and it is an interesting question why talk of fitness fanaticism is so much more common than talk of fitness extremism. However, for better or worse, my main interest here is in political extremism and fanaticism. Other varieties will only be mentioned in passing. Hegel characterized fanaticism as 'an enthusiasm for something abstract'.[11] This notably abstract characterization of fanaticism was used by Hegel to make sense of Islam, a religion that supposedly destroys all particularity and whose object of devotion is purely intellectual. In the more straightforwardly political realm, the fanatics of the French Revolution were moved by their enthusiasm for abstractions like liberty, equality and fraternity to send large numbers of their fellow citizens to the guillotine.

In reality, there is more to political fanaticism than enthusiasm for something abstract. Fanatics have unwarranted contempt for other people's ideals and interests and are willing to trample on those ideals and interests in pursuit of their own ideals and interests. They will try to impose their ideals on others, by force, if necessary. They are unwilling or unable to think critically about their own ideals and do not suffer from self-doubt. Their vice is not, or not just, excessive *enthusiasm* but excessive *certainty* about matters that are far from certain. No doubt this explains their willingness to sacrifice themselves and others in pursuit of their ideals. The relationship between fanaticism and extremism is extremely complex and requires careful unpacking. This happens in Chapter 5, the upshot being that one can be an extremist without being a fanatic but not a fanatic without being an extremist.

Philosophers who write about highly abstract, technical subjects in metaphysics or logic or epistemology often have difficulty convincing non-philosophers, and sometimes even other philosophers, that what they do is worthwhile. The outsider's question is always: why should I, or anyone else, care about that? Philosophers vary in how they respond to this challenge. Some see it as unworthy of a response, as expressive of an unfortunate philistinism or anti-intellectualism from which they can only avert their eyes. Others assert that their questions are intrinsically valuable or interesting, and that they need no further justification for pursuing them, despite their apparent lack of practical relevance. Those who say things like this are always in danger of having their bluff called by those who reject their conception of what has intrinsic value. Still other philosophers represent the eye-wateringly abstract questions that interest them as no different in kind from the questions that exercise theoretical physicists or mathematicians. Some go so far as to represent philosophy as continuous with science. Be that as it may, the impression one comes away with from such discussions is that philosophy is a subject for which justifications need to be given or excuses made.

The philosopher of extremism is in the unusual and happy position of tackling questions whose importance and interest need no explanation. It would be very unusual for someone writing a book on political extremism to be asked: 'Why should I care about extremism?' A more likely question is: 'What can philosophy possibly tell us about extremism?'. The short answer to the latter question is: read this book and tell me if you are any the wiser. Ultimately, the only way to prove the value of philosophizing about extremism is to actually do it and assess the results. Some philosophical purists might regard extremism as an unsuitable subject for philosophers precisely *because* it is of such practical importance. Such a preoccupation with philosophical purity is a type of intellectual extremism that I deplore. In my vision of philosophy, not only is there room for philosophical thinking about subjects like extremism, but such thinking is positively desirable and worthwhile. The pages that follow will put this bold proposition to the test.

As well as philosophers who question the strictly philosophical interest of extremism, there are also those who claim not to find the label 'extremism' a useful one.[12] One reason for questioning the usefulness of this label is the conviction that it does not pick out something real and only serves to delegitimize political outlooks that are at odds with mainstream thinking. Another way of expressing scepticism about talk of extremism is to describe it as a 'social construction' that does not exist independently of the practice of labelling particular ideologies, individuals and groups as 'extremist'. If something is socially constructed, then it is, to that extent, 'real', but the point of describing extremism as a social construction is to suggest that the *idea* of extremism is optional as well as unhelpful.[13] The opposing view is that the description of some ideologies, individuals and groups as extremist is *apt*, in the sense that it accurately reflects aspects of political and psychological reality, as well as being theoretically *useful*. The only sense in which the idea of extremism is socially constructed is arguably no different from the sense in which ideas generally are socially constructed: it is 'the result of social-historical events' (Haslanger 2012: 116).

The best way to demonstrate the aptness of an idea is to identify patterns of thinking and behaving that call for the use of that idea if one is to describe and make sense of them. The best way to demonstrate the usefulness of an idea is to put it to use and then reflect on whether one could just as well have done without it. To the extent that each of the following chapters puts the idea of extremism to theoretical use, each of these chapters bears on the question whether this is a useful idea or one that is, in any surprising sense, socially constructed. For the moment, it is enough to say the following: someone who seriously proposes that talk of extremism is dispensable or unhelpful is going to have to find some other way of describing the beliefs, mindset and actions of people like Breivik and KSM. It can hardly be denied that Breivik, KSM and others who figure in the following chapters have important things in common, for all their other differences. There is no better way of characterizing what they have in common than by reference to their extremism. While extremism comes in several different forms, it would be perverse to deny that thinking of the Breiviks and KSMs of this world as extremists helps us to make sense of their actions, their beliefs, and their psychology more generally. 'Extremist' is, of course, a political label, the application of which is a political act with political consequences. However, it is possible to accept this, and acknowledge that the label has sometimes been misapplied, without denying the reality of extremism. To deny its reality is to leave oneself in no position to make sense of the political world in which we now live.

Notes

1 'Terrorism police list Extinction Rebellion as extremist ideology: Prevent strategy'. *The Guardian*, 10 January 2020. Available at: www.theguardian. com/uk-news/2020/jan/10/xr-extinction-rebellion-listed-extremist-ideology-police-prevent-scheme-guidance

2 'How dare they? Extinction Rebellion responds to terrorism slur by Police', Press Release, 10 January 2020. Available at: https://extinctionrebellion.uk/2020/01/10/how-dare-they-extinction-rebellion-responds-to-terrorism-slur-by-police/. On its website, Extinction Rebellion describes itself as an 'international movement that uses non-violent civil disobedience in an attempt to halt mass extinction and minimise the risk of social collapse'. Available at: https://extinctionrebellion.uk/the-truth/about-us.

3 The events of that day are described in Borchgrevink (2013) and Seierstad (2015).

4 McDermott and Meyer (2012) give a detailed and compelling account of Mohammed's role in masterminding the 9/11 attacks, which killed approximately 3,000 people.

5 There is more about this label in the Introduction to Ruthven (2007).

6 There is much more about the concept of ideology in Chapter 2.

7 See Chapter 5 for some examples.

8 The distinction between these two conceptions of analysis is explained in Strawson (1992, Chapter 2).

9 As I argue in Chapter 3.

10 The latter conception of extremism has been described as the view that extremism is 'a characteristic of the way beliefs are held rather than their location along some social dimension; for example, if they are held rigidly or the person holding them displays a small capacity or willingness to compromise' (Breton et al. 2002: xiii).

11 See Chapter 5.

12 This is implied, though not asserted, in Coady (2021).

13 On the idea of a 'social construction', see Hacking (1999) and Haslanger (2012).

How to think about extremism

Methods extremism

The 3rd of January 2015 was the last day of Muad al-Kasasbeh's life. A mechanical fault had forced the 26-year-old Royal Jordanian Air Force pilot to eject from his F-16 during a bombing raid against ISIS.[1] He was captured near Raqqa in Syria and held for a short time before being executed by an extraordinarily cruel and sadistic method. A video showed him locked in a cage, doused with petrol and burned alive.[2] ISIS was well known for beheading its prisoners, but this method of execution took its moral depravity down to a whole new level.

It is worth remembering al-Kasasbeh's dreadful fate if it is ever suggested that it is a purely subjective matter whether a person or organization is 'extremist', or that this category owes its existence to a politically motivated decision to apply the label to some organizations but not others. This is not to deny that this label, like the label 'terrorist', is often applied for political reasons, as a way to delegitimize opposition to the established order. It is instructive that the African National Congress (ANC) was labelled a terrorist organization for its armed struggle against apartheid, and it is often said in response to this and other such examples that one person's terrorist is another person's freedom fighter. If this is true, then is it not also true that one person's extremist is another person's moderate? Doesn't it all depend on one's point of view? After all, the ANC was fighting for democracy in South Africa. In the apartheid era, were they the extremists or the South African government?

These concerns about the use of the label 'extremist' certainly need to be addressed.[3] Yet, when one thinks about Lieutenant al-Kasasbeh, it is difficult

DOI: 10.4324/9780429325472-1

to believe that extremism is relative or that it is a matter of subjective judgement rather than objective fact that ISIS is an extremist organization. One sense in which this is so is that it uses *methods* that are extreme by any reasonable standard. Indeed, they are extreme even by Jihadi standards. Some years before al-Kasasbeh's murder, Al-Qaeda's second-in-command, Ayman al-Zawahiri, wrote to the founder of ISIS urging him to avoid any action that the masses do not understand or approve of.[4] The reality of ISIS's extremism is inescapable when its methods are judged too extreme even by Al-Qaeda, with its own record of wanton killing and destruction.

Some might object to the idea that ISIS had a method. Would it not be more accurate to classify what was done to al-Kasasbeh as a random act of extreme cruelty, the kind of thing that only a psychopath would do? In a scene in the film *Apocalypse Now*, the unhinged Kurtz asks Captain Willard if he thinks that his brutal methods are unsound. Willard replies: 'I don't see any method at all, sir.'[5] With ISIS, however, there *is* a method. Savagery is the method, albeit an extreme one. Its use is explained in a document called *The Management of Savagery*, whose recommendations include terrorizing the enemy by liquidating hostages in a 'terrifying manner'.[6] The use of this and other similar methods is part of a *strategy* to create conditions in which people will eventually turn to ISIS in desperation to restore order and provide basic services.

Extreme or extremist methods do not have to be *as* extreme, *as* intentionally savage, as the ones employed by ISIS. A list of other such methods might include: car bombing, hostage taking, and assassination. These examples all involve the use or threat of physical violence. Some might regard violence against civilians as more extreme than violence against military targets. A different view is that whether a method is extreme or not depends on the nature of the method itself and not the status of the individuals targeted. It is also debatable whether only violent methods are extreme. Some forms of cyber-terrorism might deserve to be labelled as extreme even if no physical violence is involved. There is more to be said about all this but not until later in this book. There is also the issue of whether the use of extreme methods can ever be morally justified. This is another important issue that can be put to one side for the moment.

A methods extremist is an individual or group that uses extreme methods (however exactly these are defined) in pursuit of its objectives. Where these are political objectives, the use of extreme methods makes one a *political* extremist. It remains to be seen whether there are forms of extremism that are not political. For the moment, our focus is political extremism. The question now arises: why would anybody use, or want to use, extreme methods in pursuit of political objectives? Many different answers to this question are possible. One might be: because they are the most effective. This is the explanation given in *The Management of Savagery*. Another is: because there is no viable alternative. These answers, which tend to be the ones given by methods extremists themselves, are controversial, to say the least. A less controversial answer is that people use extremist *methods* because they have an extremist *ideology*.

The following chapters are organized around a distinction between three basic forms of extremism:

1. Methods extremism.
2. Ideological extremism.
3. Psychological extremism.

Each of these types of extremism will be discussed in greater detail below. The aim of this chapter is to give a brief explanation of the three-way distinction and provide an introduction to each of the three types of extremism. The methods used by ISIS justify its classification as extremist in the first of the three senses and make it vivid what methods extremism amounts to in a specific case. The fact that one is an extremist in the methods sense does not mean that one cannot also be an extremist in the other two senses. Indeed, the leaders of ISIS are plainly extremist in all three senses.

An ideological extremist is an individual or group with an extremist ideology. What is an ideology, and what makes an ideology extremist? Here is one way to think about ideology:

> Ideology is an interrelated set of beliefs that provide a way for people to understand the world. Ideologies tell people what is important, who the good guys and bad guys are, what their goals are, and how those goals should be reached. Without ideologies to help categorize and interpret information, the world would be meaningless.
>
> (Uscinski and Parent 2014: 12)

This definition brings out the extent to which ideologies are a framework for making sense of the world. A person watching the news will interpret and respond to the presented stories in a particular way but these interpretations and responses do not come out of the blue; they are grounded in the viewer's ideological framework. Ideologies aren't just sets of *beliefs*, and they influence our behaviour as well as our understanding of the world. Apart from beliefs, a person or group's ideology will also include, in Raymond Geuss's formulation, 'the concepts they use, the attitudes and psychological dispositions they exhibit, their motives, desires, values, predilections, works of art, religious rituals, gestures' (1981: 5). An ideology in this broad sense is something that everyone has, and ideologies are guides to action as well as frameworks of understanding. One's ideology tells one what to *do* as well as what to *think*.

There is much more to be said about the nature of ideology, but the immediate issue is: what makes an ideology extremist? The most straightforward answer to this question sees ideologies as arranged on a left-right spectrum.[7] Every ideology is located somewhere on the spectrum, and an extremist ideology is one that is either on the extreme left or the extreme right. This is a *positional* conception of ideological extremism. For example, if fascism is on the extreme right of the left-right spectrum, then it is an extremist ideology; it is a form of ideological extremism. Ideological extremists are more likely to be methods extremists, but the two types of extremism are nevertheless conceptually distinct. However, before taking a closer look at the relationship between them, there some other aspects of ideological extremism that need to be clarified.

Ideological extremism

The idea that ideological extremism is a position on an ideological spectrum has the virtue of simplicity. Positions in the literal sense are positions in physical space. Ideological extremism is a position in ideological space, one that in Nozick's words, 'falls somewhere near the end or fringe of something close to a normal distribution' (1997: 296) along a salient dimension. One is the left-right dimension. Moving from left to right, there is communism, socialism, social democracy, liberalism, conservatism and fascism. A fascist is an ideological extremist, and *becoming* an extremist is a matter of moving in the political sense from the centre to the far left or right. It follows on this definition that social democrats and liberals are not ideological extremists. Because they are in the middle of the left-right dimension, they are *centrists*.

The positional approach to ideological extremism raises a number of questions. Does the spectrum have to be understood in such a way that social democracy and liberalism are in the middle? Are there other equally legitimate projections of ideological space? How fine-grained is the spectrum? Which ideologies should be lumped together, and which ones distinguished on the spectrum? Is 'neo-liberalism' a form of liberalism or an ideology in its own right? Is it to the left or to the right of conservatism? Whichever dimension one chooses, there is bound to be an element of arbitrariness in the placing of ideologies. Furthermore, the left-right spectrum is not the only dimension of ideological space. Ideological space is *multi-dimensional*.

Consider ISIS once again. It is extremist not just in the sense that it uses extreme methods but also in the sense that it has an extremist ideology. However, if an extremist ideology is one that is located on the extreme left or the extreme right of the left-right spectrum, then we will be forced to classify ISIS in terms of this spectrum. Yet ISIS is neither on the extreme left nor the extreme right. It is a mistake, some might argue, to think of ISIS in left-right terms, since its extremism is *religious* rather than political. If its extremism is ideological, it is not so in the sense in which the extremism of revolutionary communists or fascists is ideological. Furthermore, the initial thought was that groups like ISIS use extreme methods because they have extremist ideologies, but the ideological conception of extremism does not explain the link between ideological and methods extremism.

The first thing to say is that the contrast between political and religious extremism is a false one because the contrast between politics and religion is a false one. As Richard English observes, 'any religion of significance necessarily involves vital relations to politics, society, culture, identity, power, economics, and other potentially secular aspects of human life' (2009: 39). To put it another way, the ideological extremism of groups like ISIS is political as well as religious. In fact, it is political *because* it is religious. And this takes us back to the challenge of locating their political ideology on the left-right scale. If ISIS has an extremist political ideology, is it on the extreme left or the extreme right? If the answer is 'neither', then where in ideological space should it be located?

There is a case for classifying the ideology of ISIS as fascist. This would make its ideological extremism 'positional' in a standard sense. The case for classifying ISIS as fascist or 'Islamofascist' has been made by those who point to its rejection of Enlightenment values, its extreme authoritarianism, virulent anti-Semitism, and conspiratorial world-view.[8] These are recognizably fascist elements of ISIS ideology, although the notion that there is such a thing as 'Islamofascism' is controversial. It is worth noting, however, that the ideology of ISIS can be viewed as extremist in an ideological sense even if one hesitates to classify it as right-wing. As Nozick observes, 'there can be many different salient political dimensions' (1997: 296). This opens up the possibility that ISIS is on the extreme end of some *other* dimension, that is, one that does not run from left to right.

What might this other dimension be? Consider what is called the Pro-Violence spectrum.[9] Political ideologies can be classified based on their views about the legitimacy, or otherwise, of using violence to achieve their political objectives. Advocating or otherwise supporting the use of violence for political ends places an ideology at the extreme end of the Pro-Violence spectrum. The stronger its advocacy of violence, the more extremist the ideology. This cuts across the left-right spectrum since ideologies at opposite ends of that spectrum – say, revolutionary communism and militant fascism – are in the same place on the Pro-Violence spectrum: they both advocate violence as a legitimate means of achieving their (very different) political objectives. On the same basis, ISIS will come out as ideologically extremist regardless of whether its ideology is a form of fascism.

One attraction of this approach is that it makes the classification of groups like ISIS as ideologically extremist completely straightforward. Furthermore, there is less arbitrariness in locating an ideology on the Pro-Violence spectrum than on the left-right spectrum. There are arguments about whether one ideology is to the left or the right of another but attitudes to the use of violence are arguably more clear-cut. Any party or group that advocates the use of violence is, by definition, extremist in an ideological sense. There is also now a clear link between methods and ideological extremism. Groups with extremist ideologies use extremist methods because their ideologies *advocate* the use of such methods. There is no mystery about the connection.

Despite its attractions, the idea of a Pro-Violence spectrum is not unproblematic. For a start, it says nothing about *why* violence is advocated in a given situation, or whether there might be circumstances in which it is *legitimate* to advocate violence. The fact that the ANC advocated violence against the apartheid regime would have made its ideology an extremist ideology on the Pro-Violence scale. One way to avoid this is to complicate the spectrum by distinguishing between the justified and unjustified advocacy of violence. The difficulties with this hardly need spelling out. The tidiest and most straightforward position is that advocacy of violence *always* makes an ideology extremist. On this account, it is a separate question whether ideological extremism is ever legitimate.

An interesting question raised by the Pro-Violence spectrum is whether it allows governments or democratically elected leaders to be classified as extremists. For example, regime change in Iraq was a key political objective of President George W. Bush. The President not only *advocated* but *ordered* violence in pursuit of this objective. This would make him an ideological extremist on the Pro-Violence spectrum as well as a methods extremist. From some standpoints, this will not be an unwelcome result. For those who wish to avoid this result, there is the option of arguing that advocating violence to remove a tyrant like Saddam Hussein does not make one an extremist. As in the case of the ANC, this confuses questions of classification with questions of justification.

These difficult issues will taken up in later chapters. Another difficult issue that will need to be tackled is whether the Pro-Violence spectrum implies that an ardent pacifist who is opposed to political violence under any circumstances is an ideological extremist. For the present, what can be said is the following: the positional view of ideological extremism has its attractions but also has to contend with a number of difficulties. When it comes to the ideologies of groups like ISIS, the idea of Pro-Violence offers a simple account of the sense in which they are ideologically extremist. However, this idea is not without its problems. These problems might lead one to look for a viable alternative to the ideological approach, which brings us neatly to the third of the three varieties of extremism: psychological extremism. For reasons that will soon become clear, this can also be described as *mindset extremism*.

Extremism in the psychological sense

Ideological approaches to extremism assume that whether an *ideology* is extremist or not depends on its ideological *content*, that is, on whether it is on the extreme left or the extreme right, or whether it advocates violence. Derivatively, whether an *organization* is extremist depends on its ideology. There is, however, another approach that bypasses difficult questions about how to classify ideologies. This alternative approach starts with the intuition that being an extremist is less about *what* one believes than about *how* one believes. The key thing that extremists lack is *moderation*. They are *fervent* believers in their own ideologies, whatever those ideologies are, and this is the key to their extremism. Moderates also have ideological commitments but their commitments are more measured.

On this account, extremism is 'a characteristic of the way beliefs are held rather than their location along some dimension' (Breton et al. 2002: xiii). The way a person believes is an aspect of their psychology. The implication is that 'extremist' and 'moderate' are points on a *psychological* spectrum that cuts across the left-right spectrum. A fervent liberal is in the middle of the left-right spectrum but at the extreme end of the psychological spectrum. In theory, a person at one end of the left-right spectrum could nevertheless be in the middle of the psychological spectrum. Their beliefs are extreme but their way of believing is not. For example, the eminent historian A. J. P. Taylor was once challenged about his political views at an interview for an appointment at an Oxford college. The President of the college said to him: 'I hear you have strong political views.' Taylor replied: 'Oh no, President. Extreme views weakly held' (1977: 8). This encapsulates the distinction between what one believes and how one believes. One version of the psychological approach says that extremism is *entirely* a matter of how one believes rather than what one believes. A milder and much more plausible version accepts that what one believes matters even if it *also* matters how one believes.

The first and most important theoretical challenge facing the psychological account of extremism is to explain its notion of a 'way of believing'. It is often claimed that beliefs do not have a distinctive 'feel'. For example, there is nothing that it feels like to believe that it is raining. However, it would be unusual to believe fervently that it is raining but not unusual to have fervent political or religious beliefs. Suppose, then, that to have the fervent belief that P (where P is a proposition with political content) is to have the strong or intense belief that P. The strength or intensity of a belief might be seen as a function of the strength or intensity of the *feelings* that accompany it. On this *phenomenological* view of belief, there actually can be something that it feels like to believe that P fervently: it is to believe that P with exceptionally strong feelings of conviction. Psychological extremists qualify as such because their political, religious or other beliefs are accompanied by such feelings. This explains why they are more likely to resort to violence than psychological moderates. They are motivated to commit acts of violence by the sheer intensity of their convictions.

An alternative to this approach is to see strong belief in dispositional terms.[10] On this view, strong or fervent beliefs are ones that the believer is disposed to hold on to, come what may. To put it another way, they are beliefs the believer is unwilling to revise or abandon. A fervent believer's commitment to his or her strong beliefs is uncompromising, and it is in this sense that they believe fervently. It is possible that fervent believers are unwilling to compromise *because* their beliefs are accompanied by strong feelings of conviction. On this interpretation, the dispositional and phenomenological approaches to fervent belief are not incompatible. However, it is also possible that a believer is uncompromising about certain matters for reasons that have nothing to do with intense feelings of conviction. It might be, for example, that the belief is too important to be easily given up because giving it up would threaten the believer's sense of self, or require too many adjustments elsewhere in their system of beliefs.

This points to the following account of psychological extremism: extremism in this sense is indeed a characteristic of the way beliefs are held rather than their location along some dimension. However, strength of belief needn't be understood as strength of feeling. Extremists are people who believe uncompromisingly, in the sense that they are unwilling to revise their beliefs or consider the possibility that they might be wrong. They are strongly disposed to hold on to their political beliefs regardless of what anyone else thinks, and 'display a small capacity or willingness to compromise' (Breton et al. 2002: xiii). As a result, they are described as dogmatic or closed-minded. Extremists in the psychological sense have intellectual dispositions that moderates lack, while moderates have intellectual dispositions that extremists lack. The key difference between moderates and extremists is a difference in their intellectual dispositions rather than a difference in their feelings.

One limitation of this approach is that it focuses entirely on extremism as a way of *believing*. As noted above, extremist ideologies include many important elements apart from beliefs so the psychological extremist's way of believing can only be part of the story. A more serious difficulty is that being uncompromising in one's beliefs is not enough to make one a psychological extremist. I am uncompromising in my belief that triangles have three sides, but this does not make me an extremist.[11] This example might be regarded as irrelevant since it does not concern a political belief. Perhaps it is only when one is uncompromising in one's *political* beliefs that one is a psychological extremist, but even that is doubtful. It depends on what one is uncompromising about. The ANC was uncompromising in its view that every adult in South Africa should be entitled to vote, regardless of race. This was a matter of principle, and it would be unsatisfactory to classify Nelson Mandela and other senior ANC figures as psychological extremists on the basis that they were unwilling to compromise on this issue. It is not irrelevant that the principle to which they were uncompromisingly committed was sound.

This example points to the difficulty of characterizing psychological extremism solely in terms of *how* one believes, regardless of whether this is understood in phenomenological or dispositional terms. *What* one believes also matters. Being uncompromising might make one a psychological extremist or it might simply make one a person with strong principles. In his essay on extremism, Nozick asks: 'how do we distinguish [a] non-compromising position from a principled one?' (1997: 297), but this is a false dichotomy. After all, being principled *requires* one to be uncompromising about certain things. The issue is whether the principles about which one is uncompromising are ones about which one *ought* to be uncompromising. The answer to this question depends on what the principles are as well as on why one believes them. Even if one's principles are sound, one's reasons for sticking to them might not be.

Unlike psychological extremists, individuals who are uncompromisingly committed to sound principles for sound reasons are neither dogmatic nor closed-minded. These labels are applied to people who are uncompromisingly committed to what are taken to be *unsound* principles. Since there are arguments about which principles are sound, there are bound to be arguments whether a person's uncompromising commitment is dogmatic. One might be unable of seeing any value in an opposing point of view – say, the point of view of a staunch defender of apartheid – because it genuinely has no value. One might be unwilling to engage seriously with an alternative to a belief one already holds because the alternative has no merit. The true psychological extremist is not just uncompromising but *dogmatic*: he is uncompromising about matters concerning which he is not entitled to be uncompromising. His unwillingness to compromise says more about his own limitations than about the actual merits of the beliefs or principles to which he is committed. However, for this view to be justified, the nature of his beliefs or principles must be taken into account.

What we are looking for, then, is an account of psychological extremism that attaches due weight both to the 'what' and the 'how' of the extremist's beliefs in the specific context of their time and place. Ideally, it should also try to capture the significance for psychological extremism of factors other than belief. As it happens, there is an idea that is tailor-made for developing a balanced and compelling account of extremism in the psychological sense. This is the idea of a *mindset*.[12] Given its importance and usefulness, I will devote a whole chapter to it at the appropriate time (Chapter 4). Now is not the time to get into the details but simply to outline the basic idea of a mindset and explain how it makes sense of psychological extremism. The basic idea can be simply stated: to be a psychological extremist is to have an *extremist mindset*. What, then, is a mindset?

Mindsets and extremism

A familiar observation is that, despite all their ideological differences, extremists on opposite sides of the political spectrum have a lot in common. There is what might be called a common extremist *style*, a way of thinking and acting that one finds in extremists with very different political agendas. Why would that be? It is hard to resist the idea that the extremist style is underpinned by a common extremist mindset. Eric Hoffer makes a closely related point in his classic text, *The True Believer*. Although he does not discuss extremism as such, he does analyse people he calls 'fanatics':

> Though they seem to be at opposite poles, fanatics of all kinds are actually crowded together at one end. It is the fanatic and the moderate who are poles apart and never meet. The fanatics of various hues eye each other with suspicion and are ready to fly at each other's throat. But they are neighbours and almost of one family … And it is easier for a fanatic Communist to be converted to fascism, chauvinism or Catholicism than to become a sober liberal. The opposite of the religious fanatic is not the fanatical atheist but the gentle cynic who cares not whether there is a God or not.
>
> (1951: 86)

What Hoffer says about fanatics is also true of extremists. They, too, are of one mind, even if they are ready to go for each other's throats. If fanaticism and extremism are the same thing, then it is, of course, hardly surprising that Hoffer's observations about fanatics also apply to extremists. There is more below about the relationship between fanaticism and extremism.

Another source of the notion of an extremist mindset is Richard Hofstadter's book, *The Paranoid Style in American Politics*. The paranoid style is a style of mind that 'has to do with the way in which ideas are believed and advocated rather than with the truth or falsity of their content' (2008: 5). The paranoid style is also identifiable by its preoccupations and emotions like anger and 'the feeling of persecution' (ibid.: 4). It is the style of 'angry minds' (ibid.: 3). The *clinical* paranoid regards himself or herself as the victim of a hostile and conspiratorial world. For the *political* paranoid, it is his or her nation's way of life or culture that is under threat. His or her feelings of righteous indignation give rise to a style that is 'overheated, oversuspicious, overaggressive, grandiose, and apocalyptic' (ibid.: 5). His or her preoccupations include conspiracy theories and the extent to which the government has been infiltrated by communists who are selling out American national interests.

The paranoid style is most evident on the extreme right but is not always right-wing in its affiliations and is not confined to American extremists. Anger and feelings of righteous indignation are common to extremists everywhere, as is the tendency to resort to heated exaggeration in making their case. Hofstadter's essay was first published in 1964, and this explains the dated reference to a preoccupation with communist infiltration. Today extremists have different preoccupations, including two that Hofstadter associated with the clinical paranoid: conspiracy theories and the insistence that one's in-group, one's own people, have been, and continue to be, victims of persecution by a hostile out-group.[13] In these respects, the extremist mindset and paranoid style are indistinguishable.

The fact that paranoia is a mental disorder might prompt the thought that extremism should itself be regarded as a mental disorder, and that this is really what the psychological conception of extremism should be emphasizing. It is easy to sympathize with this view: how could people who can do what did ISIS did to the Jordanian pilot possibly be psychologically normal? Isn't a diagnosis of psychopathy or some other mental disorder inescapable? Not so, and the pathologizing of extremism is best avoided. Even if having a mental disorder makes a person more prone to extremism, it does not follow that extremism itself is a mental disorder, as distinct from something correlated with a mental disorder. As for whether there is in fact a correlation between mental illness and extremism, there is a paucity of evidence that bears on this issue. One recent study found an association between extremist sympathies and comorbid depression and dysthymia.[14] On the other hand, studies of terrorists, many of whom are also extremists, have found little evidence of psychopathy. John Horgan summarizes the relevant evidence by noting that 'terrorist movements should be seen nei- ther as organisations of necessarily psychopathic individuals because of the brutality of behavior involved, nor likely to recruit people with psychopathic tendencies' (2003: 7).

The evidence that there is such a thing as an extremist mindset is histor- ical rather than clinical. Mindsets are sometimes understood simply as sets of beliefs but that is not what is intended here. To talk about the common mindset of extremists with different ideological agendas is to talk about their characteristic *preoccupations*, *attitudes*, *emotions*, and *ways of thinking*. If one is preoccupied by the persecution of one's in-group that must be because one *believes* that one's in-group is being persecuted. Preoccupa- tions are in this sense underpinned by beliefs but not all beliefs are preoccu- pations; it is possible to believe that it is raining without being preoccupied by that fact. Preoccupations are more like obsessions, and there is a great deal of historical evidence that extremists with very different ideological agenda have several common obsessions.

Apart from the ones identified by Hofstadter, another extremist preoc- cupation is with *purity*, that is, the dilution of the religious, ideological, or ethnic purity of one's in-group by external forces. This purity preoccupation can have lethal consequences, including campaigns of ethnic, religious, or ideological 'cleansing'. Extremists also tend to be preoccupied by the vision of a mythical past, or of a mythical future, for which they see themselves as fighting. These and other extremist preoccupations will be discussed in more detail in Chapter 4. For the moment, the important point is that preoccupa- tions are part of the extremist mindset, and that a preoccupation is not just a way of believing something. It is, or is at least based on, concrete beliefs about one's situation, beliefs that can be verified or falsified. Preoccupations can be baseless because the beliefs they are based on can be baseless.

The notion that the extremist mindset is partly constituted by attitudes should not be controversial. A basic positive attitude is liking, and a nega- tive attitude is disliking.[15] Hence, the attitudinal component of the extremist mindset can be identified by identifying the likes and dislikes that are asso- ciated with it. Dislikes include compromise, doubt, and ambiguity. Extrem- ists believe uncompromisingly because they are averse to compromise. Compromise detracts from purity. In the extremist mindset, there is no place for doubt because doubt implies the possibility that one might be mistaken. This is something that a true extremist cannot contemplate. Another possi- bility that the extremist mindset is unwilling or unable to contemplate is that the truth might be unclear, or that points of view that are different from their own might have some merit. For the extremist, there can be no grey areas. However, although extremists have strong likes and dislikes, there are also important matters about which they are indifferent. Typically, they are indifferent to the practical consequences of their actions. They see harm to others or even to themselves as a price worth paying for their ideals.

The attitude that is perhaps most commonly associated with an extremist mindset is a positive attitude towards violence. This is what the Pro-Violence spectrum tries to capture, but it is debatable whether favouring violence as a means of attaining one's political or other objectives is essential to the extremist mindset. It is certainly essential to what might be called a *militant* extremist mindset, but does extremism have to be militant?[16] It is not out of the question that a person or group might be preoccupied with persecution, purity, and myths about the past or future, but not be Pro-Violence. Such a person's mindset would be extremist but not in the militant sense. Pro-Violence without an extremist mindset is also a possibility. Nelson Mandela supported armed resistance to apartheid, but his preoccupations and attitudes did not mark him out as a person with an extremist mindset. It might still be true, however, that a person with an extremist mindset is more *likely* to be Pro-Violence than one with a non-extremist mindset.

Other dimensions of the extremist mindset will be discussed in Chapter 4. Enough has already been said here to make several things clear. To talk about a person's mindset is to talk about their psychology. A person with an extremist mindset can therefore be described as a psychological extremist, but mindset extremism is different from types of psychological extremism that see it as entirely in terms of one's mode of believing. The mindset approach is multidimensional in more than one sense: it is concerned with mental characteristics other than belief, though it does not dispute the relevance of belief, and it correctly represents the extremist mindset as depending both on the content of one's beliefs or preoccupations and one's way of believing. The mindset approach only allows centrists to count as extremists if they display extremist preoccupations, attitudes, emotions, and ways of thinking. In practice, this means that most centrists will not count as extremists since people who are ideologically middle-of-the-road are highly unlikely to have extremist preoccupations.

A mindset can be more or less extremist, depending on the extent to which it is preoccupied with persecution, purity, and so on, and on the strength of its extremist likes and dislikes. Since both individuals and groups can have an extremist mindset, there should be no concern about the mindset approach being too individualistic. This approach has no difficulty classifying a group like ISIS as extremist even if it is difficult to locate on the left-right spectrum. There is an ideological element to the extremist mindset, but this mindset is not confined to those on the extreme left or extreme right. Last but not least, the mindset approach delivers a nuanced account of the relationship between extremism and violence. To speak in such glowing terms of the mindset approach is not to imply that the ideological and methods conceptions of extremism should be abandoned. Extremism has different aspects, and the three conceptions of extremism outlined here are its three most important aspects.

The metaphysics of extremism

After distinguishing between the three different forms of extremism, it is sometimes easy to see that a specific group or individual is extremist in one or more of the three senses. For example, it is easy to see that ISIS is extremist in all three senses. In other cases, the label is more contentious. This raises a question about the objectivity of labelling ISIS or any other group or individual as 'extremist'. A deeper question concerns the nature of extremism itself. What kind of *thing* are we describing when we describe the extremism of groups like ISIS? Are we describing an objective fact about the world? This issue came up earlier when the question was raised whether extremism owes its existence as a category to a political decision to apply the 'extremist' label to some people and ideologies but not others. This is a question about the *metaphysics* of extremism, and now would be a good time to consider it.

A route into the philosophical issues in this area is via recent academic debates about the metaphysics of terrorism and the role of labelling in that related context. In their account of what they call the 'politics of labelling', Richard Jackson, Lee Jarvis, Jeroen Gunning and Marie Breen-Smyth argue that:

> Terms such as terrorism should not be thought of as neutral words we employ to refer to an independent realm of existence. Rather, they are lenses that shape or co-construct the world around us, giving it order and meaning *as* we engage in the act of observation … Because of

this, the words we use to describe political violence … and the meanings we give to those words, are never inevitable and their use is not determined or 'given' in advance.

(2011: 112)

They add that terrorist violence is a 'social fact' that 'does not exist *as* terrorist violence outside of the categories and theories we use to designate it as such' (ibid.: 119). The label is always used by 'someone speaking from somewhere and for some purpose' (ibid.: 119).

Much of what Jackson and his colleagues say about the idea of terrorism can be said with equal validity about the concept of extremism. It gives order and meaning to the world around us and is always used by someone speaking from somewhere and for some purpose. However, one might quibble with the notion that terms like 'terrorism' and 'extremism' do not refer to an 'independent realm of existence'. What ISIS did to Lieutenant al-Kasasbeh certainly took place in an 'independent realm of existence' and did not depend in any way on the labelling of the pilot's brutal execution as an act of terrorism or violent extremism.[17] It is not a 'social fact' that the pilot was locked in a cage and set alight.[18] On the other hand, if what it means for something to exist *as* an act of violent extremism is for it to be *categorized* as such, then it is trivial that the pilot's execution did not exist as an act of violent extremism outside of the categories used to designate it as such. The substantive point, however, is that the use of labels like 'terrorist' and 'extremist' places what ISIS did to the pilot in a wider pattern of belief and action. The labelling of groups like ISIS, and people like Breivik and KSM, as 'extremists' or 'terrorists' is a matter of identifying common patterns of thought, belief and action and is justified by these same patterns of thought, belief and action.

Even those who claim that terrorism and extremism do not exist outside of the categories we use to designate them as such do not deny the existence of either. For Jackson and his colleagues, 'terrorism represents a form of politically motivated violence intended to communicate a message, in part by the instrumentalization of its victims' (ibid.: 118). Since there *are* politically motivated and communicative acts of violence that instrumentalize their victims, it follows that terrorism is something real: there are acts of violence that meet the definition of terrorism. By the same token, there *are* methods, ideological and psychological extremists according to the definitions of these varieties of extremism given here. It follows that extremism is something real, and not just a figment of the theorist's imagination.

However, there is one respect in which this argument for the reality of extremism is too quick. Writing in the eighteenth century, Kant pointed out that we sometimes use concepts that are bogus or, as he calls them, 'usurpatory'.[19] For example, the concept of a *witch* is still in use in various places in the world. Users of this concept might insist that there *are* women in their communities who are, by their definition, witches. Witches exist, they might say. However, quite apart from concerns about whether anyone has ever really met the conditions for being a witch, there is the more fundamental problem that there is something wrong with the very idea of a witch. It is a bogus concept that, as Philip Kitcher puts it on Kant's behalf, 'plays no role in what, by our current lights, is the best description and explanation of the world' (1981: 224). To put it another way, it is not enough to demonstrate the reality of witches to come up with a definition according to which some people are indeed witches. It also needs to be shown that the concept of a witch is legitimate rather than usurpatory.

Could it be that the concept of extremism is usurpatory? Just as the labelling of people as witches does not establish the reality of witches, so the labelling of people as extremists does not establish the reality of extremism *if* there is something wrong with the concept of extremism. The best way to disarm this form of scepticism is to show that this concept plays a useful role in what, by our current lights, is the best description and explanation of political reality. That is the mission of this book. However, even if this mission is successful, there is a further question about extremism that flows from what Jackson and his colleagues say about terrorism: is extremism a social construct? Many things are said to be socially constructed. Examples include gender, race and illness.[20] Should extremism be added to this list? If so, what is the philosophical or practical significance of that fact?

In a helpful discussion, Sally Haslanger highlights two somewhat different forms of 'constructionism'.[21] For any X, *idea-constructionists* claim that it is the *idea* of X that is constructed. For the *object-constructionist*, it is X itself that is socially constructed. Suppose that X = extremism. If the point of saying that extremism is socially constructed is to suggest that the *idea* of extremism is socially constructed, then this is not a claim that anyone should want to deny. In its blandest form, idea-constructionism comes down to the claim that 'what concepts and so what ideas we have [are] the result of social-historical events' (Haslanger 2012: 115–16). This is as true of the idea of extremism as of any other. Idea-constructionism is more interesting if, as well as drawing attention to the historical origins of our ideas, it denies that there is anything in the nature of things that justifies the use of X. However, if X is the idea of extremism, then the obvious response to idea-constructionism is that there is something in reality that justifies its use. What justifies its use, and makes it apt, are the conduct, ideology and mind-set of groups like ISIS and people like Anders Breivik and KSM. In this sense, constructionism about the idea of extremism turns out to be either correct but trivial, or substantive but incorrect.

Object-constructionism is difficult to pin down. When it comes to gender, the point being made is that 'gender is not a classification scheme based simply on biological or anatomical differences, but should be understood as a system of social categories that can only be defined by a network of social relations' (ibid.: 130). This is a substantive and, indeed, controversial thesis. What about the thesis that *extremist* and *terrorist* are social categories? If there is resistance to this view, its source is unlikely to be the supposition that the distinction between, say, extremists and moderates is built into the natural structure of the world in anything like the way that gender differences were thought to be before the rise of social constructionism. Rather than think of *extremist* as a social category defined by social factors, one might insist instead that it is a *political* category constituted by psychological and ideological factors. This is neither a straightforward assertion nor a straight-forward denial of social constructionism. However, it is certainly not obvious that defining extremism by reference to its characteristic ideological com-mitments, methods or psychology amounts to defining it by reference to a network of *social* relations. For example, ideological extremism is defined by reference to a network of *ideological* relations, that is, by reference to where the ideological extremist's ideology stands in relation to other ideologies.

For this and other reasons, talk of extremism as a social construction con-fuses more than it clarifies, and will be avoided for the remainder of this book. This is not to deny that the concept of extremism has social-historical roots, that it is used to give order and meaning to the world around us, and that the labelling of people as extremists is always done by someone speaking from somewhere for some purpose. However, these points can all be acknowledged without describing extremism as a social construction. Extremism in the forms identified in this book is real, as real as what ISIS did to the Jordanian pilot, and the *concept* of extremism is answerable to that reality. The fact that a concept is answerable to the reality that it is used to describe has methodological implications for the study of extremism, and the next section will draw out these implications.

How to study extremism

In philosophy, there is a long tradition of answering questions of the form, 'What is x?' by conceptual analysis, that is, by analysing the *concept* of an x. So, for example, if asked 'what is knowledge?', one might answer this question by analyzing the concept of knowledge. One way to do that is to employ the *method of cases*. One considers a range of test cases in which a subject satisfies at least some putative conditions for knowing and then asks whether these are cases of knowledge. All one has to go on are one's *intuitions* about whether the concept of knowledge does or does not apply in a given case. The hope is that by drawing out our intuitions about a range of cases, the method of cases will make it possible to identify the necessary and sufficient conditions for knowing. Since the experiments that the method of cases employs are thought experiments, this allows all the analytical work to be done from the comfort of one's armchair.

This is not the correct approach for answering the question 'what is extremism?' or 'what is an extremist mindset?'. These questions cannot be answered simply by analyzing the concept of extremism. Account must also be taken of the preoccupations, attitudes and other mental characteristics of real-world extremist groups and individuals. Since these cannot be known by armchair reflection, it follows that armchair reflection alone cannot uncover the nature of extremism. If one proposes a list of extremist preoc-cupations and then discovers that ISIS or other extremist groups do not have these preoccupations, then the right response is not to conclude that these groups are not extremist after all but rather to revise one's list of extremist preoccupations. There is no substitute for knowing what real-world extrem-ists think, feel and do. This illustrates two important features of philoso-phy highlighted by the philosopher David Papineau: philosophical claims depend on empirical support and they are primarily aimed at understanding the actual world. Papineau maintains that these things are true of philosophy generally.[22] They are certainly true of the philosophy of extremism.

The discussion so far implies that what is known about actual extremists can be used to *test* proposed analyses of the extremist mindset. However, this raises another question: how does one arrive at such analyses in the first place? Suppose that one begins the process of analysis with a list of uncontroversially extremist groups or individuals and studies their attitudes, preoccupations and other characteristics. Common themes can then be attributed to a shared extremist mindset. In this paradigm, what is known about extremists is not just used to test analyses of extremism or the extremist mindset. Rather, an analysis of this mindset is *derived* from a study of the mental characteristics of actual extremists. In the same way, an analysis of the militant extremist mindset is derived from a study of actual militant extremists. For example, one notable study of the militant extremist mindset identifies no fewer than 16 themes that characterize this mindset by scrutinizing the public statements of extremist groups from seven regions of the world. The resulting model of the militant extremist mindset is described by the study's authors as an 'inductively based working model' (Saucier et al. 2009: 258). General features of a given mindset are derived by observation of these features in a range of entities that have that mindset.

The project of deriving a working model of the extremist mindset by studying the statements of extremist groups cannot succeed without philosophical input. These statements and the actions to which they give rise typically point to a wide range of preoccupations and attitudes. Which of these is essential? How are the different preoccupations and attitudes related? What is the best way of understanding them? These questions call for exactly the kind of analytical thinking in which philosophy specializes. For example, it is a fact that most uncontroversially extremist groups and individuals are Pro-Violence. In other words, they are militant extremists. It follows that if one's understanding of the extremist mindset is based on what is known about such groups, then one will find it difficult to accommodate the notion of non-militant, non-violent extremism. In contrast, the possibility of non-militant extremism comes more clearly into focus once one realizes that Pro-Violence is not entailed by the other elements of the extremist mindset. Reflection on these issues, and on what it would take to resolve them, should put paid to any notion that philosophy cannot help with the question 'what is extremism?'.

Taking these considerations into account, the obvious conclusion is that the study of extremism must be multidisciplinary if it is to cast any light on this important phenomenon. It goes without saying that a major contribution is required from political science and political theory, especially in relation to the ideological and positional issues. Psychology is another field whose contribution is clearly required, especially in relation to psychological extremism and the extremist mindset. Another relevant discipline is sociology, at least to the extent that extremism is a group phenomenon and not just something that operates at the level of the individual. Finally, there is philosophy. It is one thing to list some of the questions about extremism that philosophy might help to answer, but the real test for a philosophical analysis of extremism is whether it delivers convincing answers to these questions. This is the test for the remaining chapters of this book.

Looking ahead

Many of the issues to be discussed in the following chapters have been touched on in this chapter. Chapter 2, 'Ideological extremism', will go into whether the location of an ideology in ideological space is absolute or relative. When an ideology is described as extremist, is this just a comment about its position relative to other ideologies or about its absolute or objective location? What are the other dimensions of ideological space, and how does location on one dimension relate to location on another? My proposal is that for each dimension of ideological space, an ideology's location is determined by the answers it gives to a menu of diagnostic questions. This means that an ideology's location in ideological space is both relative to a dimension and relative to a menu.

One thing that will emerge is the futility of insisting on a sharp distinction between positional and psychological extremism. An ideology is shaped by its adherents, by how they understand it, and put it into practice. Questions about the location of an ideology are not just abstract theoretical questions but also questions of practical politics. Theories matter but so does the way they are implemented. Even with respect to a single dimension of ideological space, such as the left-right dimension, there are different ways of deciding the location of an ideology along that dimension. In addition, some ideologies give inconsistent answers to the questions that are supposed to fix its location. A case in point, and one that will come up at the end of Chapter 2, is fascism. There is no better way to bring out the difficulties of the idea of ideological location than to reflect on the peculiarities of fascist ideology.

Chapter 3, 'Methods extremism', will stress that extreme methods needn't be violent. It is also conceivable that the use of violent methods in pursuit of a political objective does not necessarily make one a methods extremist. The question whether the use of a particular method constitutes methods extremism depends on a range of factors apart from the method itself. If violent methods are used, then whether this amounts to methods extremism depends on whether the violence is in a just cause, whether there is a realistic alternative to violence, whether the violence is proportional and whether it discriminates between innocents and non-innocents. On this account, there are degrees of violence and anyone who uses, or endorses, extreme violence as a political tool is almost certainly a methods extremist because extreme violence is almost certainly – though not always – disproportionate.

Determining whether violence is in a just cause is, of course, not straightforward but people have the right to resist tyranny, oppression or gross violations of their human rights. If violence is the only way and is not excessive, then there is a case for not classifying the use of violence in these circumstances as amounting to methods extremism. In the words of Hannah Arendt, sometimes violence is 'the only way to set the scales of justice right again' (1969: 64). Questions about the proportionality of violence are especially tricky and will be addressed at some length in Chapter 3. Extremists either reject the requirement for violence to be proportional or only pay lip service to this requirement. Like Osama bin Laden in some of his pronouncements, they also endorse the killing of innocents. One lesson of Chapter 3 is that violence in a just cause is not necessarily just.

Chapter 4, 'The psychology of extremism', is the longest of the eight chapters in this book. It should be clear from the brief summary given above that the idea of a mindset raises many difficult questions. Starting from psychological accounts of the militant extremist mindset, the various different components of the extremist mindset will be identified in a way that leaves open the possibility of non-militant extremism. Apart from being preoccupied with purity and visions of a mythical past or future, extremists also tend to be preoccupied with victimhood and humiliation. Extremists not only see themselves as persecuted by their enemies but also as humiliated by their persecution. This leads to emotions like anger and resentment, which are at the heart of the extremist mindset.

A key extremist attitude that has already been mentioned is a deeply felt aversion to compromise. A difficulty here is that being principled also involves being uncompromising about certain matters, so what is the different between an extremist and a person of principle? The difference is that a person of principle is not averse to compromise *per se* but only to what Avishai Margalit calls 'rotten compromises', that is, compromises that support cruelty or injustice.[23] In contrast, extremists see *all* compromise as capitulation. In other words, they regard all compromises as rotten. This relates to another key extremist attitude: intolerance. Extremists are intolerant of those with whom they are unwilling to compromise and they are also anti-pluralist. To be a pluralist is to accept, in Isaiah Berlin's famous formulation, that 'the ends of men are many' (2013a: 239). A corollary that pluralists are also happy to accept is that 'there is no uniquely right way of living' (Lyons 2020: 7). This is anathema for those with an extremist mindset. As far as they are concerned, there is a uniquely correct set of values and a uniquely correct way to live, which they are within their rights to impose on others. This is the view if ISIS, not to mention other notorious extremists like Hitler, Stalin and Mao.

The particular ways of thinking or thinking styles that are associated with an extremist mindset include conspiracy thinking, utopian thinking, and apocalyptic thinking. Extremist who see themselves as victims of persecution may also find it easy to blame their persecution on a conspiracy. They see themselves as fighting for a utopian future, but a utopia that will only become a reality after an impending catastrophe or apocalypse.[24] Apocalyptic thinking is integral to ISIS's world-view but not all extremism is apocalyptic. This raises two further questions that will be addressed in Chapter 4: which of the elements of the extremist mindset are essential and which are inessential? On what basis is the distinction between essential and inessential components of the extremist mindset to be drawn? The answers to these questions are far from straightforward.

Chapter 5, 'Extremism, fanaticism, fundamentalism', will consider how these three notions are related. A fanatic, Churchill is reputed to have said, is 'one who can't change his mind and won't change the subject'. It isn't true, however, that fanatics can't change their minds. Those who shift from one end of the ideological spectrum to the other *have* changed their minds. It is a paradox of fanaticism that unwavering certainty about their ideals does not prevent fanatics from giving up those ideals and adopting entirely different ones. Fanatics, it will be argued, have unwarranted contempt for other people's ideals, are prepared to trample on those ideals and interests in pursuit of their own perverted ideals, and impose their ideals on others, by force if necessary. In addition, they are unwilling to think critically about their ideals even though they are willing to sacrifice themselves in pursuit of them.

On this account, fanaticism is both an intellectual and a moral failing. Fanatics are almost always methods extremists, though fanaticism without methods extremism is possible in theory. Fanaticism does not entail positional extremism on the left-right dimension. ISIS is led by fanatics who are hard to think of in terms of left and right. However, it is arguable that fanaticism does entail positional extremism on at least one dimension. Fanatics needn't have the preoccupations of mindset extremists, though they mostly do, but mindset extremists are fanatics unless they are *armchair* extremists. The extremism of the armchair extremist is purely theoretical but fanaticism is not purely theoretical. One thing that is clear is that the *concepts* of extremism and fanaticism are different regardless of whether the categories coincide in practice.

A key question about fundamentalism is whether it is a religious notion or whether non-religious uses are also legitimate. In its strict, original sense, fundamentalism originated in religious thinking in America in the early part of the twentieth century. In a broader sense, to be a fundamentalist is to revere a text from which one's core doctrines are derived, and to be inclined to favour a literalist interpretation of the text. That text might be, but need not be, the Bible. Since it is possible to be an extremist or a fanatic without revering a text, it is possible to be an extremist or a fanatic without being a fundamentalist. Committed Nazis were both extremists and fanatics but not fundamentalists. However, there are similarities between what might be called the *fundamentalist mindset* and the extremist mindset. These will be explored at the end of Chapter 5.

In what has been called the 'pejorative tradition', extremism and fanaticism have an unmissable and inescapable negative connotation. However, there is also the view that it is sometimes better to be an extremist or a fanatic than a moderate. In the words of the right-wing American politician Barry Goldwater, 'extremism in defense of liberty is no vice', and 'moderation in pursuit of justice is no virtue'.[25] An example that is often mentioned in this connection is that of the nineteenth-century abolitionists who campaigned against slavery in the U.S. If they were right to describe themselves as fanatics, then isn't this a case in which fanaticism and extremism are preferable to moderation? This question will be addressed in Chapter 6, 'Why not extremism?'.

The issues here are complex, and it is easy to be seduced by the imagined advantages of extremism as a response to injustice or oppression. However, both philosophy and history suggest that extremism and fanaticism are not the answer. Excessive moderation can be an obstacle to progress, but radicalism rather than extremism is the solution. What marked the abolitionists out as radicals was their use of extra-institutional means and their commitment to radical political change. Left and right can both be radical but being a political radical does not make one an extremist or a fanatic. Radicals need not have extremist preoccupations and are not committed to violence. However, radicals are right that moderation is an overrated virtue, and can be a liability. Pleas for moderation can end up being anti-democratic and used to limit criticism of the established order.

Chapter 7, 'Pathways to extremism' is about the so-called 'radicalization process', in other words, the process of becoming an extremist.[26] The risk factors of radicalization include the perception of grievance. According to the grievance model, the perception of grievance in the form of injustice, oppression or socio-economic exclusion can make people receptive to extremist ideas. Radicalization in this ideological sense is in turn a risk factor for behavioural radicalization, for the use of extreme methods in pursuit of one's objectives. As others have noted, it is when ideologically radicalized individuals self-categorize as soldiers that they are liable to turn violent. Radicalization is facilitated by an extremist mindset, but it is also true that an extremist mindset is promoted and reinforced by ideological or so-called 'cognitive' radicalization.

Radicalization is something that happens at the level of groups as well as individuals. It has been suggested that political extremism is often the result of group polarization and group dynamics. Socio-epistemic approaches blame radicalization on what Russell Hardin calls the 'crippled epistemology' of extremists and extremism.[27] The idea is that extremists live in epistemic bubbles or echo chambers from which dissenting views are excluded. Without any serious pushback, their views become increasingly extreme as the views of larger society are held at bay. There is much to be said in favour of this view of group radicalization but it does not explain the self-radicalization of individuals outside a group context. Much has been made of the role of social media in radicalization but the focus on social media is sometimes responsible for the misleading impression that radicalization is a passive process or the result of manipulation by others rather than one that relies on the active participation and initiative of extremists themselves.

Assuming that extremism is generally undesirable, what are the possible antidotes? This is the question to be addressed in Chapter 8, 'Countering extremism'. What is known as *counter-radicalization* seeks to prevent the radicalization of those who are supposedly at risk of radicalization but have not yet been radicalized. *Deradicalization* programmes are targeted at already radicalized individuals and groups. One of the key myths of influential models of counter-radicalization, such as the UK's *Prevent* strategy, is that extremism is analogous to a disease or contagion. However, this underestimates the extent to which people are radicalized by *arguments* and *narratives* that convey their ideology, justifications and values. Effective counter-radicalization requires serious engagement with the arguments that extremists find convincing and the devising of compelling counter-narratives. Where radicalization is driven by the perception of grievance, this perception needs to be addressed and genuine grievances acknowledged. In general, the most effective way to inoculate people against extremism is to tackle extremist arguments head-on.

Extremist narratives are exercises in sensemaking. Lawrence Freedman describes narratives as 'compelling story lines which can explain events and from which inferences can be drawn' (2006: 22). Narratives that are capable of countering extremism must have a range of features: they must have the ring of truth from their audience's perspective and do a better job of making sense of their lives and their world than the extremist narrative. They must be conveyed by credible messengers and must display narrative depth, that is, avoid shallowness and over-simplification. Where extremist grievances have deep historical roots, these must be engaged with by the counter-narrative. Counter-narratives must also be relevant, that is, both targeted and tailored. They must target the key points of extremist narratives and be tailored to different audiences. Finally, they must be accessible to those tempted by extremism. Counter-narratives that have all these features are not easy to devise and governments are especially bad at producing them. They need to change not only minds but also mindsets, and the fact that this is so hard to do explains why, in the end, extremism is something that we will always have to live with.

The following chapters will contain accounts of many organizations and individuals: the Khmer Rouge, Al-Qaeda, ISIS, the ANC, the IRA, the senior Nazi Reinhardt Heydrich, the Oklahoma City bomber Timothy McVeigh, Osama bin Laden, and others. The point of these case studies is not only to ensure that abstract philosophical theorizing has some basis but also to bring out the difficulty of determining who is and is not an extremist and whether extremism is ever justified. Literature is another source of insights about extremism. Among the best fictional accounts of extremism is Philip Roth's *American Pastoral*, which will play a key role in the account of the extremist mindset given in Chapter 4.[28] The lessons of history must also be learned in philosophical theorizing about extremism, and it is important not to lose sight of the political ramifications of a theory of extremism. The challenge is to avoid overblown criticism of extremism while also not apologizing for its worst excesses. Readers will have to judge for themselves whether the following chapters succeed in striking this delicate balance.

Notes

1 ISIS stands for the Islamic State of Iraq and al-Sham or, the Islamic State of Iraq and Syria. The group is also known as ISIL (Islamic State of Iraq and the Levant). In 2014, it adopted the name the Islamic State (IS). For more on ISIS, see McCants (2015), Gerges (2016) and Wood (2018).

2 The story of the pilot's execution is told in Wood (2018: 84–6).

3 They are addressed in the section on the metaphysics of extremism.

4 The text of Zawahiri's letter to Zarqawi is available at: www.usma.edu. The recipient of the letter was Abu Musab al-Zarqawi, the leader of Al-Qaeda in Iraq, which morphed into ISIS after Zarqawi's death in an American air strike in 2006. Zarqawi's brutality and depravity made Zawahiri and Osama bin Laden seem moderate in comparison.

5 *Apocalypse Now*, directed by Francis Ford Coppola, was released in 1979. It was loosely based on Joseph Conrad's *Heart of Darkness*.

6 Naji (2006). For an account of this document and its influence, see McCants (205: 82–4).

7 Heywood (2017: 15–17).

8 Hitchens (2007).

9 Pro-Violence has been defined as 'a belief that violence is not only an option, but it may be a useful means to achieve one's personal and social goals' (Stankov, Saucier and Knežević 2010: 75–6). It would be more accurate to define Pro-Violence as the belief that violence may not only be useful but is also a *legitimate* means of achieving one's goals. However, Pro-Violence is not just a matter of belief. It is an attitude – what philosophers call a 'pro-attitude' – towards violence. Talk of a Pro-Violence *spectrum* is justified by the supposition that Pro-Violence is a matter of degree.

10 Ramsey (1931) is a helpful and influential discussion of different views of belief. Commenting on the view that 'beliefs differ in the intensity of a feeling by which they are accompanied', Ramsey argues that 'the beliefs which we hold most strongly are often accompanied by practically no feeling at all; no one feels strongly about things he takes for granted' (ibid.: 169).

11 Katsafanas (2019) has a helpful discussion of this kind of case in relation to fanaticism.

12 See Dweck (2012). However, my conception of a mindset is different from hers.

13 The terminology of 'in-group' and 'out-group' in relation to extremism is explained in Chapter 3 of Berger (2018).

14 Bhui et al. (2020). Dysthmia is a chronic form of depression.

15 Maio and Haddock (2015: 3–4).

16 On the idea of a militant extremist mindset, see Stankov, Saucier and Knežević (2010).

17 For present purposes, an 'independent realm of existence' is one that does not depend for its existence or character on our perception or categorization of it.

18 It should be acknowledged, however, that the idea of a 'social fact' is far from straightforward.

19 Kant (1932: A84/B117). Kant's examples of usurpatory concepts are *fate* and *fortune*.

20 For a much longer list, see Hacking (1999: 1).

21 The distinction between idea-constructionism and object-constructionism is taken from Hacking (1999).

22 Papineau (2009).

23 Margalit (2010).

24 This type of thinking is fundamental to ISIS's world-view, as noted in Wood (2015).

25 This saying is discussed in Wilkinson (2016).

26 This definition of the radicalization process is from Neumann (2013: 874).

27 Hardin (2002).

28 Roth (1997).

2

Ideological extremism

Ideological space

When Khmer Rouge soldiers entered the Cambodian capital Phnom Penh on 17 April 1975, local residents were hopeful that life would return to something approaching normality after a long and bloody civil war. Little did they know. Under the leadership of Saloth Sâr, or Pol Pot, as he was better known, the Khmer Rouge had defeated the US-backed government of Lon Nol, and now they had a plan for the country they called Democratic Kampuchea. This involved the evacuation of Phnom Penh and the creation of an ethnically and ideologically pure utopia that would ultimately enslave virtually the entire population. The genocide that followed would claim the lives of at least 1.5 million people out of a total population of 7 million.[1]

In his authoritative study of the Khmer Rouge, Ben Kiernan describes the ideology that drove the genocide as 'a unique ideological amalgam of communism and racism' (2008: x), an 'explosive combination of totalitarian political ambition with a racialist project of ethnic purification' (ibid.: xxx). Khmer Rouge ideology called for the abolition of markets, money and religion, as well as the evacuation of all towns. Markets and money implied the existence of private property but under the Khmer Rouge there was to be no private property and, for that matter, no private life. Even eating had to be done communally. There were to be no schools, no hospitals and no contact with the outside world. On pain of death, people had to work for the state without payment. In a biography of Pol Pot, Philip Short argues that the Cambodian leader's aim was to make the country a 'paragon of communist virtue' (2004: 288). This was to be communism 'without compromise or concessions' (ibid.: 9), even if this meant treating the population like slaves.

DOI: 10.4324/9780429325472-2

Like actual slaves, the inhabitants of Democratic Kampuchea 'were deprived of all control over their own destinies – unable to decide what to eat, when to sleep, where to live or even whom to marry' (ibid.: 291). Such was Pol Pot's pursuit of ideological purity that even Mao Zedong, who was no ideological shrinking violet, thought that he was trying to go too far too fast.[2]

It is hard to find a more compelling example of an extremist ideology than that of the Khmer Rouge. One sense in which it was extremist is that it advocated the use of extreme methods, including genocide, in pursuit of its political objectives. It was also extremist in an ideological sense. If ideologies are viewed as occupying positions in ideological space, then an ideology counts as extremist because of where it is in ideological space. On this 'positional' account, Khmer Rouge ideology was extremist because it was on the extreme *left* of ideological space, just as fascism is on the extreme right. This chapter is about ideological extremism and the notion of an 'ideological space' in which ideologies are located. A key question is whether it is helpful to think of ideologies in general, and extremist ideologies in particular, in these terms. As will quickly become apparent, the answer to this question is far from obvious.

In physical geography there is a distinction between absolute and relative location. To say that San Francisco is west of New York is to make a point about the relative locations of the two cities. Now consider the location of a third city, say, Topeka. Relative to New York, it is to the west. Relative to San Francisco, it is to the east. These ways of specifying the location of Topeka are equally valid but in absolute terms, Topeka is neither to the east or the west. It is only east or west relative to somewhere else. However, it also has an absolute or objective location in the following sense: it has a longitude and latitude that together determine its location without reference to any other city. However, even at this level, there is an element of relativity since a city's latitude and longitude only determine its location relative to the Equator and the prime meridian.

Is the location of an ideology in ideological space relative or absolute? When an ideology is described as extremist, is this simply a comment about its position relative to some other ideological point of reference or is it a comment about its absolute or 'objective' location? In what sense could ideologies have an absolute location? Starting with relativism, one way to be an ideological relativist is to be an *egocentric* relativist. The egocentric relativist regards his or her own ideology as being at the centre of ideological space and defines extremist ideologies as ones that are well to the left or well to the right of his or her own stance.[3] This account will especially appeal to those who think of themselves as 'middle of the road'. They will assume that any ideology that is a long way from the middle of the road *must* be extremist. A more familiar version of ideological relativism says that what makes an ideology extremist in the positional sense is its position relative to other ideologies. However, unlike the egocentric relativist, a relativist of the latter type does not think that ideological space is egocentric and does not see his or her own ideology as having any special significance in determining which other ideologies are extremist. This is the form of relativism that will be our concern here.

Although ideological relativism does have its attractions, it faces several challenges. One is to explain the sense in which one ideology is 'well to the left' or 'well to the right' of another. In what sense is one ideology 'further' to the left than another? What is this notion of ideological distance and how is it measured? This is the point at which the supposed analogy between ideological and physical space breaks down, since only the latter can literally be measured. The Khmer Rouge also brings another concern about relativism into focus. The concern is that there isn't anything relative about its extremism. Its ideology is absolutely extremist, not just extremist relative to something else. However, an absolutist who says this still needs to explain the notion of an 'absolute' ideological location. What, one might ask, is the ideological equivalent of longitude and latitude?

One thing an absolutist might argue in response to these concerns is that, like physical space, ideological space has *dimensions*. One is the familiar left-right dimension. If there is what Andrew Heywood describes as a 'linear political spectrum that travels from left wing to right wing' (2017: 15), then an ideology's absolute location will be given by its location on this spectrum. However, this only raises a further question: how is an ideology's location on the left-right spectrum determined? Furthermore, there are extremist ideologies that are hard to place on the left-right spectrum. Examples of such ideologies will be given below. If they are neither on the left nor on the right, then in what sense are they *positionally* extremist? This might lead to the suggestion that ideological space has other dimensions, and that an ideology can be extremist on one dimension without being extremist on another. It remains to be seen what these other dimensions might be, but it would be peculiar for someone who is trying to make the case that extremism is an absolute matter to concede in the next breath that an ideology that is extreme on one dimension might not be extremist on another. Does this not amount to the admission that ideological extremism is relative after all, that is, relative to a dimension?

The discussion so far has raised many questions but given few answers. The rest of this chapter will answer these questions. On the issue of relativism versus absolutism, the approach to be defended here is neither straightforwardly absolutist nor straightforwardly relativist. Instead, an attempt will be made to steer a middle course. For each dimension of ideological space, an ideology's location along that dimension is determined not by a direct comparison with other ideologies but by how it answers a menu of diagnostic questions. This will be referred to as the Menu Conception of ideological location. In these terms, whether the Khmer Rouge is on the extreme left of the left-right spectrum ultimately depends not on its stance relative to other ideologies but on how it answers the questions on the relevant menu. Yet an element of relativity remains: there is relativity to a dimension (assuming there is more than one) and, of course, relativity to the menu. If, as is surely the case, there is more than one reasonable conception of the questions that are relevant to determining whether one is on the left or the right, then an ideology that is on the left relative to one set of questions might be on the right relative to another. This suggests that a good place to start is with the notions of left and right.

Left and right

In Chapter 1, an ideology was characterized as an interrelated set of beliefs, concepts, attitudes, and psychological dispositions that provide a way for people to make sense of the world. It was also suggested that an ideology in this broad sense is something that everyone has. It is not true, however, that everyone has a well-defined *political* ideology, such as fascism or communism. How, then, is the idea of ideology being understood by the positional approach to extremism? Geuss refers to the ideologies that everyone has as ideologies in the *descriptive* sense. Every human group has an ideology in this sense because 'the agents of any group will have some psychological dispositions, use some concepts, and have some beliefs' (1981: 5). A political ideology like fascism and communism is more specific. It is a political version of what Geuss calls 'world-view'.

World-views deal with central issues of human life. Political ideologies deal with the central political issues of human life. As Heywood puts it, a political ideology is 'a more or less coherent set of ideas that provides the basis for organized political action, whether this is intended to preserve, modify, or overthrow the existing system of power' (2017: 10). Accordingly, every ideology will offer an account of the existing order, advance a model of a desired future, and explain how political change is to come about. Taken together, these three components constitute the ideology's 'world-view'. In that case, in what sense is an ideology 'extremist'? One might say that extremist ideologies have, or promote, extremist world-views but what is an extremist world-view?

To answer this question, consider again the notion that ideologies are arrayed from left to right in ideological space. Where does this notion come from? For that matter, where do the ideas of 'left' and 'right' in the political sense come from? Why is conservatism on the 'right' and socialism on the 'left'? This terminology goes back to the French Revolution. In *A Place of Greater Safety*, Hilary Mantel describes the seating arrangements in the French National Assembly when it moved into a former indoor riding school in Paris a few months after the storming of the Bastille:

> Members faced each other across a gangway. One side of the room was broken by the President's seat and the secretaries' table, the other by the speaker's rostrum. The strict upholders of royal power sat on the right of the gangway; the patriots, as they often called themselves, sat on the left.
>
> (2010: 267)

Today it is of course possible to be on the right without being a royalist. Instead 'right-wing' has come to signify an acceptance of the inevitability or even the desirability of inequality, a commitment to the status quo, and, in the economic sphere, to free markets and private property.[4] Since these are among the defining commitments of conservatism, it follows that conservatism is a right-wing ideology. In contrast, 'left-wing' signifies, among other things, a negative view of inequality, a commitment to change, and support for state intervention in the economic realm.[5] Socialism counts as a left-wing ideology because these are among its core commitments. Presumably, conservatism would now be described as left-wing and socialism as right-wing had the seating arrangements in a Parisian riding school been different.

Once we accept the idea of a left-right spectrum on which ideologies are located, it becomes hard not to think of *extremist* ideologies as ones that are either on the *extreme* left or the *extreme* right. In other words, extremist ideologies are located at one or other end of ideological space, just as a seat can be at either end of a row of seats rather than the middle. Furthermore, if the *only* ordering of ideologies in ideological space runs from left to right then the *only* two ways for an ideology to be extreme are for it to be on the extreme left or on the extreme right. 'Centrist' ideologies that steer a middle course between the two extremes are, by definition, not extremist. There is no such thing as 'extremist centrism' if an ideology's extremism is determined by its distance from the centre. Ideological extremism, it seems, is a strictly positional matter.

What determines where a given ideology sits on the left-right spectrum? Consider the idea that ideologies are world-views that include a vision of the desired future. Each vision of the future raises a series of questions, and the location of an ideology in ideological space is determined by how it answers these questions. For example, is ideology X's vision of the future one in which there is still private property? If X favours the total abolition of private property in favour of state ownership of everything, then X is not just on the left but on the extreme left. If X envisages unrestricted private ownership with a minimal role for the state, then X is not just on the right but on the extreme right in this respect. Many ideologies avoid such extremes. The post-war British Labour Party favoured state ownership of public utilities but did not favour the abolition of private property. An ideology that allows both private and state ownership is, by definition, less 'extreme' than one that favours one to the exclusion of the other. A model of ideological space that places the Khmer Rouge on the extreme left and the Labour Party closer to the centre is more accurate than one that places the Khmer Rouge at the centre and Labour on the extreme right. If Pol Pot had argued that the Labour Party was extremist because it was so far to the right of the Khmer Rouge or, what comes to the same thing, so far to the right of his own ideology, he would have been wrong. It is not in *this* sense that ideological location is relative, and any notion that the Khmer Rouge's ideology was only extremist relative to other ideologies should be rejected. There is, in this sense, an element of objectivity to questions of ideological location.

Nationalism is another core issue with respect to which there is a non-arbitrary middle position. At one extreme is the ultra-nationalism of various twentieth-century fascist movements.[6] At the other extreme are forms of internationalism that deplore all national or patriotic sentiment. In between are mildly nationalistic ideologies that reject ultra-nationalism but do not regard patriotism as the last refuge of the scoundrel. Again, there is a sound and obvious rationale for regarding this type of nationalism as closer to the centre of ideological space than ultra-nationalism. The hard question here is not whether ultra-nationalism is a form of extremism but whether it belongs on the left or the right. If it belongs on the right, then that raises a question about the location of ideologies that combine nationalism with a left-wing stance on other issues. There is more on this below.

To sum up, the Menu Conception of ideological location says that the location of an ideology at a specific point on the left-right spectrum is determined by its response to a menu of diagnostic questions. These include questions about the size and role of the state, private property, freedom, human rights, democracy, justice, equality, nationalism, and free speech. The answers that a given ideology provides to these questions determine whether it is on the left or the right. They also determine how *far* to the left or right it is located. This is because, with respect to each item on the menu, an ideology can adopt a more or less extreme position. Left-wing extremism adopts an extreme left-wing position on the core issues. Right-wing extremism adopts an extreme right-wing position on these issues.

How does the Menu Conception measure ideological distance? On what basis can one ideology be described as 'further' to the left or right than another? The examples of the Khmer Rouge and the British Labour Party point to a range of possible metrics, some of which are quantitative while others are qualitative. Take the case of state ownership. Both parties are in favour to some extent, but the Khmer Rouge wanted much *more* of it than the Labour Party ever has. If being in favour of state ownership places an ideology on the left, then being in favour of *more* state ownership places an ideology further to the left. This is a quantitative measure of ideological distance. A qualitative measure is, to put it crudely, not how much of something one wants but how badly one wants it. The Khmer Rouge was unequivocal in its commitment to state ownership, much more so than the Labour Party. In this qualitative sense, it is more extreme than the Labour Party. One's position in ideological space is fixed not only by the *nature* or *content* of one's commitments but also by their *quality* or *mode*.

One thing that this view of ideological distance brings out is the futility of insisting on a sharp distinction between ideological and psychological extremism. Part of what placed Khmer Rouge ideology so far to the left was the extent to which its ideological commitments were 'unequivocal', but what exactly does this mean? What type of measure of ideological distance is equivocality? Unequivocal commitments are firm and unambiguous. Strictly speaking, however, it is not ideologies that are firm. Firmness is a psychological property of the person whose ideology it is. Firm commitments tend to be uncompromising but being uncompromising is also a psychological property of ideologues rather than of ideologies. It follows that if an ideology counts as being further to the left on account of being unequivocal in its commitments, then this measure of ideological distance is psychological. At this level, there is no neat dividing line between the psychological and the positional, or between the ideology and the people whose ideology it is. The ideology is shaped by its adherents, by how they regard it, understand it, and put it into practice.

There is one final feature of Khmer Rouge ideology that is worth highlighting for what it reveals about ideological distance. That ideology was above all a *totalizing* ideology. It had an extremist position on a wide range of issues, including ones that would not normally be regarded as political. An example is the Khmer Rouge's insistence on communal eating. Its ideological extremism might therefore be described as *broad*. It is also possible to imagine narrower forms of ideological extremism, that is, ideologies that are silent on many questions but that give extremist responses to the questions that they do choose to address. Other things being equal, totalizing ideologies are more extreme than non-totalizing ideologies, and broad ideological extremism is more extreme than narrow ideological extremism. However, other things might not be equal. Suppose that X and Y are both extremist ideologies but only X is totalizing. However, Y gives more extreme answers to the smaller range of questions it addresses than X gives to a much wider range of questions. Overall, which of X and Y is the more extreme? The answer to this question might not be clear. One might take the view that the mere fact that an ideology chooses to comment on how people should eat is an extremist feature of that ideology, regardless of what it in particular says about how people should eat. In ideological matters, moderation partly consists in not having a position about every aspect of human life, however mundane.

Where does this leave the debate between absolutism and relativism? The lesson of the discussion so far is that there is little to be said for egocentric relativism. An ideology is not extremist by virtue of being well to the left or right of *my* ideological stance. If, contrary to what I believe, I am well to the right, then ideologies that are well to the left of mine might in fact be in the middle of the left-right spectrum and so not positionally extremist.

The actual location of an ideology on this spectrum is determined by its actual answers to the questions on the menu, and these answers determine its location without reference to any other ideology. The only relativity that remains is relativity to the menu. Hence, the role of the menu is some-what analogous to the role of latitude and longitude in the determination of geographical location. The menu is the point of reference for ideological location in the way that the Equator and the prime meridian are points of reference for geographical location. If this is really relativism, it is relativism of the most benign kind, one that is consistent with the intuition that the Khmer Rouge's extremism was, in an important sense, absolute rather than relative.

Unfortunately, the discussion cannot end here, since there are still a number of major unanswered questions. Once these questions are identified and addressed, a more substantive relativism starts to look like a serious option. Although the three main questions are closely related, it will be helpful to list them separately:

1. Where do the diagnostic questions on the menu come from, and how are disputes about these questions to be settled? In geography, there are no arguments about the location of the Equator or its relevance for determining the location of places but in the ideological sphere there *are* arguments about the questions that are relevant for placing an ideology on the left or right.
2. How should we classify ideologies that give ideologically inconsistent answers to questions on an agreed menu? Answers to two questions are ideologically inconsistent if one places the ideology in question on the left or extreme left while the other places the ideology on the right or extreme right. What happens in these cases? Where on the left-right spectrum does the ideology go?
3. What should we make of intuitively extremist ideologies that are neither left-wing nor right-wing? In what sense can they be ideologically extremist if the concepts of left and right simply do not apply to them? How is it possible for these concepts not to apply to something that is recognizable as an ideology?

The next section will address these questions in turn and show how they might prompt more substantive concessions to relativism than we have made so far.

The truth in relativism

Some of the ideological commitments of the left and right have already been noted. In his *Dictionary of Political Thought*, Roger Scruton argues that while terms like 'right' and 'left' are 'without precise meaning', each of them is used to suggest some combination of views, 'no one of which is necessary and each of which admits of degrees' (2007: 385). This is Scruton's list of the views associated with the term 'left':

   (i) Hostility to private property.
  (ii) Hostility towards classes judged to be favoured by the political system.
 (iii) Hostility towards the establishment in all its forms.
 (iv) Desire for a classless society.
  (v) Belief in democracy or at least in government by consent.
 (vi) Belief in certain natural or human rights.
(vii) Belief in progress, to be furthered by revolution or reform.
(viii) Egalitarian leanings.
 (ix) Anti-nationalist tendencies.
  (x) Belief in a welfare state.

This list can be used to generate a menu of diagnostic questions for determining whether a given ideology is left-wing and, if so, how far to the left. For example, corresponding to (i) is the question: is the ideology under discussion hostile to private property? The greater the hostility, the further to the left the ideology, at least on this issue.

Where does Scruton's list come from? What is the justification for including one item while excluding another? The justification is partly historical. Since the French Revolution, the left has generally been defined by its commitment to the various items on Scruton's menu. 'Left-wing' is not a natural kind and has no ahistorical essence. What it means to be 'on the left' is what history tells us it means, and the main difference between left-wing ideologies is in their degree of enthusiasm for the various items on Scruton's menu. Beyond that, the only other relevant factor is how terms like 'left' and 'right' are used today. Meaning, as Wittgenstein noted, is use,[7] and the meaning of 'left-wing' is given by its past and present use in specialist and non-specialist discourse.

According to Scruton, 'the right' signifies 'several connected and also conflicting ideas' (2007: 601). These include conservative or authoritarian doctrines concerning the nature of civil society, theories of political obligation framed in terms of obedience, piety and legitimacy, reluctance to countenance too great a divorce between law and morality, cultural conservatism, respect for the hereditary principle, belief in private property, a belief in the value of the individual as against the collective, belief in free enterprise, and varying degrees of belief in human imperfectability. Whatever the merits of this account of 'the right', it is not an adequate basis for understanding the sense in which some ideologies are not just on the right but on the *extreme* or *far* right. The extreme right today has ties to white supremacism and is defined more by its views on race than the issues highlighted by Scruton.

On this point, recent work by Cynthia Miller-Idriss is much closer to the mark. On her account, the far right is defined not just by its anti-government and anti-democratic ideals and practices but also by its exclusionary beliefs, conspiracy theories and apocalyptic fantasies.[8] Its key goals are 'the establishment of white ethno-states, the re-migration and deportation of non-whites or non-Europeans, and the reduction of rights for ethnic minorities' (Miller-Idriss 2020: 5). For Miller-Idriss, 'all far-right ideological beliefs share exclusionary, hierarchical, and dehumanizing ideals that seek to preserve the superiority and dominance of some groups over others' (ibid.: 8). The far right embeds its dehumanizing ideologies 'within a framework of existential threat to the dominant group' (ibid.: 9), namely, white men. Modern far-right ideologies promote the so-called 'Great Replacement' conspiracy theory, according to which global elites are conspiring to bring about the replacement of white Christians by non-white Muslims. Some on the far right believe that 'the only way to prevent this process is through an apocalyptic race war, which will result in the rebirth of a new world order and restored white civilization' (ibid.: 13).

The differences between Scruton and Miller-Idriss bring out the fluidity of terms like 'left' and 'right'. Political ideologies are, as Heywood notes, capable of 'almost constant re-invention'. This means that our notions of left and right must be 'regularly updated' (2017: 16). Scruton's is a 'classical' account of 'left' and 'right', and the corresponding diagnostic questions make no mention of issues that, at least in present-day America, are regarded as fundamental to determining whether an ideology is on the left or liberal side of the left-right divide or on the right or conservative side. For example, according to a typology published by the Pew Research Center in 2017, being a liberal or conservative in the American sense depends on one's attitude towards social issues such race, homosexuality, and environmental regulation.[9] Key diagnostic questions in this context include whether homosexuality should be accepted, whether racial discrimination is 'the main reason why black people can't get ahead these days', and whether stricter environmental laws are worth the cost. Indeed, there is remarkably little overlap between the Pew Research Center's list of diagnostic questions and what a person influenced by Scruton's typology might regard as the key issues.

Despite this, it would be wrong to conclude that one of the typologies must be objectively better than the other. Each can be justified by how left and right are understood in specific contexts, and both are consistent with the dictum that meaning is use. The Pew Research Center's list captures how the notions of liberal and conservative are interpreted in one historical and cultural context while Scruton's list is faithful to how the notions of left and right are used and understood in a different historical and cultural context. In principle, this opens up the possibility of what might be called the *menu-relativity* of extremism. Measured by its response to one menu of diagnostic questions, a given ideology might be on the extreme left or right. Going by its responses to a different set of diagnostic questions, the same ideology might end up in a different spot on the left-right spectrum.

Notice that the issue here is not whether the left-right dimension is the only dimension of ideological space but whether, even along this dimension, ideologies have an absolute location. The location of an ideology at a specific point on the left-right spectrum is indeed determined by its response to a menu of diagnostic questions but the multiplicity of menus is a problem for any attempt to represent an ideology's location on the left-right spectrum as an absolute matter. It cannot be an absolute matter if there is more than one left-right spectrum. It might be that, in practice, an ideology that is on the left, according to Scruton, is unlikely to be on the right, according to the Pew Research Center. However, this is not guaranteed. There is no *essential* connection between an ideology's attitude to private property and its attitude towards, say, homosexuality.

Another way to make the point that our notions of left and right must be regularly updated is to think about the so-called 'Overton Window'.[10] The Overton Window, named after Joseph Overton, a vice-president of a US think tank, is the idea that at any given time there is a set of ideas and policies that are widely accepted throughout society. Politicians who propose policies that are well outside the window risk defeat for being too radical.

However, the window can shift over time for a variety of reasons, including the slow evolution of societal values and the actions of lobbyists and politicians. For example, the idea of female suffrage was outside the Overton Window at one time. Today, this idea is squarely within the window and opposition to female suffrage is a fringe position. By the same token, ideas that would once have been regarded as well to the left of the window – for example, the idea of free universal healthcare – are inside the window in the UK today, though not in the US. Although shifts in the Overton Window are usually gradual, rapid shifts can also happen, for example, because of 'the mainstreaming of extremism', that is, 'the process through which previously extreme ideas become normalized as part of the acceptable spectrum of beliefs within democratic societies' (Miller-Idriss 2020: 46).

This might seem to point to another sense in which ideological location is relative in relation to the left-right dimension. Ideas or ideologies that are well to the left of the Overton Window at a given time might be in the middle of the window at a later time. However, it is important not to exaggerate the significance of shifts in the Overton Window. To say that the window has shifted is to say that ideas that were once *seen* as well to the left or the right of the window might be *seen* as centrist. It does not follow that these ideas are *actually* centrist after the window has moved. In Nazi Germany, extremist ideas and policies that once would have been beyond the pale became widely accepted. In other words, there was a significant shift in the Overton Window but that does not alter the fact that these ideas were *actually* on the extreme right of ideological space according to the Menu Conception of ideological location. What the Nazis did was to make the previously unthinkable thinkable, and this is a classic extremist tactic. There is more on this tactic in Chapter 7.

The next question concerns the proper classification of political ideologies that give ideologically inconsistent answers to questions on a *single* agreed menu. This issue is brought into focus by the Khmer Rouge's stance on a Scruton-inspired menu of diagnostic questions. On many of these questions, the Khmer Rouge is not just on the left but on the extreme left. Yet on the issue of nationalism, the Khmer Rouge was far from being on the 'left' in Scruton's sense. Not only did it *not* display anti-nationalist tendencies, it was rabidly nationalistic and racist. These are respects in which it was not on the left at all, and so not on the extreme left, any more than it was on the extreme right. Yet its ideology was extremist. So, it is false that the only way for an ideology to be extremist is for it to be on the extreme left or the extreme right. In the real world, people's ideological commitments are rarely neat and tidy. As in the case of the Khmer Rouge, they tend to be a hodgepodge. In such cases, it is often misleading to think in terms of left and right.

This brings us to the third of the three questions raised at the end of the last section: What should we make of intuitively extremist ideologies that are neither clearly left-wing nor clearly right-wing? In what sense are they ideologically extremist? A controversial example of this possibility is an ideology that, unlike the Khmer Rouge's ultra-communism, is still influential today. The name of that ideology is fascism. Only a passing acquaintance with this ideology is needed to recognize that placing it on the extreme right of the left-right spectrum is not straightforward. Its location on this spectrum is far from clear and, for what it is worth, prominent twentieth-century fascists have insisted that they made the distinction between left and right obsolete. *If* they are right about this, then it is not by being on the far right that fascism qualifies as an extremist ideology.

Accounts of fascism might take the form of the search for the 'fascist minimum', a set of core doctrines that constitute its underlying essence. Confusingly, there are almost as many accounts of the fascist minimum as there are scholars of fascism. In his influential discussion, Roger Eatwell argues that the fascist minimum has four key elements: (1) nationalism (the belief that the world is divided into nations); (2) holism (the insistence that the collective predominates over individual rights and interests); (3) radicalism (a rejection of the existing society and the power of establishment groups); and (4) a commitment to the so-called 'Third Way' (hostility to both capitalism and socialism combined with a willingness to draw on aspects of both).[11] The idea that the collective predominates over individual rights and interests is usually associated with ideologies on the left rather than on the right. Its radicalism is another feature that makes it problematic to place fascism on the right, especially when it takes the form of hostility to the established order. As for its hostility to both capitalism and socialism, this is the single most persuasive argument in favour of the conclusion that it is difficult to place fascism on the left-right ideological map.

One response to these concerns about the location of fascism in ideological space would be to argue that, as fascism scholar Robert O. Paxton puts it, 'what fascists *did* tells us at least as much as what they said' (2004: 10). When fascists are in power, they rarely carry out their anti-capitalist threats. Instead, they attack the left, ban strikes and cut wages. In each of these respects, fascism *in practice* has always been on the right. Further-more, fascists are not just nationalists, they are ultra-nationalists and, in many cases, ethnonationalists who promote the interests of a particular eth-nic group which they regard as superior to all others. Their ethnonationalism is indistinguishable from the dehumanizing ethnonationalism of the twenty-first-century far right groups described by Miller-Idriss. These groups are the true heirs to twentieth-century fascism, and they can hardly be described as seeking a middle way between left and right, socialism and capitalism. However, even if fascism's commitment to the Third Way is, at least to some extent, fraudulent, this does not refute the notion that there are extremist ideologies that are difficult to place on the left-right ideological spectrum.

None of this invalidates the idea of a left-right ideological spectrum. There could be such a spectrum, even if it is not clear where on the spec-trum fascism belongs. The same goes for other ambiguous ideologies, if any. However, there is still the question of what the extremism of such ideolo-gies consists in, if it is not a matter of their being on the extreme left or the extreme right. The obvious and basically correct answer to this question is to insist that ideological space has more than one dimension, and that the positional extremism of fascism can only be properly understood by reference to where it is on a dimension *other* than the left-right dimension. It remains to be seen what these other dimensions might be but the fact that ideological space is multi-dimensional brings out another truth in rel-ativism: extremism is not just menu-relative but also *dimension-relative*. In other words, it is possible in principle that an ideology that is neither on the extreme left nor the extreme right is still extremist on another dimension. Equally, an ideology that is not extremist relative to that other dimension might come out as extremist on the left-right dimension. The next challenge, therefore, is to identify other relevant dimensions of ideological space and show how ideologies that seem ambiguous when viewed in terms of left and right are unambiguously extremist along at least one other dimension.

A spectrum of spectrums

Instead of thinking of ideologies in terms of left and right, there is also the option of sorting them according to their views regarding violence in poli-tics: extremist ideologies are in favour of violence in a way that other ideol-ogies are not. This points to the possibility of a *Pro-Violence spectrum*, with fascism coming out as extremist because of where it stands on this spectrum. There is also the *Authoritarianism spectrum*, which sorts ideologies on the basis of their actual or supposed authoritarian tendencies. This is the classic argument for lumping fascism together with communism: because they are both authoritarian in outlook, they are at the extreme end of the Authoritarianism spectrum. From this perspective the key contrast is not between fascism and communism but between authoritarian and anti-authoritarian ideologies.

Questions about how to understand the notion of violence will be addressed in Chapter 3. For the moment, the more pressing question is: what does it mean to be 'Pro-Violence'? On a minimal reading, an ideology is Pro-Violence just if it views violence as justified in some circumstances as a means to an end. This type of justification is *instrumental*. However, most ideologies, and most people, would agree that violence is justified in *some* circumstances. Ideologies that are higher up the Pro-Violence spectrum can be differentiated from those that are lower down by their responses to the following questions:

1. What are the *circumstances* in which violence is justified?
2. What are the *ends* in pursuit of which violence is potentially justified?
3. What is the nature of the *violence* that is potentially justified?

Relative to this menu, the 'high' end of the Pro-Violence spectrum is occupied by ideologies that see violence as justified in a wide range of circumstances and for a wide range of ends. However, the most extreme form of Pro-Violence does not confine itself to thinking of violence as instrumentally justified. This version of extremism sees violence, including extreme violence, as *non-instrumentally* justified in some situations, and not just as a means to an end. At the opposite, lowest end of the Pro-Violence spectrum are ideologies that view violence as, in virtually all circumstances, neither instrumentally nor non-instrumentally justified. There is a familiar label for this view: pacifism.

It seems odd, on the face of it, to classify pacifism as a form of extremism. However, if Pro-Violence is a spectrum, and extremism is a function of proximity to *either* end of a spectrum, then pacifism must be classified as a form of extremism. Resistance to this idea is explained by the intuition that extremism and enthusiasm for political violence go hand in hand. If only positions at *one* end of the Pro-Violence spectrum – the high end – are extremist, then this would represent a structural difference between this spectrum and the more familiar left-right spectrum. In the latter case, there is no suggestion that positions at one end are more or less extremist than positions at the other. On the other hand, the idea that violence is never justified, even in self-defence, is arguably *extreme*, even if one is reluctant to describe those who endorse it as extrem*ists*. A way to overcome this reluctance is to accept that extremism can take benign forms.

Going back to the first question on the Pro-Violence menu, the 'moderate' position is that violence is only ever justified as a last resort, when there is no practical alternative. In other words, violence is not just a means to an end. For it to be justified, it must be the *only* remaining option to attain a desirable end after all other means have been exhausted. A more extreme view is that violence can be legitimate even if it is not strictly the last resort and there are alternative pathways to one's objective. Violence may be preferable on account of the speed with which it delivers results when compared with non-violent alternatives. This is a potentially serious consideration when violence is a response to suffering or oppression. A further consideration is that it is often impossible to tell whether violence is the last resort. As Michael Walzer notes, 'it is not so easy to reach the "last resort"' (2004b: 53) and it is by no means clear when all other options have been exhausted. For Walzer, this is part of an argument for the moral impermissibility of terrorism. The Pro-Violence extremist draws a different conclusion: if the last resort has what Walzer calls 'only a notional finality' (ibid.: 54), then it is better to accept that violence is always elective and be prepared to defend it on that basis.

Regarding the ends of violence, the minimal view is that self-defence is the only legitimate end of violence. Positions higher up the Pro-Violence spectrum endorse violence for a wider range of objectives, including the promotion of one's economic and strategic interests. Thus, the American 'neo-cons' who endorsed violence as a means of bringing about regime change in Iraq in the early 2000s thereby placed themselves at the higher end of the Pro-Violence spectrum, given that their primary objective was to advance US strategic and economic interests in the Middle East. Furthermore, a full-scale military invasion of Iraq was not the only viable means of overthrowing the Saddam Hussain regime. Economic sanctions were already in force and might have delivered the same result, albeit more slowly. Neocon violence against Iraq was elective violence.

Positions higher up the Pro-Violence scale also have a much broader conception of what counts as 'self-defence' than positions lower down the scale. For example, Pro-Violence extremists count the use of violence in defence of one's culture or 'in-group' as a legitimate form of self-defence. A less dubious example of defensive violence is anti-colonial violence. According to Frantz Fanon, colonialism is 'violence in a natural state, and it will only yield when confronted with greater violence' (2001: 48). He even describes anti-colonial violence as a 'cleansing force' (ibid.: 74), although he was well aware of its dangers. Even if anti-colonial violence is defensive, it can take more or less extreme forms. This brings us to the third item on the Pro-Violence menu: what is the nature of the violence that can be justified in pursuit of worthy ends?

While it is easy to see that violence can take more or less extreme forms, it is not easy to explain the distinction between more and less extreme violence. The Jordanian air force pilot who was locked in a cage by ISIS and then set alight was the victim of extreme violence in a qualitative sense, that is, as measured by the pain and unpleasantness of such a fate. By this measure, is setting fire to a person in a cage a more or less extreme form of violence than, say, beheading or electrocuting them? This question is hard to answer, but it adds to the sense of a person as having been subjected to extreme violence when, as in the case of the pilot, their grisly demise is turned into a public spectacle. The most extreme forms of violence are the most revolting and sadistic, but what is viewed as revolting and sadistic in one context might be viewed differently in a different historical context. The guillotining of aristocrats after the French Revolution was not seen as revolting or sadistic but the use of the same method of execution today would be beyond the pale.

A quantitative measure of extreme violence is the number of people against whom it is directed. The Norwegian mass murderer Anders Breivik's violence against his victims was extreme not because of his method of killing them but because of the sheer number of people he killed – 77 – within the space of a few hours. On this basis, the most extreme violence is violence that is extreme in both quantitative and qualitative terms. A further consideration is the extent to which the violence at issue is indiscriminate. Indiscriminate violence might be deemed more extreme than targeted violence but much depends on the nature of those against whom the violence is targeted. Justifiably or not, violence against civilians or non-combatants is regarded as more extreme than similar violence against combatants.

On this basis, an example of extreme violence on *all* counts was the Allied bombing of German cities during the Second World War.[12] It involved the relentless bombing from the air of residential areas of German cities in order to demoralize the population. The killing was indiscriminate and on a large scale. The targets were civilians and the *de facto* method of killing was incineration. On all measures this was extreme violence, and illustrates something important: the perpetrators of the most extreme forms of violence tend to be states rather than sub-state actors. Positions at the low end of the Pro-Violence spectrum will view the bombing of German cities as criminal. Positions at the higher end are likely to take a different view. From this perspective, even extreme violence might be justifiable in a so-called 'supreme emergency', that is, 'when our deepest values and our collective survival are in imminent danger' (Walzer 2004a: 33).[13]

Whether or not fascism is on the extreme right of ideological space, it is extremist on the Pro-Violence spectrum. The same goes for the ideology of ISIS. Both ideologies glorify violence to the extent of almost seeing it as an end in itself. In the words of one expert, fascism 'not only promotes violence but relishes it, viscerally so' (Griffiths 2017). Relatedly, Paxton draws attention to the way that fascism regards violence as 'redemptive' (2004: 218) and even beautiful (ibid.: 218). For fascist and ISIS ideologues, violence is a first rather than a last resort, and the legitimate use of violence is not confined to self-defence. Both kinds of Pro-Violence extremist see violence, or the threat of violence, as ways of imposing their views and priorities on the politically or theologically recalcitrant. Fascist and Nazi violence in the 1930s and 1940s was certainly extreme and ISIS takes pride in its savagery.

The authoritarianism spectrum can be dealt with more briefly. Cas Mudde defines authoritarianism as 'the belief in a strictly ordered society, in which infringements on authority are to be punished severely' (2019: 29). Authoritarian political systems are ones in which the legitimate exercise of authority is not seen as requiring either the explicit or the tacit consent of those over whom it is exercised. Authoritarian regimes rule by compulsion and fear. Individuals, political parties and governments can be more or less authoritarian in outlook and practice. Authoritarianism is a matter of degree, and this opens up the possibility of an authoritarianism spectrum on which individuals, political parties and governments can be placed, depending on their ideas and their behaviour. In these terms, ideologies that are not on the extreme left or right of the left-right spectrum, or that are hard to classify in terms of left and right, can still be classified as extremist on account of their authoritarian tendencies. The belief in a strictly ordered society in which infringements of authority are to be punished severely is as much a part of fascist ideology as it is of the ideologies of ISIS and, indeed, the Khmer Rouge.

If being at the high end of the authoritarian spectrum is a way for an ideology to be extremist, are ideologies at the other end of this spectrum also extremist? The other end of the authoritarianism spectrum is occupied by ideologies that are staunchly anti-authoritarian. Anarchism is one such ideology. In his classic *In Defense of Anarchism*, Robert P. Wolff fails to find any theoretical justification for the authority of the state and concludes that there is no justification. This is the crux of *philosophical* anarchism. The problem is that the authority of the state cannot be reconciled with the moral autonomy of the individual. Since the latter is non-negotiable, the only remaining option is to 'embrace philosophical anarchism and treat *all* governments as non-legitimate bodies whose commands must be judged and evaluated in each instance before they are obeyed' (Wolff 1998: 71). Is this 'extremism'? The resistance to calling anarchists extremists is similar to, though possibly not as strong as, the resistance to calling pacifists extremists. Yet on the spectrum of possible views of the authority of the state, it can hardly be denied that philosophical anarchism is an *extreme* position, that is, an outlier. It is, in this sense, a form of extremism, albeit a relatively benign form.

The position at which we have arrived is the following: ideological space has turned out to be multi-dimensional, and it is therefore not true that the only way to be an extremist is to be on the extreme left or right of the left-right spectrum. In addition, positions that are not extremist on one dimension might be extremist on another. This is the dimension-relativity of extremism, which is additional to its menu-relativity. Although only three dimensions have been identified here, there might be others. There is arguably no fixed number of dimensions since there is no fixed number of issues or concerns in relation to which it might be helpful to locate different ideologies. In the same way, there is no fixed set of questions by reference to which it might be illuminating to locate ideologies within a given dimension.

This is, in some ways, a messy account of ideological extremism, certainly far messier than the simple left-right conception with which we began. Is there any way to tidy things up so as to unify the different dimensions into a single overarching conception of the structure of ideological space? To ask the same question in a different way, is there a single theme on which the different dimensions of ideological space can be viewed as local variations? There is a suggestion along these lines in Scruton's account of extremism. He argues that extremism involves, among other things, 'taking a political idea to its limits' (2007: 237). Although Scruton himself does not use this label, this might be called a *limitationist* conception of extremism. On this conception, *all* forms of political extremism, regardless of their specifics, are distinguished by their penchant for taking political ideas to their limits.

There is something in this. Being on either end of the left-right dimension is certainly a matter of taking a political idea to its limits. The Khmer Rouge took the idea of communism to its limits. ISIS does the same thing with its core ideas, even if it is difficult to say whether these ideas are left-wing or right-wing. The authoritarianism spectrum can also be regarded in the same way. Anarchists take doubts about the legitimacy of the state to their limit, just as authoritarian ideologies take the notion of the authority of the state over the individual to its limit. The Pro-Violence spectrum is more of a challenge for limitationism. Being Pro-Violence is not a matter of taking the idea of *violence* to its limits, but there is a sense in which Pro-Violence ideologies take to the limit the idea that violence is a legitimate means of pursuing one's political objectives. The fewer the restrictions on the nature, targets and extent of what a given ideology sees as justified violence, the closer it comes to taking to the limit the idea of justified violence.

Among the attractions of a limitationist interpretation of ideological extremism, one is that it offers an answer to what would otherwise be a difficult question: what is it about ideological extremism that attracts? The attractions of ideological extremism can now be seen to include the attractions, such as they are, of taking an idea to its limits. Taking an idea to its limits means embracing it in its purest and most unadulterated form. This points to a link between limitationism and the purity preoccupation of the extremist mindset. There is more about this mindset and its purity preoccupation in Chapter 4. The link between limitationism and a preoccupation with purity is one more illustration of the futility of insisting on a sharp distinction between ideological and psychological extremism. The Khmer Rouge's ideological extremism was underpinned by its obsession with taking communism to its limits, and that obsession was in turn underpinned by its obsession with the purity of its ideology. This ideology, as well as extremist ideologies more generally, gives expression to an extremist mindset. There is more to be said about all of this, but before tackling the extremist mindset, there are further questions about the role of violence in political extremism that need to be addressed. This is the subject of Chapter 3.

Notes

1 The exact number of people who lost their lives in the Cambodian genocide is disputed. It is not disputed that it was a very large number.

2 According to Short, Mao urged the Khmer Rouge to 'abandon their early extremism' (2004: 299) at a meeting in 1975. Short claims that at the end of his long life Mao 'was lucid enough to realize that the new world the Cambodians dreamed of would prove to be a mirage' (ibid.: 300).

3 This is the ideological analogue of Gareth Evans' conception of egocentric space. As Evans puts it, 'the subject conceives of himself to be in the centre of a space (at its point of origin), with its co-ordinates given by the concepts "up" and "down", "left" and "right", and "in front" and "behind"' (1982: 153–4). This is egocentric space.

4 See below for more on the meaning of 'left-wing' and 'right-wing'.

5 See Scruton (2007: 384–5).

6 In the present century, fascist ultra-nationalism has morphed into extreme ethno-nationalism, defined as advocacy or support for the interests of a particular ethnic group. See Stern (2019: 57).

7 Wittgenstein (1978). Wittengenstein says in section 43 of the *Investigations* that 'the meaning of a word is its use in the language'.

8 Miller-Idriss (2020: 4).

9 Pew Research Center, 'Political typology reveals deep fissures on the right and left', 24 October 2017, available at: www.pewresearch.org/politics/2017/10/24/political-typology-reveals-deep-fissures-on-the-right-and-left/

10 See www.mackinac.org/OvertonWindow.

11 Eatwell (1996).

12 For an account, see Garrett (2004).

13 This is not to imply that the bombing of German cities in the last months of the Second World War can be justified on these grounds. The 'supreme emergency' defence was only applicable, if at all, when the outcome of the war was still in doubt.

3

Methods extremism

Extreme methods

In the spring of 1978, IRA prisoners at the Maze Prison near Belfast, began a 'no wash' protest against the brutality of their warders. It was not a pleasant experience. In his history of the IRA (the Irish Republican Army), Richard English describes the protest as follows:

> Fights began with prison officers over the emptying of chamber pots from the cells: their contents were thrown though spy-holes and windows, and the warders sometimes threw them back; the openings were then blocked, and so prisoners poured urine through any available cracks and put their excrement on the walls. The 'dirty protest' had begun.
>
> (2003: 191)

At issue was the status of IRA prisoners. Having previously been accorded special status in the prison system, IRA inmates found themselves categorized and treated as common criminals from 1976 onwards. Yet they saw themselves as prisoners of war and demanded recognition as political prisoners. In 1980 and again in 1981, they went on hunger strike in pursuit of political status. In the event, the 1981 strike transformed the fortunes of the IRA even though it ended in defeat for the strikers.

One of the hunger strikers was a young man called Bobby Sands. He refused food on 1 March 1981 and died on 5 May, his sixty-sixth day without food. He was one of ten prisoners who perished before the strike ended. Although the strike was eventually called off without its objectives having

DOI: 10.4324/9780429325472-3

been achieved, it proved a Pyrrhic victory for the British government. The strikers' sacrifice revitalized the republican movement and made Sands, who was elected to the British Parliament before he died, a hero from a republican perspective. English notes that the hunger strikers were 'essentially ordinary men, whose zealous conception of their struggle led them to extremity' (ibid.: 201). Prime Minister Margaret Thatcher conceded that it was possible to admire the courage of Sands and the other hunger-strikers who died, without sympathizing with their cause. Thatcher's grudging admiration of Sands makes an important point: while the use of extreme methods is often met with disapproval, especially by political moderates, there are circumstances in which the use of such methods is seen in a much more positive light.

In Chapter 1, 'methods extremists' were defined as individuals, organizations or groups that use extreme methods (however these are defined) in pursuit of their objectives. How, then, should 'extreme methods' be defined and understood? The usual assumption is that extreme methods are violent, and that a methods extremist is a *violent* extremist. The connection with ideological extremism is that extremists in the ideological sense are often Pro-Violence. The link with psychological extremism is that Pro-Violence is typically, though not invariably, an element of the extremist mindset. Yet the example of Bobby Sands shows that extreme methods need not be violent. Sands chose an extreme but arguably non-violent method of pressurizing the British government to restore the political status of republican prisoners.[1] Extreme in what sense? At least in the sense that starving oneself to death for a political cause is something that only very few people would ever dream of doing, or be capable of doing even if they wanted to. The dirty protest was another extreme but essentially non-violent method of making a political point. This is not to deny that the IRA was a violent group. It clearly was, and Sands was in jail for possession of a gun. Still, the fact remains that extreme methods do not have to be violent, and that methods extremists do not have to be violent.

Is it nevertheless the case that anyone who *does* use violence in pursuit of a political objective *is* a methods extremist? Regardless of whether extreme methods have to be violent, are violent methods necessarily extremist? This is a hard question, not least because the idea of violence is so difficult to pin down. The *Oxford English Dictionary* tells us that violence involves the exercise of physical force but what counts as physical force? In January 1969, Jan Palach set fire to himself in Prague as a protest against the Soviet invasion of

Czechoslovakia the previous year. Palach's death by fire was terrible but did he use physical force against himself? Is self-immolation an act of violence? Intuitions about this are likely to vary, though it has to be said that violence is usually assumed to be directed at other people and that Palach's patently extreme method of making his point was not violent in an other-directed sense.[2]

In his reflections on violence, Slavoj Žižek distinguishes between subjective, symbolic and systemic violence. The first is 'direct physical violence' (2009: 8). It is 'directly visible' and 'performed by a clearly identifiable agent' (ibid.: 1). Symbolic violence is linguistic. Thus, hate speech might be construed as symbolic violence. Finally, systemic violence is built into social relations of domination and exploitation. This violence is not attributable to concrete individuals but is 'purely "objective", systemic, anonymous' (ibid.: 11).[3] For present purposes, violence means what Žižek calls 'subjective' violence. It might be hard to define direct physical violence, but it is not hard to recognize examples of it: beatings, bombings, shootings, water-boarding and other forms of physical torture are examples of subjective violence. Hunger strikes and dirty protests are not. The question whether violent methods are necessarily extreme will be understood here as the question whether subjectively violent methods are necessarily extreme. Is it possible to use such methods in pursuit of a political objective and *not* be a methods extremist?

The obvious answer is that it depends on the type of violence. There are many different varieties of subjective violence, and some are more extreme than others. Car bombing a busy street is an extreme form of subjective violence. Getting into a fight with one's jailers or vandalizing government property are milder forms. This suggests that it is possible to use violent methods for political ends and not be a methods extremist *as long as the violent methods used are not extreme*. On the other hand, anyone who uses *extreme* violence for political ends is a methods extremist. On this view, which might be called *intrinsicalism*, the extent to which a person counts as a methods extremist is determined by the intrinsic qualities of their methods. If their methods are extreme in and of themselves, then they are methods extremists.

A different approach is *contextualism*. For the contextualist, the question whether the use of a particular method constitutes methods extremism cannot be answered on the basis of the intrinsic qualities of the method itself. It depends, rather, on a range of contextual factors. Presented with what looks like an act of extreme violence for political ends, the key questions are: was the violence in a just cause? Was there an alternative to violence? Was the violence proportional? Did it discriminate between innocents and non-innocents? These are questions about the ends or *objectives* of violence, its *necessity, proportionality* and *targets*. Violent extremists are guilty of one or more of the following:

- using violence for unjust causes;
- using violence when there are viable alternatives;
- using disproportionate violence;
- using violence against innocents.

On this account, anyone who uses extreme violence is likely to be a methods extremist because extreme violence is likely to be disproportionate. But not necessarily. For example, there is an interpretation of proportionality on which the use of extreme violence by concentration camp inmates against their Nazi persecutors would not have been disproportional and would not necessarily have satisfied any of the other conditions for methods extremism. The lesson that the contextualist draws from this is that it is not possible to read off from the intrinsic nature of a given method, however brutal or extreme, whether those who employ it are methods extremists. It depends.

On one issue, the intrinsicalist and contextualist are in agreement: it is possible to use violent methods without being a methods extremist. Where they disagree is over whether it is possible for someone to use *extreme* methods, including extreme violence, without being a methods extremist. For the intrinsicalist, this is not possible. For the contextualist, it is possible, at least in theory. There is something to be said for both approaches, although it will turn out that the distinction between them is less clear-cut than it might initially seem. In any case, the plan for the rest of this chapter is: the next section will discuss the relevance, if any, of the extremist's objectives. This is followed by the idea that violent extremists use unnecessary violence. Then the next section will discuss the idea that the violence of violent methods extremists is disproportionate, followed by a discussion of the sense in which extremist violence targets innocents. Finally, the chapter will briefly return to the intrinsicalism/contextualism contrast.

The discussion will abide by the following terminological conventions: to be a methods extremist in the primary sense is to use extreme methods (violent or non-violent) in pursuit of one's objectives. Where these objectives are political, one's extremism is also political. Then there are those who support the use of extreme methods by others but do not themselves use extreme methods. This is methods extremism in a secondary or derivative sense. An extremist whose extreme methods are violent is a *violent methods extremist*. Violent methods extremism (VME) in the primary sense consists in the use of violent methods. A violent methods extremist in the secondary sense is someone who supports but does not use violent methods. For the most part, the discussion here will concentrate on VME in the primary sense.

What violence is for

A method is always a method *for* doing or achieving something. Bobby Sands' hunger strike was a method for putting political pressure on the British government. For the IRA, violence was another method for achieving its political objectives. As noted in Chapter 2, there are some extremist ideologies that regard violence as 'redemptive' or 'cleansing'. To regard violence in this way is almost, but not quite, to see it as an end in itself. Redemptive violence is a means to redemption, but it is hard in this case to separate the end from the means by which it is supposedly achieved. However, it is more usual for practitioners of political violence to regard their violence in straightforwardly instrumental terms. For them, violence is simply a means to some *other* end. They would deny practising violence for its own sake.

The many ends or objectives of political violence include resistance to oppression and national liberation. One form of liberatory violence is anti-colonial violence. The IRA fought what it regarded as an anti-colonial war of national liberation against the British. The ANC's fight against apartheid was a fight against racist oppression. It is generally accepted that people have the right to resist tyranny, oppression, or gross violations of their human rights. There are also circumstances in which there is a right to resist using armed force. As Christopher J. Finlay puts it, there is a *prima facie* case for armed resistance where:

> it is directed against an unjust regime that uses credible threats of unjustified lethal force to try to prevent people from exercising rights. On this account, violence may be justified against regimes that are either systematically and unjustly violent in the first place, or where

they employ excessive violence in an attempt to suppress a legitimate, peaceful resistance movement.

(2015: 10–11)

This is exactly how the IRA and ANC saw their own and each other's armed
struggles. As far as they were concerned, they were both resisting, by force
of arms, systematically and unjustly violent regimes that either directly
violated the rights of the people they claimed to represent or connived in
such rights violations. The IRA and ANC saw themselves as defending their
communities and as correcting major historical injustices. They would have
wholeheartedly agreed with Hannah Arendt's observation that sometimes
violence 'is the only way to set the scales of justice right again' (1969: 64).

The question whether the IRA and ANC were right to see themselves as
fighting for justice and human rights need not be pursued here. For present
purposes, the key issue is this: *if* they were right, then is it still correct to
classify them as violent methods extremists? Their methods included acts
of extreme violence. For example, in 1983, the military wing of the ANC
planted a car bomb on Church Street, Pretoria, outside the headquarters
of the South African Air Force (SAAF). Predictably, the explosion killed
many civilians, as well as a smaller number of SAAF personnel. In 1987,
the IRA detonated a bomb at a Remembrance Day ceremony in the town
of Enniskillen, thereby murdering 11 civilians. These were, by any reasonable standard, acts of extreme violence and brutality. From an intrinsicalist
perspective, such acts of extreme violence had to be the work of violent
methods extremists, especially when account is taken of the fact that they
were not isolated incidents. Is there any reason to disagree with this verdict?

There would be a reason to disagree if it is stipulated that only those fighting for unjust causes are extremists. It is not clear, though, why one should
accept this stipulation. The point that it is possible to be an extremist for
good as well as for evil was well made by Martin Luther King Jr. when he
asked whether we will be extremists for the preservation of injustice or for
the extension of justice.[4] Both kinds of extremist can be methods extremists,
and the fact that extreme violence is used to set the scales of justice right
again has no bearing on whether those who use it are extremists. From an
intrinsicalist perspective, there are three separate questions: are those who
employ a specific tactic like car bombing violent methods extremists? Is the
use of such tactics morally justified? Is the tactic employed in a just cause?
The fact that one's cause is just does not entail that everything one does

in pursuit of that cause is just. The ANC was morally justified in fighting against apartheid, but the Church Street bombing was morally unjustified. Furthermore, even if the use of a given tactic is morally justified, it *still* does not follow that it is not an extremist tactic or that those who employ it are not violent methods extremists. A car bombing is a form of extreme violence regardless of whether it was planted by the ANC or white supremacists.

So far, the case for intrinsicalism looks strong, though questions remain. If the extent to which one is a violent methods extremist depends on whether one's tactics include extreme violence, then it should be possible to determine whether the violence of a car bombing is more extreme than, say, the violence of a targeted assassination. There is not a straightforward way of making such comparisons. In practice, one violent act is judged more extreme than another if it causes more casualties, but this brings in considerations of luck. By sheer good fortune, a car bomb on a busy street might cause no fatalities and so would be judged a less extreme form of violence than the targeted assassination of a single individual. Yet the car bomb could easily have caused more fatalities, and this is surely also a relevant factor. On the other hand, the burning alive by ISIS of one of its hostages, as described in Chapter 1, might strike many readers as a more extreme form of violence than the Church Street car bombing even though the latter killed more people. The intuition is that ISIS's violence was more extreme because it was more cruel, not because it was more lethal.

Such examples also bring in an element of historical relativity. In Tudor England, the punishment for heresy was burning, while traitors were hung, drawn and quartered. Beheading was seen as comparatively merciful. Viewed in this light, the various tactics employed by ISIS are no more extreme than judicial killings in the reign of Henry VIII, though it would be odd to describe Henry VIII as a 'methods extremist'. The truth is that there is no simple rule for ranking different types of violence in respect of how extreme they are. Still, the intrinsicalist insists that in practice we have no difficulty in recognizing some kinds of violence as extreme, and that in deciding whether a violent political actor's methods are extreme, it is irrelevant whether their methods are employed in a just cause. One might be more *understanding* of extreme violence in a just cause or less inclined to condemn in such cases, but this does not alter the fact that even warriors for justice can be violent methods extremists.

In his autobiography, Nelson Mandela defends the ANC's tactics not just on the basis that they were fighting for a just cause but also on the basis that 'violence was the only method that would destroy apartheid' (1994: 182).[5] Non-violent passive resistance 'is effective as long as your opposition adheres to the same rules as you do. But if peaceful protest is met with violence, its efficacy is at an end' (ibid.: 182–3). For Mandela, 'non-violence was not a moral principle but a strategy; there is no moral goodness in using an ineffective weapon' (ibid.: 183). These remarks are intended to explain and justify the ANC's armed struggle against apartheid on the basis that there was no alternative. Violence was necessary, according to Mandela, and this gives the contextualist an opening: the ANC's violence did not make them violent methods extremists because they had no choice. Extremists use violence when there *is* a choice, when non-violence is a realistic alternative. The next question, then, is how to understand the notion of 'necessary' violence and whether it is helpful to think of violent methods extremists as those who use unnecessary violence in pursuit of their objectives.

The need for violence

How should the distinction between necessary and unnecessary violence be interpreted? Suppose that an organization O has a political goal G. If O uses violence in pursuit of G, then one question is whether G could be achieved by O without using any violence. Suppose that the answer to this question is 'yes'. In that case, O's violence is unnecessary. The fact that O uses violence when there was no need for violence makes O's violence extremist. By the same token, O is guilty of violent methods extremism. This labelling of O is appropriate not, or not just because, O's violence is extreme but because its violence is unnecessary. So, if Mandela was right about there having been no way to overthrow apartheid without *some* violence by the ANC, then this counts against labelling the ANC a violent methods extremist organization. The ANC's violence was not the violence of an extremist group if it had no choice.

The fact that some violence was necessary to overthrow apartheid does not tell us how much violence was necessary, or what level of violence was necessary. Suppose that the ANC used *more* violence than was strictly necessary to achieve its goal, or that it used more extreme forms of violence than were strictly necessary. This would make its violence *excessive*. If the ANC was excessively violent relative to its goal, then this would be a reason to think of it as committed to violent methods extremism. Thus, one might agree with Mandela that some violence was necessary to overthrow apartheid but disagree that tactics such as those employed by the Church Street bombers were necessary. Their violence was excessive, and any organization that is excessively violent is an extremist organization. Its extremism takes the form of violent methods extremism.

It should be obvious that this approach to violent methods extremism conceals or sets aside many complications. For example, it ignores questions of timing. Suppose that O's goals would be achievable without violence, but it would take a century. With violence, G would be achievable in a handful of years. Is this a situation in which violence is necessary? Yes, if this means that it is necessary for the achievement of G in a relatively short space of time. Suppose also that the time can only be shortened through the use of extreme violence. Would it still be correct to classify such violence as excessive in the circumstances? Again, it depends on how the goal is specified. Speed might be of the essence if G is urgent because achieving G quickly would save many more lives relative to achieving it slowly.

A further obvious complication is that it can be hard to know these timings with any certainty. It is not even clear *in retrospect* whether the ANC's armed struggle made a decisive contribution to the downfall of apartheid, or whether and by how much it speeded up a process that would have unfolded anyway. How much more difficult, then, to know *in advance* whether violence is necessary. The same goes for liberatory violence in other contexts. In *The Wretched of the Earth*, Frantz Fanon asserts that colonialism is 'violence in a natural state, and it will only yield when confronted with greater violence' (2001: 48). How can he be sure? It is not true that violence was needed to end Britain's colonial presence in India. Gandhi showed that violence is not *always* necessary, and Fanon's assumption that only violence can put an end to colonialism is itself a form of extremism. The most one can say is that violence is *probably* necessary in a given situation. There is nothing definite about it, and the greater violence recommended by Fanon can backfire.

One response to these challenges is to reflect further on what it would take to *know* or *prove* that violence is necessary. One way to do this is by actually trying non-violent methods and only turning to violence once non-violent alternatives have been tried and seen to fail. This is how Finlay expresses this idea:

[V]iolence can be deployed only once *all* other alternatives have been tried without success (perhaps repeatedly). The intuition behind this idea is that violent methods ought to be adopted only if proven strictly *necessary*; it is then assumed that only once other methods have been entirely exhausted can this proof be claimed.

(2015: 132)[6]

This is unrealistic. The idea is to connect the necessity of violence with its being *the last resort* but how many other resorts are there and how can one be sure that all of them have been tried? This is what leads Walzer to object that it is not so easy to reach the last resort, which has only a 'notional finality' (2004b: 54).

These difficulties are caused by the insistence on *proof* that violence is necessary. A more moderate alternative suggested by Mandela is concerned with the balance of probabilities. The ANC tried non-violence in the form of its 1952 Campaign for the Defiance of Unjust Laws. This was a campaign of non-violent civil disobedience, with small numbers of non-white volunteers using Whites Only facilities such as toilets and railway compartments. At this stage, Mandela saw *non*-violence as a 'practical necessity' (1994: 147) since any attempts at violence against apartheid would be devastatingly crushed. It was only after the failure of non-violence that Mandela came round to the view that armed struggle was unavoidable if the objective was to free South Africa from the curse of apartheid. Although the failure of the Defiance Campaign did not constitute absolute *proof* that there was no alternative to violence, it did constitute strong *evidence* that there was no alternative. To establish the necessity of violence, it was not necessary to try every conceivable non-violent alternative to the armed struggle. The increased government repression triggered by the Defiance Campaign justified Mandela's conclusion that the government would 'ruthlessly suppress any legitimate protest on the part of the African majority' (ibid.: 182). To put it another way, it justified the conclusion that *in all probability* violence was the only way forward for the ANC.

The contrast with violent methods extremism could not be clearer. True violent methods extremists have no real interest in establishing that violence is necessary. They take the need for violence for granted and do not seriously explore alternatives. For them, violence is closer to being a first rather than a last resort, and they make no effort to minimize their violence. If it were really the case, as has been claimed, that 'nonviolence has lost the debate' and that 'nonviolence does not work' (Gelderloos 2016: 11), then those who turn to violence as a means of achieving their objectives need not be extremists on account of choosing violence. Rather, they would only be doing what had to be done. But is it true that non-violence doesn't work?[7] If it is true, *why* is it true?

Going back to the example of Gandhi's successful non-violent campaign against the British in India, the fact that non-violence was viable in that context does not mean that it would be viable in other contexts. As Arendt notes, 'If Gandhi's enormously powerful and successful strategy of nonviolent resistance had met with a different enemy – Stalin's Russia, Hitler's Germany, even prewar Japan, instead of England – the outcome would not have been decolonization, but massacre and submission' (1969: 53). The lesson is that there is no *general* answer to the question whether non-violence does or does not work. It depends on the context and the nature of one's opponent. The British in India were very different from the Afrikaners in South Africa, in that the latter were much less amenable to non-violent resistance. Just as pacifists misguidedly take the success of non-violence in very specific political, historical and geographical contexts as an indication that it is a viable strategy in other contexts, extremists misguidedly take the failure of non-violence in some contexts as an indication that violence is always necessary.

In his account of why the ANC had to resort to violence, Mandela refers to the nature of the South African regime. The non-viability of non-violence as a means of achieving the ANC's political objectives had nothing to do with lack of popular support, as its post-apartheid election landslide proved. In other cases, however, the reason that methods extremists turn to violence is that they don't have the popular support that would be needed to succeed without violence. In these cases, the need for violence reflects the extremists' own weakness. Where their cause is only supported by a minority of the population at large, or a minority of the people they claim to represent, violence becomes necessary *de facto*. However, the attempt to impose one's political objectives by violence in these circumstances is itself a mark of VME. It is not in dispute, in such cases, that violence is necessary, but what *makes* it necessary – a lack of popular support – also makes the resort to violence a form of violent methods extremism.

Another consideration is the following: in the case of some violent methods extremists, the need for violence is not, or not just, a reflection of lack of public support but also a reflection of the nature of the objective. Some extremist political objectives are so outlandish that it is perfectly true that extreme violence is the only conceivable means of achieving them. Yet the use of extreme violence to achieve such objectives is itself a form of VME even if it is true that there is no non-violent route to the objective in question. The argument that violence is the only way only carries weight if the ultimate objective is realistic. In many cases in which violence is used, there is no chance of the objective being achieved without violence and little chance of success even with violence. The charge that those who use violence in these circumstances are violent methods extremists is based on the idea that their violence is more likely than not to prove futile because of the nature of their objective. The probability of success always needs to be considered when violence is represented as a means to an end.

To recap: it is possible to use extreme methods in pursuit of one's political objectives and *not* be a violent methods extremist if one of the following is true:

1. One's extreme methods are non-violent.
2. Although one's extreme methods involve some degree of violence, the violence involved is not extreme.
3. The specific circumstances in which one employs violent methods are ones in which one is justified in believing that (a) some violence is necessary for the achievement of one's objectives; (b) the level of violence used is, however extreme, not excessive relative to what is necessary in the circumstances. In other words, one's violence must be proportionate; (c) the need for violence is not a reflection of lack of popular support for one's cause; and (d) the violence used is unlikely to prove futile. That is, there is a reasonable probability of success.

Being a violent methods extremist is not just a matter of using extreme violence for political ends. It involves using violence when at least one of the conditions listed under 3 is not met. Whether these conditions are or are not met is clearly a matter of judgement, but that is what one would expect. In some cases, it is clear that the conditions have not been met by a particular organization. In other cases, the verdict will be less clear-cut.

One aspect of the discussion so far remains puzzling. The case against intrinsicalism so far is that the use of extreme violence need not mark one out as a violent methods extremist as long as various other conditions are met. One of these conditions is that the violence used is not excessive. As has already been noted, extreme violence is likely to be excessive so it looks as though there will be little difference in practice between intrinsicalists and contextualists. In theory, their verdicts might be different but what would extreme violence, that is not excessive, and does fall foul of any of the other conditions set out above, even look like? One way to think about excessive violence is to think of it as disproportionate. The next question, therefore, is: how should the notion of proportionality be understood? What makes the violence of a violent act disproportionate?

The issue of proportionality

Violent methods extremists don't just fail to explore non-violent alternatives, and don't just use violence when it isn't necessary. They also use or endorse the use of disproportionate violence. How should the notion of proportionality be understood? In his highly influential discussion of this issue, Jeff McMahan observes that:

> Proportionality is a constraint on action that causes harm. In most cases, for an act that causes harm to be justified, it must be instrumental to the achievement of some valuable goal against which the harm can be weighed and assessed. If the assessment is favorable, the harm is proportionate; if it is unfavorable, the harm is disproportionate.
>
> (2009: 19)

McMahan gives the example of Bernard Goetz, who shot four men on the New York subway who were menacing him and demanding money. The men were liable to certain forms of harm that Goetz might have inflicted in self-defence. However, since the harm that Goetz inflicted exceeded that to which the men were liable, his action was disproportionate in what McMahan calls the 'narrow' sense.

For McMahan, *liability* to harm is instrumental: 'a person is liable to be harmed only if harming him will serve some further purpose' (ibid.: 8), such as self-defence. Relative to that purpose, what Goetz did was disproportionate because the harms he inflicted were not necessary for self-defence. This brings out the close connection between proportionality and necessity.[8] *Desert* of harm is non-instrumental: 'if a person deserves to be harmed, there is a moral reason for harming him that is independent of the further consequences of harming him. Giving him what he deserves is an end in itself' (ibid.: 8). The infliction of deserved harm is 'not governed by a requirement of necessity, since the value of a person's getting what he deserves is not instrumental and hence not necessary for anything beyond itself' (ibid.: 9). Nevertheless, the infliction of deserved harm must still be proportionate. Thus, in the example of concentration camp inmates using extreme violence against their Nazi persecutors, a natural thought is that the latter deserved to be harmed, independent of the further consequences of harming them. Furthermore, even extreme violence would be proportionate since the Nazis subjected to such violence would (arguably) be getting what they deserve, on account of their previous conduct.

What is the extremist perspective on proportionality? The claim that extremists use or endorse the use of disproportionate violence needs to be qualified in one respect: it is not that violent methods extremists necessarily reject the proportionality requirement *in theory*. It is common for extremists to pay lip service to this requirement and insist that their violence *is* proportionate. The problem is that they have a perverse or unrealistic concept of proportionality and that *in reality* their violence tends not to be proportionate. There is no better illustration of this than the pronouncements of Osama bin Laden. In his 1998 *fatwa*, he declared that it is an individual duty incumbent upon every Muslim 'to kill the Americans and their allies – civilian and military' (Lawrence 2005: 61). Yet bin Laden was fond of representing the violence he recommended as defensive and reactive. Hence, the violence was not disproportionate by his own lights, and he is especially keen to emphasize that the terror to which the United States was subjected on 9/11 was fully deserved by its actions in the Middle East. Because America killed Muslims in Iraq, its own soldiers and citizens deserved to be killed by Al-Qaeda. As bin Laden puts it: 'As they kill us, without a doubt we have to kill them, until we obtain a balance in terror' (ibid.: 114).

The idea that the 3,000 civilians working in the World Trade Center on 9/11 deserved to die on account of American actions in the Middle East is, of course, preposterous. The same is true of the idea that the 9/11 attacks were carried out in self-defence or that they were in any reasonable sense instrumental to the achievement of Al-Qaeda's strategic goal of getting U.S. forces out of the Middle East. Predictably, the 9/11 attacks had the opposite effect, and resulted in the subsequent American military action in Afghanistan. Those harmed on 9/11 were neither liable nor deserved to be harmed, and this is illustrative of the sense in which extremist violence is excessive: it presents itself as proportionate but, in reality, is disproportionate. In some cases, the extremist's theoretical commitment to proportionality is sincere.

In other cases, it is just for show. Either way, disproportionate violence is the result.

This is not to say that the proportionality of an act of violence is always clear-cut. It is easy to say that the harms inflicted by Goetz were disproportionate, given that he caused one of his assailants to suffer brain damage and paralysis. It is no less clear that the harms suffered by the civilian victims of the Church Street bombing were undeserved. Could it nevertheless be argued that the ANC's violence in Pretoria was proportionate to the achievement of its goal of overthrowing apartheid? A crude way to answer this question is to do a simple piece of cost-benefit analysis. On the one side are the costs of the bombing, in the form of the harms caused to its victims. On the other side are the benefits of its overall objective being achieved, namely, the ending of apartheid. Given the suffering caused by apartheid, is it not highly plausible that the benefits of overthrowing this system far outweighed the costs of the bombing?

One objection to this type of calculation is that the victims of the bombing were not in a position to enjoy its supposed benefits. Their deaths were treated by the ANC as means to its own political ends, and this raises obvious ethical questions. Aside from these questions, there is also the following concern: even if the benefits of ending apartheid clearly outweighed the costs of the bombing, it still does not follow that the harms were proportionate in the instrumental sense. For there is the further question whether and how much the bombing contributed to the ending of apartheid. It is implausible that apartheid would not have ended, or would have ended later, if the ANC hadn't bombed Church Street in 1983. In this sense, the bombing itself hardly contributed anything to the achievement of the valuable end. Once this is taken into account, it is far from clear that its harms were outweighed by any benefits attributable to it.

A possible response to this line of reasoning would be to insist on not looking at acts of violence in isolation. The ANC engaged in a long *campaign* of violence, and the Church Street bombing was one part of that campaign. The relevant question, it might be argued, is whether apartheid would have ended without such a campaign. If not, then it is appropriate to weigh the costs of the Church Street bombing against the benefits of dismantling apartheid. The right question is not what the bombing contributed *in isolation* to attaining the ANC's objectives but what it contributed as an integral part of its overall campaign. But exactly why is this the right question? Although the bombing was part of a campaign of violence, no single violent act was essential to the campaign as a whole. This means that the questions about the proportionality of individual acts of violence cannot be bypassed by talking about the bigger picture. It is a fallacy to argue that the violence of the Church Street bombing was proportionate because the campaign of which it was a small element was proportionate.

As noted above, one of the difficulties with seeing proportionality in cost-benefit terms is that the alleged benefits of acts of violence are not enjoyed by those who bear their costs, at least if the cost is death. This is one source of the worry that such acts of violence are unjust. In the case of the civilian victims of extremist violence, there is also the worry that they do not deserve to be harmed at all, and therefore that *any* harms they suffer are disproportionate. Yet extremists like bin Laden operate with a view of desert on which some civilians deserve to be killed. Violent methods extremists don't just have an expansive conception of what counts as proportionate violence. Notoriously, they also have an expansive conception of the legitimate *targets* of their violence, and they rely on this expansive conception to justify their actions. This is the last feature of VME that needs unpacking.

The targets of violence

The operational commander of the Church Street bombers, both of whom died in the attack, was Aboobaker Ismail. In evidence given to the South African Truth and Reconciliation Commission (TRC), Ismail declared that 'We did not target civilians.' However, in line with the policy of the ANC at the time, he would not be prevented from striking at apartheid 'for the sake of saving a few lives'.[9] The TRC judged that the bombing was a political act and not merely an act of anarchy or terrorism. On this basis it granted Ismail an amnesty. What is of interest for present purposes, however, is Ismail's attitude towards the victims of the attack. Despite his insistence that civilians were not the target, he was clearly aware of the possibility of civilian casualties. He did not regard this as a reason not to proceed. He was, in this sense, indifferent to civilian casualties, and this attitude is entirely characteristic of one variety of VME. This type of extremist does not target civilians and expresses regrets about killing civilians but their tears about harming civilians are crocodile tears. Many felt this way about statements of regret about harming civilians issued by the IRA. These statements did not deter it from continuing military operations that would endanger the lives of innocents.

It supposedly cared about harming people who did not deserve to be harmed, but it did not care enough not to harm them.

At least the ANC and IRA recognized that some of their victims were innocents and did not deserve to be harmed. There is a more virulent form of VME that either blurs the distinction between legitimate and illegitimate targets or explicitly targets people who, *even by its own lights*, are innocent. Both tendencies are apparent in various statements made by Osama bin Laden concerning the casualties of Al-Qaeda operations. In one statement, he declared that Al-Qaeda did not distinguish between military and civilians; they were all targets. American civilians were legitimate targets, he argued, because they had chosen their government despite knowledge of its 'crimes' and so were 'not exonerated from responsibility' (Lawrence 2005: 47). In other statements, bin Laden accepted that some of Al-Qaeda's victims were genuinely innocent but justified their killing on the basis that the United States had killed innocent people in Iraq. Asked whether this was a case of 'an eye for an eye', he replied: 'Yes, so we kill their innocents – this is valid both religiously and logically' (ibid.: 118).

The discussion so far has not been careful to distinguish the targeting of civilians from the targeting of innocents. These are not necessarily the same thing. If there are circumstances in which military personnel are guilty of wrongdoing that makes them legitimate targets, then perhaps civilians who work for the military are also legitimate targets, though much would depend on the exact nature of the work that such civilians do for the military. A general question that needs answering is: what makes a victim of political violence 'innocent', and how should the distinction between legitimate and illegitimate targets be drawn if it is not simply identical with the distinction between military and civilian? One view is that *no* victims of political violence, military or civilian, are harmed legitimately if the cause for which they are harmed is itself unjust. But what about harms inflicted in a *just* cause, such as ending apartheid or colonial occupation? According to just war theory, as interpreted by McMahan, to say that a person is *innocent* in this context is to say that 'he has done nothing to make himself *morally liable to military attack*' (McMahan 2009: 8). In addition, to say that a person is *not* liable to attack is that he or she would be *wronged* by being attacked. Crucially:

> For liability to be an issue, the goal sought must usually be a solution to a problem. The principal condition of a person's being liable to be

harmed in pursuit of that goal is that he or she be implicated in some way in the existence of the problem. If a person is implicated in the existence of a problem in such a way that harming him in a certain way in the course of solving the problem would not wrong him, then he is liable to that harm.

(ibid.: 19)

According to what McMahan calls the *requirement of discrimination*, 'combatants must confine their intentional attacks to legitimate targets' (ibid.: 13). In these terms, VME is often characterized by a willingness to flout the requirement of discrimination.

For example, when Osama bin Laden justified the killing of innocents, he was justifying harming people, such as children, who had done nothing to make themselves liable to attack, even by his own lights. The intentional harming of such people was a clear violation of the requirement of discrimination. Even if the United States harmed innocents in Iraq, as bin Laden was never slow to point out, the harming of innocents in the United States by Al-Qaeda was still a breach of this requirement. In contrast, when bin Laden argues that American civilians were morally liable to harm, he was attempting to respect the discrimination requirement. Suppose that the problem to which Al-Qaeda's violence was a response was U.S. policy in the Middle East. According to bin Laden, American civilians were morally liable to be harmed because they were implicated in the existence of the problem. In what way were they implicated? By voting for President Bush.

This doesn't explain the liability to harm of American civilians who didn't vote for Bush and were opposed to his administration's foreign policy. More to the point, bin Laden's argument illustrates a pattern of argument that is often employed by proponents of VME. They believe that one can make oneself liable to attack simply by voting for someone whose policies the extremist finds objectionable. In effect, the extremist exploits the wiggle room that is built into McMahan's account of liability to harm. His account implies that a person is liable to harm as long as they are 'implicated in some way' in the problem to which the extremist is reacting with violence. The hard question is: implicated in what way, or in which ways? The extremist has a maximally broad view of what makes a person implicated. For bin Laden, simply having an American passport implicates one in the misdeeds of the American government, even if one is a staunch critic of that government.

There is a parallel with the extremist view of the necessity of violence. Just as violent methods extremists are prone to assuming that violence is necessary when it isn't, they are also prone to thinking that people are legitimate targets when they aren't. Extremists don't just have an expansive view of when violence is necessary, they also have an expansive view of who is liable to be harmed by their violence. What is missing in both cases is self-restraint and sound judgement. Violent methods extremists find it all too easy to convince themselves that their way is the only way, and that the people they harm deserve to be harmed. Even when they harm people whom they recognize as undeserving of harm, their capacity to be distressed by this or to modify their tactics is limited. Like Ismail's response to the prospect of innocents being harmed by car bombings, their view of the likelihood of harming innocents by their actions is, in effect, to say: shit happens. And that is a fundamental difference between people who are extremists and people who are not. The difference isn't the difference between being willing and unwilling to use violence, but a difference in their conceptions of *when* and what *kinds* of violence are to be used and against *whom*.

Conclusion

When people are classified as extremists because they believe in the use of extreme methods to attain their political objectives, the idea sounds simple and intuitive. Extremists use extreme methods; what could be simpler than that? We can think about how a willingness to use extreme methods relates to a person's ideology or their psychology but why a person uses extreme methods is less important than the fact that they use them. Or so one might suppose. It turns out, however, that methods extremism is just as difficult to pin down as ideological or psychological extremism. The key points to have emerged in this chapter are: (1) extreme methods needn't be violent; and (2) using violence for political ends does not necessarily make one an extremist. It depends on the answers to a whole host of further questions, including the following:

1. Was violence employed in a just cause?
2. What was the nature of the violence employed?
3. Was violence necessary to attain the objective for which it was employed?

4. If it was necessary, what made it necessary?
5. Was the violence proportionate?
6. Was violence likely to be an effective means of achieving its objective?
7. Were those against whom violence was directed legitimate targets?

The answers to these questions are themselves not straightforward, as we have just seen in relation to the last question. However, if there is an archetypal methods extremist, then it is someone who uses unnecessary or disproportionate violence in pursuit of an unjust but hopeless cause, and directs their violence against illegitimate targets. Extremists can also be extremists for just causes. If, as in the case of the Church Street bombers, they target innocents, then they commit an injustice in pursuit of justice. The fact that they were extremists for justice did not make their methods just. There are several ways in which those who use extreme violence for a just cause can be violent methods extremists: by using disproportionate violence, unnecessary violence or violence against innocents. Any one of these failings is enough to make one guilty of VME.

Regarding the dispute between intrinsicalism and contextualism, there are many cases in which these approaches will deliver identical verdicts. Methods that are regarded by the intrinsicalist as violent in and of themselves are also likely to involve disproportionate or indiscriminate violence. This raises a question about how to understand the intrinsicalist's talk of the 'intrinsic qualities' of a person's method. When a car bomb is detonated on a busy shopping street, do the intrinsic qualities of this method of making a political point include the fact that the bomb was detonated on a busy street, or is its only intrinsic quality that it was a car bomb? The contextualist sees the fact that the bombing harmed innocents as a contextual factor but perhaps that isn't right. Detonating a car bomb in the middle of the night on an empty street is a very different thing from detonating a car bomb on Church Street in the middle of the day. The methods are 'intrinsically' different, precisely because setting off a car bomb on a deserted street is much less likely to harm innocents than setting off a car bomb on a busy street. If this is right, then the distinction between intrinsicalism and contextualism starts to look distinctly hazy, at least in this case; so-called 'contextual' factors can be reinterpreted as intrinsic. What does and does not count as an 'intrinsic' quality of a method is hard to say with any confidence, and this makes the intrinsicalist/contextualist contrast less compelling than it seemed at the outset. What matters is to have a clear idea of the factors that bear on whether a method is extreme or not. It matters much less whether these factors are called 'contextual' or 'intrinsic'.

There is one final issue that the discussion in this chapter has not confronted head on but that cannot be avoided any longer. The question is: is violent methods extremism morally objectionable? Although this question has not received a direct answer so far, it should be fairly obvious to the attentive reader that VME, as represented here, is morally suspect. The factors that bear on whether a person is a violent methods extremist also bear on the moral qualities of their actions and methods. To target innocents is to harm people who are not morally liable to be harmed. To use disproportionate or unnecessary violence, especially in an unjust cause, is a moral failing that causes unwarranted harms to other people. To describe a person as a violent methods extremist is therefore, by implication, to censure them for such failings. When Martin Luther King Jr. talked about being an extremist for justice or love, he was not endorsing the use of violence for love or justice. His methods were powerful, effective but non-violent.

This takes us back to where we began, and Bobby Sands' hunger strike. Presented with an argument for the moral unacceptability of extremist violence in response to the violence of colonialism, someone like Fanon might ask: what is the alternative? Sands and Luther King proved that there is an alternative in many cases. The alternative is politics. As English notes, 'while republicans recognized that their dead hunger-strikers had politicized for them a section of Irish people, they certainly did not – at the time – draw the lesson that politics rather than violence offered the way forward' (2003: 205). Years later, however, they did draw this conclusion, and the result was peace. In this sense, the hunger strike was the beginning of a process that led to the ultimate victory of politics over violence. There is a lesson in this for methods extremists: do not jump to the conclusion that violence is the only way. Use your imagination to look for another way.[10] You just might find that there is one. If you don't, then at least make sure that your violence is proportionate and discriminating, as well as necessary. Above all, don't kid yourself that the fact that your cause is just guarantees that your methods are just. There is no such guarantee.

Notes

1 Was Sands' method non-violent? Given the damage to his body caused by his refusal to eat, some might argue that he subjected himself to a form of violence. See Pickard (2015) for a defence of the view that suicide and self-harm are forms of violence. The idea that what Sands did to himself was *non*-violent relies on what C.A.J. Coady calls a 'restricted' definition of violence. These are definitions which, in keeping with the *Oxford English Dictionary*, take violence to require 'the exercise of physical force so as to inflict injury on or damage to persons or property' (Coady 1986: 5). The concept of force is not straightforward but the intuition that Sands' hunger strike was non-violent is the intuition that it did not involve the exercise of force. As Coady notes, the restricted definition is not perfect since it rules out the possibility of psychological violence. However, for my purposes here, it is close enough to the truth about violence.

2 However, as Hanna Pickard notes, the standard definition of violence as involving physical force does not stipulate that the perpetrator and victim of violence cannot be identical. See Pickard (2015: 71).

3 Žižek's distinction between subjective and objective violence corresponds to Galtung's distinction between personal and structural violence. In structural violence, which Galtung refers to as social injustice, 'there may not be any person who directly harms another person' (1969: 171).

4 See his *Letter from Birmingham Jail* (Luther King Jr. 2018).

5 It is, of course, a further question whether Mandela was right about this or whether, in general, violence is more effective than non-violence. For a contrary view, and further discussion of this important question, see Chenoweth and Stephan (2011).

6 To be clear, this is not Finlay's own view. As he sees it, 'Necessity demands that agents choose that strategy for achieving the just cause that offers the best possible balance between morally relevant anticipated costs and morally relevant anticipated gains' (2015: 132). On this account, necessity is a form of proportionality.

7 For further discussion of this question, see Chenoweth and Stephan (2011).

8 Finlay (2015: 133).

9 A transcript of Ismail's testimony is available at: www.justice.gov.za.

10 Chenoweth and Stephan (2011) offer another useful corrective.

4 | The psychology of extremism

Psychological extremism

In 1968, when Lyndon Johnson was U.S. president, a teenager called Meredith ('Merry') Levov planted a bomb in the post office and general store of Old Rimrock. The bombing, which was an act of protest against Johnson's Vietnam War policy, killed an innocent bystander. Merry went into hiding and carried out more bombings. Several years later, she was found by her father, Seymour. By this time, Merry had become a Jain and subscribed to its doctrine of non-violence. She even wore a veil in order to avoid harming airborne microscopic organisms. She did not wash and did not walk about after dark for fear of crushing any living creature. Merry has gone from being the Rimrock Bomber to someone who, quite literally, wouldn't hurt a fly.

When questioned about the Rimrock bombing by her father, Merry admits that she was responsible. He is baffled by Merry's transformation from terrorist to pacificist. He can see no connection at all between her old and new world-views but Merry assures him that there is one. Here is her account of the logic to her conversion to Jainism:

> We are a religion founded in the sixth century BC. Mahatma Gandhi took from us this notion of *ahimsa*, nonviolence. We are the core of the truth that created Mahatma Gandhi. And Mahatma Gandhi, in his nonviolence, is the core of the truth that created Martin Luther King. And Martin Luther King is the core of the truth that created the civil rights movement. And, at the end of his life, when he was moving

DOI: 10.4324/9780429325472-4

beyond the civil rights movement to a larger vision … he was opposing the war in Vietnam.

(Roth 1997: 246)

Seymour doesn't buy it. He returns to the bombing and asks her who made her do it. Her answer: Lyndon Johnson.[1]

In case it isn't obvious, Merry is fictional, a character from Philip Roth's (1997) novel *American Pastoral*. However, the novel alludes to real events, including an anti-war bombing campaign by a group called the Weather Underground in the early 1970s. For present purposes, however, Roth's most striking achievement is the way he identifies and makes vivid what might be called the 'mindset' of an extremist – Merry's mindset. His insight is that extremism is not, or not just, a set of doctrines but a state of mind, an outlook, or way of being. A person like Merry is drawn to extremist causes because she thinks that if a cause of worth supporting, then it is worth supporting uncompromisingly, in its purest, strongest form. Moderation and compromise are not for her; it is always all or nothing. Her attempt to explain the logic of her transition from one extreme to another is an expression of her extremist mindset. This mindset often manifests itself in the realm of politics but needn't be political. In the end, Merry's diet is as extreme as her politics. As she says at one point to her all-too-conventional father, 'Limits. That's all you think about. Not going to the extreme. Well, sometimes you have to fucking go to the extreme' (ibid.: 105).

The idea that extremism is a mindset is also implicit in Hoffer's *The True Believer*, cited in Chapter 1.[2] Hoffer talks about fanatics rather than extremists, but the basic point is the same: it is the extremist and the moderate who are poles apart. Extremists and fanatics of all kinds are 'crowded together at one end' (1951: 86). Hoffer draws on anecdotal evidence of communists who converted to fascism and fascists who moved in the opposite direction. These conversions make sense if there is a common extremist mindset that is drawn to extremist ideologies on account of their extremism rather than their ideological content. More recently, the notion of an extremist mindset has been also defined, tested and validated empirically by social psychologists, whose work will be discussed below. 'Mindset' has a colloquial use but can also be understood as a technical or quasi-technical term that needs to be made more precise.

Apart from reading *American Pastoral*, the most straightforward way to arrive at the idea of an extremist mindset is to remember the initial distinction between ideological, methods and psychological extremism. To be a methods extremist is to use or support the use of extreme methods in pursuit of one's political objectives. Ideological extremism is a matter of where one stands on an ideological spectrum. Finally, psychological extremism is defined not by *what* one believes but by 'the way in which ideas are believed' (Hofstadter 2008: 5). Considerable effort has already gone into refining the methods and ideological conceptions of extremism. The psychological account of extremism is no less in need of refinement. As noted in Chapter 1, the main theoretical challenge facing this account is to explain the notion of a 'way of believing'.

An initial thought is that extremists are *fervent* believers, whose beliefs are held with particularly strong feelings of conviction or certainty. Alternatively, psychological extremists are people who believe uncompromisingly, where this is understood as a statement about their dispositions to believe rather than about their feelings. However, the idea that extremists are uncompromising in their beliefs raises more questions than it answers since the same is true of people who are said to be *principled*. Presumably, one would not wish to classify every principled person as an extremist. One might say that extremists are uncompromising about the wrong things, but what counts as the 'wrong things'? One conclusion one might draw from this is that there is little hope of characterizing extremism in the psychological sense without also taking account of the content of a person's beliefs. When a person is uncompromising, there is the further question whether this attitude is appropriate in this instance. *If* this is the right conclusion to draw, then being an extremist in the psychological sense is not just a matter of how one believes. What one believes also matters. There is more on this complex issue below.

Extremism in the psychological sense is a cast of mind but one's cast of mind is only partly a function of what one believes. Other mental states also matter, especially if Hume is right that beliefs are motivationally inert.[3] People are motivated to act by their desires and emotions, along with their beliefs. The implication is that extremism in the psychological sense must include these elements. Empirical studies also support the idea that extremists have characteristic attitudes and preoccupations. For example, they tend to have a negative attitude towards compromise and a preoccupation with their own victimhood. Some studies also point to extremist thinking patterns, that is, modes or styles of thinking that are closely associated with, and partly constitute, extremism in the psychological sense.

These reflections should be seen as invitations to develop a broad and multi-layered conception of the extremist mindset, one that does justice to the texture and complexity of this mindset. What makes Merry an extremist in the psychological sense is not just one aspect of her psychology – her beliefs, for example – but several different aspects. Furthermore, the fact that she has an extremist mindset will not be sufficient to explain her commitment to a specific political or religious doctrine, even if the doctrine is one to which people with her mindset are particularly susceptible. Exposure to the doctrine is also required. However, once she has been exposed to and captivated by a particular set of ideas, her extremist mindset helps to explain the nature of her commitment and her ability to move from one extreme to another. However, if the notion of a mindset is to carry such a heavy explanatory burden, it needs be clear what a mindset is and what counts as an 'extremist' mindset. Providing the necessary clarity is the task of the next section.

Mindsets

The idea of a mindset was popularized by Carol Dweck in her bestseller *Mindset*, which is a self-help book rather an analysis of extremism. According to Dweck, mindsets are 'just beliefs' (2012: 16), albeit powerful beliefs. If there is such a thing as an extremist mindset, it is not just a belief, so Dweck's work is not the answer for anyone looking for an understanding of the extremist mindset. Of greater relevance is the work of Gerald Saucier and his colleagues on the *militant* extremist mindset (MEM). Their starting point is the same as Hoffer's: the attempt to 'unconfound the phenomenon of militant extremism from any specific kind of ideology, movement, or culture' (2009: 258). The rationale for this starting point is the assumption that militant extremism is a pan-cultural phenomenon. For Saucier, Hoffer's insights are 'based on a scholarly observer's intuition rather than on scientific research' (ibid.: 257). Saucier and his colleagues use empirical psychology to vindicate and develop Hoffer's insights.

Saucier assumes that militant extremism is a 'mentality or mind-set' (ibid.: 257) rather than a personality trait. A mindset is 'a pattern of thinking and motivation that tends to be affectively mobilized and has major effects on behavior' (ibid.: 257). Under the right conditions, 'anyone is capable of adopting components of this mind-set because it draws on certain natural human tendencies' (ibid.: 257). Nevertheless, 'holding the context constant, some individuals may be more prone than others to take on this mind-set' (ibid.: 257). Even if the militant extremist mindset is not a stable personality trait, there remains the question whether certain stable personality traits contribute to and predict MEM. This possibility has also been explored in the psychological literature, about which there is more below.

What are the core components of MEM, and how are these components identified? On the second of these questions, Saucier and his colleagues 'examined materials arising from a diverse range of regions, religions, and political orientations to obtain a "sufficient range of sources" for making generalizations about the militant-extremist mind-set' (ibid.: 258). The result is 'an inductively based working model of the major components of the militant-extremist mind-set' (ibid.: 258). A total of 16 components or 'themes' were identified:

1. The necessity of unconventional and extreme measures.
2. Use of tactics that function to absolve one of responsibility for the bad consequences of the violence one is advocating or carrying out.
3. Use of military terminology in areas of discourse where it is otherwise rarely found.
4. The perception that the ability of the group to reach its rightful position is being obstructed.
5. Glorifying the past, in reference to one's group.
6. Utopianizing, that is, frequent references to a future paradise or promised land.
7. Catastrophizing, that is, the perception that great calamities have occurred, are occurring or will occur.
8. Anticipation of supernatural intervention.
9. A felt imperative to purify the world entirely from evil.
10. Glorification of dying for the cause.
11. Duty and obligation to kill or make offensive war.
12. The belief that true believers are entitled to use immoral means to ensure the success of their cause.
13. An elevation of intolerance, vengeance, and warlikeness into virtues.
14. Dehumanizing or demonizing of opponents.
15. Viewing the modern world as a disaster.
16. Viewing civil government as illegitimate.

These themes 'represent ways of framing or interpreting events' (ibid.: 265). They also indicate that 'militant extremism represents not just one, but an orchestra of responses working in concert' (ibid.: 265).

Different studies focus on different elements of MEM. A 2010 study by Stankov, Saucier and Knežević concludes that an extremist militant mindset consists of three main ingredients: (1) Pro-Violence; (2) a vile world (the belief that there is something seriously wrong with the world we live in); and (3) divine power (the belief in an all-powerful divinity who sanctions violence). These elements of MEM are linked to, and predicted by, psychopathy, sadism and disintegration, that is, 'a proneness to see and feel connections among factually unrelated phenomena' (Međedovic and Knežević 2019: 93). On this account, militant extremism is closely related to other personality traits even if it is not a personality trait in its own right. This might help to explain why some individuals are more prone than others to developing or acquiring MEM.

What is the significance of these findings for a *philosophical* analysis of mindsets in general and the extremist mindset in particular? On the one hand, it would plainly be foolish for philosophers to ignore psychological accounts of extremism. These accounts contain a number of insights and provide philosophers who employ the concept of a mindset in their analyses of extremism with the assurance that they are talking about something that is psychologically real. On the other hand, it is also necessary to proceed with caution in drawing conclusions from the psychological research. The studies cited so far are specifically concerned with the *militant* extremist mindset, that is, 'a pattern of beliefs, feelings, thoughts and motivation that tends to be mobilized under facilitating conditions – that may lead to violent behavior' (Stankov, Saucier, and Knežević 2010: 70). However, not all extremism is militant and a satisfactory analysis of the extremist mindset must take account of this. A person can have an extremist cast of mind but not be Pro-Violence. At the end of *American Pastoral*, Merry is an extremist but against violence.

As noted in Chapter 1, armchair reflection of the kind favoured by many philosophers cannot, on its own, uncover the nature of the extremist mindset. Philosophical claims about extremism require empirical support, including studies such as the ones that have just been cited. One might worry that if the characteristics of the extremist mindset are derived by induction from the statements of actual extremists, then there is very little for philosophy to contribute. Why not leave it to psychologists to analyse the extremist mindset, if necessary by broadening their investigations to include non-militant forms of extremism? There are several reasons not to accept this assessment of the role of philosophy. One is that, as Hoffer shows, empirically informed armchair reflection *can* contribute to our understanding of extremism. Being empirically informed is not equivalent to being based on the findings of psychologists; thinking that exploits the thinker's own political experiences or casual observation can still be described as empirically informed. For that matter, works of fiction like Roth's novel can also provide illumination. Psychological studies are not necessarily a better guide to the extremist mindset than *American Pastoral* or other works of fiction. Furthermore, the features of the extremist mindset that psychologists list need to be categorized, ordered and interpreted if they are to be useful. There are questions about the nature these features, their relative importance, and the relationship between them. It is in relation to these questions, which have conceptual as well as empirical elements, that philosophy can make a useful contribution.

Consider again the 16 MEM themes listed above. They are a jumble of perceptions, beliefs, feelings, attitudes, thinking patterns and tactics. The list is incomplete and some omitted characteristics, such as extremism's view of compromise, are at least as important as those listed. This points to a different methodology for delineating the extremist mindset, one that tries to impose order and structure on empirically generated lists of characteristics. Some elements of MEM are preoccupations: extremists are preoccupied with purity, catastrophe and a mythical past. Preoccupations can be more or less intense, and those at the most intense end of the scale are obsessions. The extremist mindset is partly constituted by obsessions that different extremists with different ideological agendas have in common.

A person's preoccupations are related to, and expressive of, their attitudes. So, for example, a person might be preoccupied with religious, ideological or racial purity because of their attitudes towards purity and impurity. The philosophical interest in 'attitudes' tends to be an interest in so-called *propositional* attitudes, mental states that are ascribed by means of a 'that' clause. In the philosophical sense, the belief that it is raining and the hope that it is raining are different 'attitudes' to the same proposition. The attitudes that form part of the extremist mindset are attitudes in the psychological sense. In this sense,

> evaluation is *the* predominant aspect of the attitude concept. In other words, reporting an attitude involves making a decision of liking versus disliking, or favoring versus disfavoring a particular issue, object,

or person. As such, attitudes summarize different types of information about an issue, object, or person … Thus, we define *attitude* as an overall evaluation of an object that is based on cognitive, affective, and behavioral information.

(Maio and Haddock 2015: 4)

To put it another way, one's attitude towards something is one's evaluative posture towards it. For example, to say that extremists deplore compromise is to make a point about their attitude or posture towards compromise: they are against it. In contrast, the belief that it is raining is not an attitude towards rain. Changing a person's beliefs about something does not necessarily change their attitude towards it.

With this account of the nature of attitudes in place, the next step for a philosophical account of the extremist mindset is to identify the *particular* attitudes that are associated with an extremist mindset. The emphasis should be on identifying the most significant extremist attitudes, and exploring the relationship between them and between extremist attitudes and extremist preoccupations. So, for example, one might expect deep hostility to compromise to be closely related to a preoccupation with compromise. It also needs to be recognized that some postures have an affective quality. Extremists are contemptuous of compromise, as well as hostile to it, but contempt is something that is *felt*, and the affective quality of this posture is *aversion*. This points to another key element of the extremist mindset that needs unpacking: the feelings or emotions that are characteristic of this mindset.

The idea that the extremist mindset has affective components might come as a surprise to those who are used to thinking of it in doctrinal terms, or simply as a position in ideological space. However, it is hard not to notice the anger of extremists. Extremism is the mindset of 'angry minds' (Hofstadter 2008: 3). It is significant that Roth represents Merry as enraged by her life and her country. Others see the rise of extremism in the twentieth century as a reflection of the fact that ours is an 'age of anger'.[4] Resentment and self-pity also play a key role in the extremist mindset, and it is the strength of these feelings that moves extremists to act in ways that moderates find so alarming. If, as Saucier et al. put it, the extremist mindset tends to be 'affectively mobilized' (2009: 257), then we need to be clear which affects, which feelings or emotions, do the mobilizing.

Saucier's own focus is on extremist thinking patterns or, as they might also be called, extremist 'thinking styles'. Utopianizing and catastrophizing are thinking styles. Conspiracy thinking is not on Saucier's list of 16 MEM themes but plays a highly significant role in the extremist mindset. The notion of a thinking pattern requires some explanation. The thinking that is at issue in the present context involves including or excluding possibilities, evaluating evidence, and drawing conclusions.[5] Thinking patterns or thinking styles are different ways of doing these things.[6] If there are extremist thinking styles, then these styles are part of the extremist mindset. Different ways of thinking are different ways of interpreting events. They are, in this sense, also different ways of *seeing*. For example, when catastrophizing is defined as the perception that great calamities have occurred, are occurring or will occur, the implication is that it is a way of understanding reality. However, this is not sense perception but intellectual perception.

There may be more to the extremist mindset than preoccupations, attitudes, emotions and thinking patterns but the reminder of this chapter will focus on these four core elements of the extremist mindset. It would be futile to attempt to produce a complete list, but the examples given below are among the most striking characteristics of the extremist mindset. A person who has all of these characteristics has an extremist mindset, but no one characteristic is necessary. A person's mindset will count as extremist as long as it has a sufficient number of these characteristics but what counts as a sufficient number cannot be precisely stated. When a person has some of the relevant characteristics but not others it is a matter of judgement whether to classify their mindset as extremist. There may well be borderline cases where it is not clear whether a particular person's mindset is extremist. Extremism, like the individual components of the extremist mindset, is a matter of degree. It is possible to be more or less extremist but it is important that a theoretical account of extremism delivers the right judgements in actual cases. What follows, therefore, is not just an abstract theoretical account of core components of the extremist mindset but one that has some basis in what is known about the mindset of actual extremists.

Extremist preoccupations

An extremist preoccupation that has come up several times is purity.[7] The purity that preoccupies extremists can take different forms: racial, religious, or ideological. As noted in Chapter 2, the Khmer Rouge's pursuit of ideological purity was also part of a racialist project of ethnic purification. For

ISIS, the purity that matters is religious. It sees itself as defending a pure and unadulterated form of Islam, grounded in a supposedly literal reading of the Koran. Lack of purity is seen as justifying the targeting of the polluted and impure by all available means, including extreme violence. Given the extent to which extremists are preoccupied with purity, it comes as no surprise to find many of them engaged in acts of ethnic, ideological or religious 'cleansing'.

Among the dictionary definitions of 'pure' are the following: 'unmixed, unadulterated, of unmixed origin or descent, chaste, morally or sexually undefiled, not corrupt, guiltless, not discordant'. Purity is defined as 'pureness, cleanness and freedom from physical contamination or moral pollution'. On this account, purity looks like a worthy ideal. Impurity is adulteration, which sounds like a bad thing. The opposite of clean is dirty or soiled, and lack of cleanliness is not usually admired. When these seemingly innocuous observations are applied to matters of ideology, race or religion, the results have been disastrous. These are domains in which the purity that extremists value is bogus. However, this doesn't alter the fact that extremists tend to be preoccupied with it and that large numbers of people have been killed on account of it.

In the twentieth century, racial purity laws in Germany in the period from 1933 to 1935 were the ultimate expression of the extremist preoccupation with purity. These laws had two main objectives: to define 'Jew' and 'Aryan' and preserve racial purity by prohibiting sexual intercourse and intermarriage between Jews and so-called 'Aryans'. Different Nazi statutes set out different standards of racial purity, despite the fact that race was seen as biological.[8] To become a member of the SS,[9] the applicant had to prove Aryan ancestry back to 1750. In other contexts, a less demanding definition was adopted. However, the prevention of racial mixing was always a key concern since 'miscegenation undermines the very premise of racial purity laws, which is that the blood of Aryans or white people must be kept pure' (Scales-Trent 2001: 271). Intermarriage between members of so-called 'inferior' and 'superior' races would lead to the dilution and disappearance of the latter, and this was Hitler's ultimate rationale for the ban on racial mixing.

The focus on racial purity also plays a prominent role in twenty-first-century extremism. White supremacist groups have racial purity requirements on membership. As Julia Ebner notes, their mission is to create 'homogeneous societies' where 'different races and cultures do not mix'

(2020: 28).[10] The aim of one group studied by Ebner is to found an Aryan nation, the 'Northwest American Republic', whose residence and citizenship

> shall be restricted, absolutely and for all time, to those persons of unmixed Caucasian racial descent from any of the historic family of European nations, who shall have no known or identifiable non-White ancestry, and no visibly non-White element in their genetic makeup.[11]

A preoccupation with purity is evident in the manifesto of the young man who in 2019 massacred 51 worshippers at a mosque in Christchurch, New Zealand. He subscribed to the so-called 'Great Replacement' conspiracy theory, according to which mass immigration and fertility rates among immigrants will 'ultimately result in the complete cultural and racial replacement of the European people'.[12]

Racial purity is one thing, ideological purity is another. As noted in Chapter 2, the Khmer Rouge was obsessed with both. To the extent that communist ideology is against private property, a pure or purified form of communism will be one in which there is literally *no* private property. Since markets and money imply the existence of private property, neither markets nor money were permitted in Democratic Kampuchea. The ultimate stage in Pol Pot's pursuit of communist virtue was the abolition of private life. In Democratic Kampuchea, the state decided where one ate and who one married. Each of these impositions flowed from the Khmer Rouge's obsession with not being outdone in the ideological purity stakes. There were to be no concessions, however trivial, to private property and private life because Kampuchean communism was to be undiluted and unadulterated. In reality, of course, the party elite enjoyed privileges that were incompatible with their principles, but this did not prevent them from glorying in their supposed ideological purity.

As for religious purity, enough has already been said in this connection about ISIS and what one scholar describes as its project of 'purifying the Islamic lands of all alien and infidel influences' (Gerges 2016: 30). However, a preoccupation with purity is by no means unique to Islamist extremists or, indeed, to extremists. A version of the same preoccupation has played a part in the history of Christianity, especially in the rise of Puritanism. Hindu extremists in India have a preoccupation with religious purity that mirrors the same preoccupation in the mindset of Muslim extremists. In a study of the RSS, a Hindu extremist organization in India, Martha Nussbaum points to its preoccupation with 'ideas of purity and pollution' (2008: 87).[13] This is not surprising, given the extent to which Hindu supremacism is influenced by Nazi ideology.[14] The RSS pledge recited by its members includes the following line: 'I take the oath that I will always protect the purity of the Hindu religion, and the purity of Hindu culture, for the supreme progress of the Hindu nation.' It is hard to imagine a more explicit manifestation of the extremist's purity preoccupation.

Why is such a high value attached to purity? What is it about purity that appeals to the extremist mindset? One possibility is that the extremist's pre-occupation with purity is in reality a preoccupation with *im*purity. To be impure is to be defiled, and the undesirability of being defiled is taken as obvious. It also needs to be said that the purity preoccupation flows from a narrative of superiority and inferiority. Nazis and other white supremacists see the mixing of Aryan with non-Aryan blood as undesirable because they see Aryan blood as superior. For religious extremists who see their religion as superior to all others, religious 'impurity' is a diversion from the one true path. Aggressive measures against other religions, unbelievers and apostates is seen by them not as a sign of extremism but as an indication of their per-sonal virtue. This points to another, perhaps surprising, extremist preoccupa-tion: a preoccupation with virtue.

For the extremist mindset, purity and virtue are closely related, and no account of this mindset can afford to ignore its preoccupation with virtue. Purity implies incorruptibility, and incorruptibility is a form of virtue. In *Choosing Terror*, her study of the Terror after the French Revolution, Marisa Linton notes that 'for the revolutionary generation politics was about some-thing very different from ambition or egoism – it was about virtue' (2013: 1). Virtue meant selfless devotion to the public good, and the living embod-iment of virtue, in his own eyes and also the eyes of his fellow revolu-tionaries, was Maximilien Robespierre. In a biography of Robespierre, Ruth Scurr highlights the extent to which he was 'personally invested in the pub-lic image of himself as incorruptible' (2007: 183) and never in the wrong. He saw the Terror as a form of justice and an 'emanation of virtue' (Robes-pierre 2017: 115), not just virtue in the abstract but his own personal virtue.

Robespierre's preoccupations and personal style bring into focus several aspects of the extremist mindset. The way that an excessive preoccupation with purity and virtue led to the use of terror by Robespierre and his fellow Jacobins is especially revealing. What came to be known as 'terrorism' is seen by extremists as a legitimate means of imposing their values on those who need some persuading, as well as a method for weeding out those whose professed commitment to virtue is inauthentic. In the mind of the extremist, it is always in question whether a person's virtue is authentic, and this is another extremist preoccupation that Robespierre exemplified. Robespierre cultivated an ascetic and frugal personal style that was seen as a sign of virtue, hence his nickname: the Incorruptible. It is also no accident that modern-day extremists like Osama bin Laden go out of their way to project an image of asceticism. In the extremist mindset, virtue is closely connected to abstinence and self-denial. In the case of Robespierre and other extremists, the conviction of their own virtue made them self-righteous. What Amos Oz calls 'uncompromising righteousness' (2012: 57) is integral to the extremist style, if not the extremist mindset.

Two further extremist preoccupations are victimhood and humiliation. The extremist sees himself or herself and members of their in-group as victims of injustice and persecution. What Jason Stanley calls 'victimology' plays major role in the ideology and tactics of extremist parties and movements all over the world.[15] For example, Hindu extremists see themselves as victims of persecution, first by the Mughals and then the British. Their story is not just one of humiliation but also of what Martha Nussbaum calls 'humiliated masculinity' (2008: 85). In their victimology, 'Hindus have been subordinate for centuries, and their masculinity insulted, in part because they have not been aggressive and violent enough' (ibid.: 85). Pacifism was seen as part of the problem, according to this narrative, and this led to the assassination of Gandhi by former RSS member Nathuram Godse. In the West today, fantasies of persecution and humiliated masculinity are the driving force behind so-called 'Incels', a movement of involuntarily celibate men who think they are entitled to sex and trade on 'a sense of male victimhood' (Ebner 2020: 64).

Incels raise an interesting question for the present account of the extremist mindset. In their case, there is no real persecution to justify their complaints. Is this a general feature of the extremist preoccupation with persecution and victimhood, or is it possible that extremists are responding to genuine persecution and that their feelings of humiliation are not baseless? Are there cases in which extremists feel humiliated because they *have* been humiliated? This raises a further question: if a group of people are the victims of genuine persecution, then why should their preoccupation with it mark them out as extremists? The simple answer is that it does not: on its own, a preoccupation with real persecution does not make one an extremist. Talk of extremism is only appropriate when there is either a preoccupation with imaginary persecution, or a disproportionate or otherwise inappropriate response to real persecution. What counts as a disproportionate or inappropriate response needs spelling out, but in the extremist mindset a preoccupation with persecution will be combined with other extremist preoccupations and mindset features.

Enough has been said here about the extremist preoccupation with purity, virtue, and victimhood for several interim conclusions to be drawn: preoccupations are indeed a part of the extremist mindset even though no attempt has been made here to present an exhaustive list. Not all extremists have all the preoccupations listed here, and it is possible that someone with an extremist mindset will have a quite different set of preoccupations. In identifying a given extremist preoccupation, it is important that one's selection has some empirical basis. That is the reason for the extensive use of examples in the account given above. If there were no examples in the history of extremism of a preoccupation with purity, virtue or victimhood, then there would be no reason to see these are having any special relevance for an account of the extremist mindset. Furthermore, different extremist preoccupations generally go together in intelligible ways. Philosophical reflection on the notions of purity and virtue shows how the two are linked. People who are preoccupied with their own victimhood can be expected to be preoccupied with their humiliation. These preoccupations might be fuelled, in turn, by other extremist preoccupations, such as a preoccupation with a mythic past. Extremists like the RSS mythologize the past in an attempt to justify their feelings of humiliation. Reference to such feelings highlights the extent to which the extremist's preoccupations are motivated by feelings or emotions. This affective component of the extremist mindset is the next item on the agenda.

Extremism and the emotions

According to Hume, people are motivated to act by their emotions. Emotions, or what Hume calls *passions*, are the ultimate sources of human motivation. Among the passions by which we are motivated are: pride, fear, ambition, vanity, malice, aversion, and resentment. Hume also distinguishes between 'calm' and 'violent' passions. The calm passions 'cause no disorder in the soul' (2007: 268). Violent passions are stronger. For example, 'when I receive an injury from another, I often feel a violent passion of resentment, which makes me desire his evil and punishment, independent of all considerations of pleasure and advantage to myself' (ibid.: 268). This makes such passions sound irrational or unreasonable but Hume's view is that a passion is unreasonable only to the extent that it is based on a false judgement. For example, a violent feeling of resentment is irrational in a case of mistaken identity, where the resented person is not the person from whom an injury was received.

Hume's description of violent resentment making one person desire another person's evil and punishment sounds like an apt description of the extremist mindset. Although it is in the nature of humans to experience and be moved by violent passions, one might wonder whether extremists are *especially* susceptible to violent passions. Are they disproportionately influenced by such passions? Are there specific violent passions by which extremists tend to be moved? Is it the case that *irrational* emotions play a larger role in the extremist mindset than in non-extremist mindsets? Saucier and his colleagues do not make much of the emotions in their account of MEM but casual observation of extremists suggests that this mindset is one in which certain violent passions are indeed especially influential. How should such emotions be understood?

According to Bernard Williams, the emotions 'must be regarded both as productive of action and also as states to which we are subject' (1973: 223). Far from being mere blank occurrences, like some bodily sensations, emotions have an inbuilt reference to an object and involve thought. In Hume's example, the object of one's resentment is another person, and the underlying thought is that one has been wronged by that person. The role of rational thought in relation to the emotions is 'that of convincing one that a given object is no proper or appropriate object of that emotion' (Williams 1973: 224). Irrational emotions are ones that are unchecked by the realization that the grounding judgement is false. To feel an emotion towards a given object is to see it in a particular light. Ideally, the emotion will go away at the point at which one realizes that it is inappropriate to see the object in that light. However, 'when considerations which show the emotion to be inappropriate fail to displace it, this is not because it is an emotion but because it is an irrational emotion' (ibid.: 224). Irrational emotions are *recalcitrant* emotions.

Two emotions that play a significant role in the extremist mindset have already been mentioned: anger and feeling humiliated. To this list, one might add resentment and self-pity. Why these emotions? Because they are closely related to extremist preoccupations: it stands to reason that extremists who are preoccupied with their victimhood will also be subject to feelings of humiliation and self-pity, as well as resentment and anger towards their supposed persecutors. In the extremist mindset anger, resentment, self-pity and humiliation are often disproportionate. Extremist resentment is *extreme* resentment and extremist anger is *extreme* anger, regardless of whether such extreme emotions are justified by the facts. Extremists fail to recognize the extent to which their emotions are inappropriate and fail to modify emotions whose inappropriateness they recognize. They are not only subject to violent passions but their violent passions are also highly recalcitrant.

This sketch of the emotional component of the extremist mindset conceals a number of complexities. Consider the emotions of ANC activists in apartheid-era South Africa. Many felt intense anger and resentment at their treatment. However, the intensity of their anger did not make them extremists in the psychological sense because their anger was justified. The same goes for their resentment. In his influential essay 'Freedom and Resentment', Strawson stresses 'how much we actually mind, how much it matters to us, whether the actions of other people … reflect attitudes towards us of goodwill, affection, or esteem on the one hand, or contempt, indifference, or malevolence on the other' (2008a: 5–6). It is in the latter case that we feel resentful. The resentment of the ANC was intelligible and justified because apartheid reflected contempt, indifference *and* malevolence. A violent passion of resentment was not evidence of an extremist mindset because it was *appropriate* resentment. In contrast, there was little evidence of self-pity in the ANC's stance even if self-pity would also have been justified. The ANC responded not by feeling sorry for itself but by armed resistance.

Did the victims of apartheid feel humiliated? In his autobiography, Nelson Mandela recounts attempts by the warders on Robben Island to humiliate black prisoners. They referred to their prisoners as 'boy' and insisted on being called 'boss'. Prisoners were made to wear short trousers because 'short trousers for Africans were meant to remind us that we were "boys"' (1994: 455). To humiliate a person is to injure their dignity or self-respect. Forcing ANC prisoners to wear shorts was clearly an *attempt* to humiliate them but it does not follow that Mandela and his fellow prisoners *were* or *felt* humiliated. What they felt was justified resentment about the attempt to make them feel small. Mandela's response was to protest against the Robben Island dress code. When he was offered long trousers, he refused to wear them unless all the other prisoners were treated the same way.

At the opposite end of the scale is the so-called Men's Rights Movement (MRM), of which Incels are a part. Anger, resentment, humiliation and self-pity are among the emotions that motivate men's rights extremists. In this case, unlike that of the ANC, the fact that these individuals experience extreme anger, resentment, humiliation and self-pity *is* one of the factors that marks out their mindset as an extremist mindset. The sociologist Michael Kimmel identifies several features of the MRM mindset that support its classification as extremist. Kimmel argues that 'white men's anger comes from the potent fusion of two sentiments: entitlement and a sense of victimization' (2017: x). The entitlement is 'aggrieved entitlement', the sense that 'those benefits to which you believed yourself entitled have been snatched away from you by unseen forces larger and more powerful' (ibid.: x). The MRM sees white men as the victims of oppression and discrimination at the hands of the liberal elite and women they call 'Feminazis'. Men's rights activists are unmoved by statistics suggesting that American white men are 'still among the most privileged group of people on the face of the earth' (ibid.: 45). Their anger and resentment at their supposed victimization are kept at fever pitch by radio talk shows that specialize in the manufacturing of rage and self-pity.

In deciding whether the MRM's feelings about the white male predicament indicate an extremist mindset, there are several issues to take into consideration. The nature and intensity of these feelings are certainly relevant, but of much greater significance is the extent to which these feelings are irrational and disconnected from reality. In one sense they are not. The MRM can be seen as a reaction to the *actual* political and economic marginalization of sections of American society. The sense in which it is nevertheless disconnected from reality is that it is based on a series of myths about American history and society, including myths about the causes of their own marginalization. People with an extremist mindset are resentful about non-actual persecution or towards social groups who are in no way responsible for their real marginalization.

Before moving on, there is one more factor to consider. Recent accounts of the so-called 'age of anger' not only refer to the various violent passions discussed above but also to *ressentiment*. In his book, *Age of Anger*, Mishra defines this as 'an existential resentment of other people's being, caused by an intense mix of envy and sense of humiliation and powerlessness' (2018: 14). For Kimmel, the ressentiment of angry white men is 'a personal sense of self that is defined always in a relationship to some perceived injury and whose collective politics mixes hatred and envy of those who they believe have injured us' (2017: 38). The idea of ressentiment, which is associated above all with Nietzsche, captures several elements of the emotional component of the extremist mindset. The task of giving an analysis of ressentiment and its role in extremism will be undertaken in Chapter 7. Meanwhile, the discussion here can be summarized as follows: to have an extremist mindset is to be motivated by certain violent passions or emotions that are linked to extremist preoccupations. These natural emotions become problematic when they are exaggerated, irrational or based on false beliefs about the nature of reality. These defects are evident in extremist anger, resentment, humiliation and self-pity. These emotions reflect extremist preoccupations but that is not all. They are also expressive of the attitudinal component of the extremist mindset. What are the attitudes that are associated with an extremist mindset, and how are they related to extremist preoccupations and emotions? These are the questions to which answers are now needed.

Extremist attitudes

In the psychological literature on the militant extremist mindset, one attitude stands out: Pro-Violence. *Militant* extremism involves a favourable attitude towards violence as a means to one's political ends. However, the mere fact that one is Pro-Violence in certain cases does not make one an extremist. It depends on the ends for which violence is to be used and whether there is an alternative to violence. Militant extremists almost always *claim* that they are not in favour of violence for its own sake and that they have no alternative. If they are taken at their word, and their ends are worthy, then the fact that they are 'Pro-Violence' in a limited sense might make them *militants* but does not make them *extremists*. The charge of extremism would have to be justified on other grounds. As the case of Merry illustrates, it is also possible to have an extremist mindset without being Pro-Violence. Pro-Violence is part of the *militant* extremist mindset, but extremism need not be militant.

One thing that extremists *are* in favour of is being totally uncompromising, at least in some domains. Extremists were described above as people who believe uncompromisingly, where this is understood as a statement about their dispositions. It is also an account of their *attitude* towards compromise. Their attitude to compromise is not just implicitly but often also explicitly hostile. If challenged to justify their attitude, it is likely that they will describe those matters about which they are unwilling to compromise as matters of principle. This raises an obvious question: what distinguishes an extremist's unwillingness to compromise from that of a person of principle? In what circumstances does hostility to compromise indicate an extremist mindset as distinct from what might be called a 'principled mindset'?

Compromise is a subject that has attracted surprisingly little philosophical interest. There is, however, one notable exception to the neglect of this subject, Avishai Margalit's *On Compromise and Rotten Compromises*.[16] This is how Margalit summarizes the message of his book:

> On the whole, political compromises are a good thing. Political compromises for the sake of peace are a very good thing. Shabby, shady, and shoddy compromises are bad but not sufficiently bad to be always avoided as all costs, especially when they are concluded for the sake of peace. Only rotten compromises are to be avoided at all costs.
>
> (2010: 16)

A compromise in the 'anaemic sense' is any feasible agreement between two or more parties. A sanguine compromise is an agreement that also involves recognizing the other side and its point of view as legitimate. A sanguine compromise 'may even involve a measure of sacrifice from the strong side, not driving as hard a bargain as it could to get what it desires' (ibid.: 41). The aim is to 'dispel an image of domination' (ibid.: 41). Sanguine compromises 'must be based on mutual concessions: on splitting the difference' (ibid.: 48). An important form of sanguine compromise is 'for both sides to give up on their "dreams" so that what remains to negotiate is a range of possible agreements' (ibid.: 46). Lastly, and most importantly for present purposes, a *rotten* compromise is 'an agreement to establish or maintain an inhuman regime, a regime of cruelty and humiliation, that is, a regime that does not treat humans as humans' (ibid.: 2). A rotten compromise should be avoided '*come what may*' (ibid.: 90; emphasis added). A compromise in support of a racist regime is 'the epitome of rottenness' (ibid.: 4).

One of Margalit's observations is that the notion of a political compromise is caught between two pictures of politics: the economic and the religious. In the first picture, everything is subject to compromise. In the second picture, 'there are things over which we must never compromise' (ibid.: 24). Most of us recognize that some aspects of politics are covered by the economic picture while others are better thought of in terms of the religious picture. In other words, most of us have a 'stereoscopic political perception' (ibid.: 148). What Margalit calls 'sectarians' are in the grip of the religious picture and nothing else:

> Sectarianism is a mode of operation and a state of mind … The state of mind is that of keeping your principled position uncompromised, come what may. Sectarianism is a disposition to view any compromise as a rotten compromise … [The sectarian] finds compromise a capitulation, a betrayal of the cause … There is more to the sectarian cast of mind than just a negative attitude to compromise. But in my view the refusal to compromise is its main feature.
>
> (ibid.: 148–9)

Whereas sanguine compromise involves a willingness to compromise on a dream, sectarians regard their dreams as non-negotiable and sacred. It is their belief that they can 'have it all' that 'encourages the view that compromise is surrender' (ibid.: 47).

Although Margalit talks about 'sectarianism' rather than 'extremism', much of what he says about the former is applicable to the latter. In the first place, what he refers to as a sectarian *cast of mind* can be understood as a mindset. One of its main features is an *attitude*, an attitude to compromise. Furthermore, Margalit rightly links hostility to compromise with an obsession with purity. Purity is based on the fear of mixing categories. In his obsession with purity, the sectarian 'regards compromise as an act of pollution' (ibid.: 156). 'Shit is the negation of the pure' and 'the sectarian craves life without shit' (ibid.: 157). Most usefully of all, Margalit offers at least a partial solution to the challenge of distinguishing a person of principle from an extremist.

A non-extremist person of principle will not subscribe to a purely economic view of politics. They will not regard everything as negotiable and subject to bargaining. They will be prepared to make compromises, especially compromises for the sake of peace, but they will not be prepared to make rotten compromises. For them, the ban on rotten compromises is a genuine matter of principle. Extremists are not just uncompromising about the *wrong* things but uncompromising about *everything* in the political realm. They see '*any* compromise [as] a shameful capitulation' (ibid. 10). To put it another way, they see all compromises as rotten, including ones that are made for the sake of peace and that do not establish or maintain an inhuman regime. Extremists are so preoccupied with purity that for them not even keeping the peace justifies sanguine compromises. They would literally rather die or go to war than compromise. This explains why extremists are often violent and fits in with Roth's account of Merry as someone who would rather starve than compromise about not harming other living creatures.

These considerations should help to alleviate the worry that being an extremist is, at least as far as attitudes to compromise are concerned, indistinguishable from being principled. A person of principle is not preoccupied with purity, does not have a purely religious view of politics, and does not regard all compromises as rotten. True extremists are preoccupied with purity, have a purely religious view of politics and regard all compromises as rotten. They are not prepared to compromise on their dreams, and would rather die than compromise, even on relatively trivial matters. Extremists, like sectarians, have a one-track mind. They suffer from a form of monomania that makes them incapable of distinguishing between areas in which compromise and bargaining are appropriate and areas in which they are not.[17] Because they regard all compromises as rotten, they do not accept that some compromises are better than others.

Where does this leave the idea that extremism in the psychological sense is not just a matter of *what* one believes but also of *how* one believes? It has been suggested that extremists believe uncompromisingly but it is possible to believe uncompromisingly without having an extremist mindset. For example, an unwillingness to compromise about a narrow range of questions does not indicate a negative attitude to compromise as such. Nor does being unwilling to compromise about a much wider range of questions if this unwillingness is grounded in the belief that the rejected compromises are rotten. Extremists reject what they regard as rotten compromises but so do people of principle. Whether an unwillingness to compromise points to an extremist mindset depends crucially on why the uncompromising believer believes that the compromises he rejects are rotten, whether this belief is justified, and whether the compromises he rejects are in fact rotten. His belief that the compromises he rejects are rotten will be based on other things he believes, so what he believes is again relevant. What is problematic is not the belief that the compromises one rejects are rotten but a general tendency to detect rottenness in compromises that aren't rotten. The sense in which people with an extremist mindset 'believe uncompromisingly' is that they are insufficiently discriminating about what counts as a rotten compromise and have other unjustified beliefs about the nature and implications of the compromises they reject. They tend to believe, on inadequate grounds, that the compromises they reject represent a capitulation or betrayal of a supposedly non-negotiable principle.

Even this already complex discussion is too simple. Consider the case of a person whose belief that the compromises he or she rejects are rotten is *false* but still *justified* by the limited information at his or her disposal. Suppose that person is the victim of misinformation or propaganda. He or she is still insufficiently discriminating about what counts as a rotten compromise, but through no fault of his or her own.[18] Does unwillingness to compromise indicate an extremist mindset? Is it also relevant whether a person is uncompromising in his or her belief that he or she only rejects rotten compromises? Is Margalit's view of a rotten compromise too narrow? Can a compromise be genuinely rotten even if it does not establish or maintain a regime of cruelty and humiliation? A compromise to establish or maintain a racist regime is the epitome of rottenness but what about a compromise to establish or maintain a regime that discriminates against women or impoverishes large numbers of its citizens? There is clearly scope for a wider conception of rottenness than Margalit's. However, this does not affect the main point of the discussion so far: the sense in which extremists have a negative attitude to compromise is not straightforward and cannot, in any event, be understood without taking account of what else the extremist believes. It isn't just a matter of 'how' they believe.

A negative attitude to compromise is closely related to three other attitudinal elements of the extremist mindset: indifference, intolerance and anti-pluralism. The indifference that is a component of the extremist mindset includes indifference to any adverse consequences of their unwillingness to compromise.[19] If the extremist's uncompromising posture is harmful to them or to other people, their attitude is: that's just too bad and a price worth paying if the alternative is capitulation. The extremist mindset is a mixture of concern and indifference. When it comes to whether their own principles are put into practice, there is no lack of concern. Extremist indifference is indifference to any unfortunate repercussions of their principles. In much the same way, extremists are indifferent to evidence that their objectives are impractical. They believe in the power of creative destruction for the sake of a higher good, and this implies an indifference to the fate of those affected by their policies. This was the form of indifference displayed by two of the twentieth century's most prolific mass murderers. Neither Stalin nor Mao was disturbed by the notion that their policies would result in the death of millions of their fellow citizens. Unlike Hitler, mass extermination was not their primary objective, but they were supremely relaxed about the fact that their policies would in fact end up killing millions. They simply didn't care.

Extremists are often described as intolerant, but what form does their intolerance take and what is its rationale? They have a Manichaean world-view, a strong sense of dualism 'between the realm of light and goodness (us) and the realm of darkness and evil (them)' (Margalit 2010: 153–4). This is the world-view that underpins extremist intolerance. One form of extremist intolerance is intolerance of the Other, based on the supposed evil of the Other. In this context, 'the Other' is any member of a despised 'out-group'. A perspective in which 'there is no twilight, no room for compromise' (ibid.: 154) is one in which intolerance looks inevitable and justified. After all, why should we tolerate others who are part of an axis of evil? By the same token, extremists see no reason to tolerate what they regard as misguided ideas, especially if these are ideas associated with, and promoted by, the Other.

The playing up of the division 'us' and 'them' and the identification of one's opponents as the Other are a form of *othering*, that is, 'the attribution of relative inferiority and/or radical alienness to some other/out-group' (Brons 2015: 83). Othering, understood as a practice that is expressive of a hostile attitude towards specified Others, is so integral to the extremist mindset that some scholars *define* extremism in these terms. According to J.M. Berger, for example, an 'in-group' is a group of people who share an identity – the 'us' in 'us versus them'. The out-group consists of people who are excluded from the in-group – the 'them' in 'us versus them'. People have a natural tendency to esteem their own in-group but extremists amplify this tendency. Accordingly, Berger defines extremism as 'the belief that an in-group's success or survival can never be separated from the need for hostile action against an out-group' (2018: 44). Different extremists vilify different out-groups – people of colour, immigrants, women, Jews, atheists, and so on – but the structure of their extremism is similar. Political extremism is the politics of us and them in an exaggerated form.[20]

No simple definition of extremism in terms of belief is likely to be adequate. Extremism is not one belief and not just a matter of belief. Even if one concentrates on the psychological dimension of extremism and ignores its methods, the extremist mindset is more complex than a belief about the need for hostile action against an out-group. Still, Berger is partly right: the othering and vilification of selected out-groups are an important element of the extremist mindset. They are linked to other elements of this mindset, including its intolerance, attitude to compromise and preoccupation with purity. The extremist mindset is a package of interlocking elements, and the links between these elements make sense on their own terms. Berger's analysis also brings out another important element of the extremist package, its attitude to pluralism. As he notes, 'pluralistic societies accept and even celebrate differences between individuals' (ibid.: 25). Extremism is anti-pluralist, and this is the next and last extremist attitude to be considered here.

Pluralism is characterized by Isaiah Berlin as the view that 'the ends of men are many, and not all of them are in principle compatible with each other' (2013a: 239). This means that 'the possibility of conflict – and of tragedy – can never be wholly eliminated from human life, either personal or social' (ibid.: 239).[21] This 'pluralism of values' implies that 'there are many ends that men may seek and still be fully rational, fully men, capable of understanding each other and sympathizing and deriving light from each other' (ibid.: 11). Elsewhere Berlin points to a deep difference between human beings in general. On the one side are those who relate everything to a single central vision, a single universal organizing principle in terms of which they understand, think and feel. On the other side are those who pursue many ends and don't try to fit them all into a single all-embracing vision. The first kind of personality is that of the hedgehog while the second kind is that of the fox. In these terms, 'pluralism has a legitimate claim to be regarded as the philosophy of the fox in its purest form' (Lyons 2020: xvii).

If pluralism is the philosophy of the fox, monism is the philosophy of the hedgehog and an integral part of the extremist mindset. The monist finds it impossible to accept that 'there is no uniquely right way of living' (ibid.: 7). Lenin, Stalin, Mao and Hitler were not known for their openness to different values, different ends and different ways of living. The ideology of ISIS and the RSS is the ideology of people for whom diversity of belief and values is anathema. This is partly the result of their Manicheanism. If 'we' are good and 'they' are evil, then our way is the right way and their way is the wrong way. If there is an objective truth about the way human beings should live, a truth to be found in the Koran, or the Bible or the works of Marx or wherever, then the fact that the ends of men are many is neither here nor there. Those with different ends must be re-educated or crushed. In this way, monism is tied to what might be called *impositionism*, the conviction that it is legitimate and perhaps even essential to impose one's vision of the ideal form of life on other people. The monist thinks that everyone must be made to share his or her vision if they don't already subscribe to it.

Paradoxically, what makes value monism so lethal is not just its impositionism but its idealism: its conviction that every genuine question has only one true answer, that there is a dependable way of knowing what that answer is, and that true answers to different genuine questions must be compatible with each other. As Berlin puts it, monists are convinced that

> somewhere, in the past or in the future, in divine revelation or in the mind of an individual thinker, in the pronouncements of history or science, or in the simple heart of an uncorrupted good man, there is a final solution.
>
> (2013a: 237)

This is a final solution to the central problems of life. This one belief, more than any other, 'is responsible for the slaughter of individuals on the altars of the great historical ideals' (ibid.: 237), such as progress, justice or the happiness of future generations:

> For if one really believes that such a solution is possible, then surely no cost would be too high to obtain it: to make mankind just and happy and creative and harmonious forever – what could be too high a price to pay for that? To make such an omelette, there is surely no limit to the number of eggs that should be broken – that was the faith of Lenin, of Trotsky, of Mao, for all I know, of Pol Pot.
>
> (2013b: 15–16)

Even when the ideals for which militant extremists fight remain unrealized, their victims are no less dead; 'the eggs are broken, and the habit of breaking them grows, but the omelette remains invisible' (ibid.: 17).

Extremism's idealism is closely related to its utopianism. The place of utopianism in the extremist mindset is noted by John Gray. He gives the example of Lenin, who 'never gave up on the belief that, after a period of revolutionary terror, the state would be abolished' (2007: 8–9). Similarly,

Trotsky defended the taking and killing of hostages as a necessary stage on the way to a 'Bolshevik utopia' (ibid.: 9). Someone with a utopian mindset – and this includes not just Bolsheviks but also Nazis and Islamic extremists – sees history as 'a prelude to a new world' (ibid.: 3) that can only be brought into being through a process of creative destruction. According to Gray, the belief that 'a better type of society than any that has ever existed can be brought into existence by the systematic use of violence' is a 'uniquely modern pathology' (ibid.: xix). It is also a belief shared by many early twenty-first-century American neo-conservatives ('neocons'), and this is a respect in which their mindset is an extremist mindset.

Is it possible to be an extremist but not a monist? The focus so far has been on 'big picture' extremism, that is, versions of extremism that incorporate a picture of the ideal form of life. This type of extremist has views about many different aspects of human life, including what would be regarded by pluralists as aspects of a person's private life. However, there are also 'single-issue' extremists who care about only one thing and have no interest in the idea that there is a uniquely correct way of living, except insofar as one's way of living affects the issue the extremist cares about. For example, so-called 'animal rights extremists' care about the welfare of animals, and some use violent methods to prevent experiments on animals. If such people are properly described as extremists, it is on account of their *methods* rather than their commitment to a particular picture of the ideal form of life. They may be quite happy to accept the fact that the ends of human beings are many as long as the achievement of these ends does not involve cruelty to animals.

This suggests that anti-pluralism is not a necessary element of the extremist mindset. However, as noted above, the mindset analysis does not try to identify individually necessary elements of the extremist mindset. The project is rather to identify a range of psychological elements that bear on whether a person has an extremist mindset. A person has an extremist mindset only if they have a sufficient number of extremist preoccupations, attitudes, and so on. Given that no one attitude is necessary, the fact that single-issue extremists are not anti-pluralist leaves it open whether their mindset is extremist. This matter can only be resolved by examining other aspects of their psychology and working out whether, *taken together*, they add up to an extremist mindset. If not, then what we have here is not a true mindset extremist who is not anti-pluralist but a methods extremist who is not a mindset extremist.

Extremist thinking

Are there distinctive ways of thinking that are associated with the extremist mindset? In order to answer this question, one would need to know what thinking is and what counts as a way of thinking. According to the psychologist Jonathan Baron, thinking is a goal-directed activity that involves, among other things, the evaluation of possibilities and the weighing up of evidence.[22] The *goal* is to answer a question, the *possibilities* are answers to the question implicit in the goal, and *evidence* is used to evaluate possibilities. On this account, thinking is a 'method of choosing among potential possibilities' (Baron 1985: 90), and particular ways of thinking are particular ways of doing that. That is, they are distinctive ways of including or excluding possibilities, of evaluating evidence, and drawing conclusions. The particular ways of thinking that are associated with an extremist mindset are conspiracy thinking, apocalyptic thinking, and catastrophic thinking (sometimes called 'catastrophizing'). Each of these can be understood in terms of Baron's framework.

A standard goal of extremists who see themselves as victimized is to understand their situation. Among the possible explanations they focus on are conspiratorial explanations, that is, ones that blame their victimization on conspiracies by the Other. Confirmation bias then leads to a positive evaluation of evidence of conspiracy and a negative evaluation of contrary evidence. As a result, the extremist's method of choosing among possibilities results in the endorsing of a conspiracy theory to explain their situation. In this way, the extremist mindset is also a conspiracist mindset. What Margalit says about sectarians is also true of extremists: they believe that 'nothing is what it appears and that everything important is hidden' (2010: 160).

Psychologists have written extensively about the so-called 'conspiracy mentality'. Their starting-point is a paper by Goertzel which argues that conspiracism is a *monological* belief system in which 'each of the beliefs serves as evidence for each of the other beliefs' and 'the more conspiracies a monological thinker believes in, the more likely he or she is to believe in any new conspiracy theory which may be proposed' (1994: 740). Monological thinkers 'do not search for factual evidence for their theories. Instead, they offer the same hackneyed explanation for every problem' (ibid.: 741). It is worth noting that the same hackneyed explanation favoured by many extremists is one that blames the Jews. This feature of conspiracism is best explained in ideological rather than psychological terms. The ideologies to which people with an extremist mindset are attracted are not only conspiracist but also, in many cases, anti-Semitic. Why that should be so is an issue that cannot be tackled here.[23]

How is conspiracy thinking related to other elements of the extremist mindset? On the face of it, there are very few direct connections. For example, there is no obvious connection between being anti-pluralist and being a conspiracy theorist, or between conspiracy thinking and a preoccupation with purity. This opens up the possibility of a person who has most or all of the other features of the extremist mindset but not conspiracism. The latter is not required for a person to be an extremist even if, as a matter of historical and political fact, extremism and conspiracism generally go together. It remains an open question how to explain this link, not to mention the connection between extremism and anti-Semitic conspiracism. However, conspiracism can be a part of the extremist mindset even if it is not an indispensable part. The generalization that extremists tend to be conspiracy theorists can be correct and relevant for the purposes of describing the extremist mindset, even if there is no contradiction in the hypothesis of a psychological extremist with no interest in conspiracy theories.

Apocalyptic thinking, which includes the type of thinking in which ISIS specializes, is preoccupied with the end of the world. Catastrophic thinking, or catastrophizing, is the 'perception that great calamities either have occurred, are occurring, or will occur' (Saucier et al. 2009: 261). Apocalyptic and catastrophic thinking are related and many extremists engage in both. For example, in 2014, ISIS fought for control of Dabiq, an obscure village in Syria, because of a prophecy identifying it as the 'unlikely setting for one of the final battles of the Islamic apocalypse' (McCants 2015: 102). The battle would result in the defeat of the infidels by a Muslim army and be followed by the Day of Judgement. For white supremacists, the impending catastrophe is the 'white genocide', the replacement of the white population by 'immigration, integration, abortion and violence against white people' (Davey and Ebner 2019: 7). The defeat of these forces will reverse the genocide and establish a racially pure white utopia. ISIS also claims to offer its fighters a ticket to paradise as a reward for their religious purity. Paradoxically, catastrophizing and its preoccupation with utopia are two sides of the same coin in the extremist mindset.

The inclusion of apocalyptic thinking in the extremist mindset might be questioned on the basis that it is not just *possible* for extremists not to engage in this type of thinking but also that there is no shortage of *actual* extremists who are not apocalyptic. It is noteworthy, for example, that Osama bin Laden was dismissive of ISIS's apocalyptic thinking and saw it as an affectation.[24] This is one key difference between conspiracy and apocalyptic thinking. The former is much more prevalent in extremist thinking than the latter. This might count against including apocalyptic thinking in the extremist mindset. The issue is not whether it is possible to be an extremist without engaging in apocalyptic thinking – it is – but whether extremists from a diverse range of regions, religions and political orientations display a tendency to think in apocalyptic terms. If not, then Saucier's inductive approach will not justify its inclusion in the extremist mindset.

This discussion crystallizes some of the methodological issues with which this chapter began. The strength of the inductive model developed by Saucier and others is that it provides a simple methodology for identifying the extremist mindset. The essence of this methodology is generalization from a suitably diverse sample of extremist groups. Common elements are included while elements that are less common are excluded. No attempt is made to rank different elements of the extremist mindset in order of importance or to determine whether a given element is essential. So far in this chapter it has been assumed that no one component of the extremist mindset is indispensable. A person's mindset will count as extremist as long as it has a sufficient number of the elements identified by empirical study of the psychology of actual extremist groups.

In the light of the recent discussion, one might wonder whether this is quite right. Even in the case of ways of thinking, like conspiracy thinking, that are common to various different extremists, we have no difficulty in conceiving of an extremist mindset from which this type of thinking is absent. However, the same is not true of all extremist mindset components. Some are much harder to imagine away than others. Is it possible to conceive of an extremist who is willing to compromise and live and let live? The natural reaction to such imaginings is to say that the mindset of a person who is both compromising and tolerant of different ways of living is, by definition, not an extremist mindset. In contrast, the mindset of a person with no interest in the apocalypse or conspiracy theories could still be extremist. The implication is that some of the extremist mindset elements identified by the inductive method are more important than others. The other is that some specific elements are necessary. If there is anything to this, then the extremist mindset is not an undifferentiated collection of mindset components. It has both core and peripheral elements, and the difference between the two is of considerable interest and importance.

Among the strongest candidates for the status of core elements of the extremist mindset are its characteristic attitudes. Thinking styles are among the weakest. Intuitively, this seems right. While there is an association between psychological extremism and specific ways of thinking, this association is less compelling than that between the extremist mindset and specific attitudes. When it comes to psychological extremism, intolerance, indifference as understood here, and hostility to compromise are hard to view as optional extras. They are, in some sense, constitutive of an extremist mindset. Emotions like anger and resentment have a less strong, but still respectable claim to core status. Preoccupations are more of a mixed bag. Virtue and purity are common enough extremist preoccupations, but not clearly essential. On the other hand, a preoccupation with victimization is closer to the core, though there is room for debate about this.

To sum up. I have argued in this chapter that psychological extremism is not simply a matter of what a person believes or even of how they believe. Exclusively belief-based views of extremism are in danger of missing several key components of the extremist's psychology. This psychology is best understood as a mindset, and the components of this mindset can be divided into different, though related, categories. These mindset components can be viewed in two ways: as a collection of equally important elements, no one of which is indispensable, or as differing in importance and dispensability. Having started with the first of these views, the discussion has moved gradually towards the second, with certain attitudes taking priority over other extremist mindset components. There is plenty of scope for further discussion of these issues but the crucial point is this: while extremism can be understood as a matter of doctrine or methods, it is in many ways most illuminating to understand it as a cast of mind or mentality. This is the conception of extremism that talk of the 'extremist mindset' attempts to capture.

Notes

1 Lyndon B. Johnson was the 36th President of the United States. He was in office from 1963 to 1969 and presided over America's growing involvement in Vietnam.
2 Hoffer (1951).

3 On Hume's theory, see Smith (1987).

4 Mishra (2018).

5 Baron (1985).

6 There is more on this conception of a 'way of thinking' in Chapter 3 of Cassam (2019a).

7 See Fraser (2021: 106–30) for a theological defence of the purity preoccupation. For Fraser, this preoccupation is tied to the sense of there being a proper order of things that should be respected. For the anthropologist Mary Douglas, 'purity is the enemy of change, of ambiguity and compromise' (2002: 200). This insight points to a connection between extremism's purity preoccupation and its rejection of compromise.

8 Scales-Trent (2001).

9 'SS' was an abbreviation of 'Schutzstaffel', a Nazi paramilitary organization founded by Hitler in 1925.

10 See, also, Miller-Idriss (2020: 49).

11 For the source of this quotation, see Ebner (2020: 19).

12 1 See Davey and Ebner (2019) for further discussion of this theory and its role in mainstreaming extremism.

13 RSS stands for Rashtriya Swayamsevak Sangh (National Corps of Volunteers), a militant organization at the heart of the Hindu right.

14 As Nussbaum (2007: 5) notes, the founders of the Hindu right in the 1920s and 1930s were great admirers of Italian and German fascism. M. S. Golwalkar, a key RSS ideologue, expressed his admiration for Nazi ideas in *We, Or Our Nation Defined*, a book he published in 1939. On this, see Nussbaum (ibid.: 160) and pp. 7–8 of the report by the Coalition Against Genocide (CAG) on ethnic violence in Gujarat in 2002 (CAG 2005).

15 See Chapter 6 of Stanley (2018) for an illuminating account of the politics of victimhood in relation to fascism. As Stanley puts it, 'the exploitation of the feeling of victimization by dominant groups at the prospect of sharing citizenship and power with minorities is a universal element of contemporary international fascist politics' (ibid.: 95).

16 Margalit (2010).

17 On the link between extremism and monomania, see Salmon (2002).

18 Such a person has what Hardin (2002) calls a 'crippled epistemology'.

19 Scruton (2007: 237).

20 The sub-title of Stanley's book on fascism (Stanley 2018) is 'the politics of us and them'. This points to one sense in which fascism is a form of extremism regardless of concerns of where it is on the left-right ideological spectrum.

21 This quotation, like the previous one, is from Berlin's essay 'Two Concepts of Liberty' (Berlin 2013a).

22 Baron (1985).

23 There is more on this in Byford (2011), Chapter 5, and Cassam (2019b).

24 McCants (2015: 27–8).

5 Extremism, fanaticism, fundamentalism

The fanatic

When Heydrich's Mercedes slowed down at a hairpin bend on the route to his office in the centre of Prague, his assassins were lying in wait. Josef Gabčík's gun jammed but a grenade thrown by Jan Kubiš exploded against the car's rear wheel. At first it appeared that Heydrich had survived. He jumped out and chased Gabčík but collapsed before he was able to finish him off. Heydrich had been fatally wounded by shrapnel and died a week later, on 4 June 1942, at the age of 38.[1]

Reinhard Heydrich's death ended the life of a man who, in the words of his biographer, is widely recognized as 'one of the great iconic villains of the twentieth century, an appalling figure even within the context of the Nazi elite' (Gerwarth 2011: xiii). Heydrich had been the head of the Reich Security Main Office, which included the Gestapo, and the Reich Protector of Bohemia and Moravia. A few months before his death he had chaired a meeting at Wannsee at which he outlined the so-called 'Final Solution to the Jewish Question'. The purpose of the meeting was, in the words of one historian, to 'discuss the logistics of extermination' (Evans 2008: 265).

It is hard to be a moderate Nazi but Heydrich's fanaticism was off the scale. Even other senior Nazis feared him. He was the perfect Nazi, described by Himmler as someone who 'from the deepest reaches of his heart and his blood ... felt, understood and realized the world view of Adolf Hitler'.[2] Heydrich was an implementer rather than a theorist of Nazism.

DOI: 10.4324/9780429325472-5

He is sometimes represented as having been consumed by ambition rather than by ideology:

> Yet anyone who reads his written memoranda and statements must surely be impressed by their mindless and total assimilation of Nazi ideology, their permeation by the thought-patterns of Nazism, their lack of recognition of any possible alternative to the Nazi world-view ... Nazi ideology appeared to be for Heydrich something utterly impersonal, an unquestioned set of ideas and attitudes that it was his ambition to put into effect with cold, passionate efficiency.
>
> (ibid.: 276)

Nevertheless, he was a relatively late convert to Nazism. In an early naval career, he was seen by colleagues as apolitical or even liberal. He was converted by his future wife, Lina von Osten, who was already a 'convinced Nazi and a vehement anti-Semite' (Gerwarth 2011: 41) when she first met him in 1930. It was thanks to her connections that Heydrich landed a job working for Himmler. After that, there was no looking back, despite unfounded rumours that he was, in fact, a Jew.[3]

Heydrich was the fanatic's fanatic, a true fanatic in every sense. Yet there are aspects of his fanaticism that are hard to reconcile with historically influential accounts of fanaticism. That is one reason for focusing on him. The image of the fanatic today is that of the hot-headed, passionate religious zealot, the self-flagellating maniac who glorifies self-sacrifice and delights in the physical destruction of his enemies. Yet Heydrich was anything but hot-headed. His fanaticism was cold rather than hot, politically rather than religiously inspired. The fanatic, it has been suggested, adopts one or more 'sacred values' and 'needs to treat a value as sacred in order to preserve the unity of the self' (Katsafanas 2019: 13). Heydrich's fanaticism seemingly had little to do with sacred values or a need to preserve his unity.

What, then, is a fanatic? What is the relationship between fanaticism and extremism? Is it possible to be a fanatic but not an extremist, or an extremist but not a fanatic? Is it helpful to think of fanaticism as a mindset, a methodology or as a position in ideological space? The notion of a fanatic is often related to that of a fundamentalist. It has been argued, for example, that fundamentalism 'can be viewed as regression to the spirit of fanaticism' (Laqueur 1999: 98). What is the relationship between the concepts of fanaticism, fundamentalism and extremism? Are they one and the same concept, different concepts that pick out the same property, or different concepts that pick out different properties? These are among the questions to be addressed in what follows.

A common complaint about philosophical and other accounts of fanaticism is that they ignore the possibility that fanaticism might be praiseworthy in certain circumstances. In what Joel Olson calls the 'pejorative tradition' (2007: 686), fanaticism is represented as 'an irrational aberration' (Toscano 2017: xxiv), that 'knows no limits' and 'effaces all traces of pity and compassion' (Craiutu 2012: 168). Yet fanaticism can also be emancipatory. Olson argues that 'sometimes fanatical tactics are necessary to let the light of reason in' (2007: 691), and notes that leading lights of the radical wing of the nineteenth-century American abolitionist movement were 'self-defined fanatics with an unyielding commitment to the immediate and unconditional emancipation of the enslaved' (ibid.: 686). In this context, fanaticism was a genuine virtue and moderation a vice that became a 'bulwark of oppression' (ibid.: 689).

Although radical abolitionists were zealous in their pursuit of freedom for the enslaved, there is a sound rationale for not regarding their zealotry as a form of fanaticism. They were uncompromising but the compromises they rejected were, in Margalit's (2010) terminology, rotten. Regardless of the tendency of radical abolitionists to describe themselves as 'fanatics', it would be more accurate to characterize them as *radicals*. Radicalism has been defined as 'contention that is outside the common routines of politics present within a society, oriented towards substantial change in social, cultural, economic, and/ or political structures, and undertaken by any actor using extra-institutional means' (Beck 2015: 18). It is debatable whether all fanatics are radicals but clear that not all radicals are fanatics. Radical abolitionists were radicals rather than fanatics.

The question whether there is a legitimate non-pejorative use for labels like 'fanaticism' and 'extremism' will be addressed in greater depth in Chapter 6. The main task for this chapter is to develop an account of fanaticism that builds on the strengths of existing accounts. There is also the task of explicating the notion of fundamentalism and forming a view about how fanaticism and fundamentalism are related to extremism. Among the constraints on a theory of fanaticism are the following: it should both explain and justify the labelling of people like Heydrich as fanatics; it should explain why fanaticism and extremism are closely related, and it should make sense of the role of fanaticism in promoting violence. Fanatics need not be violent but often are, and a theory of fanaticism should explain this fact. Finally, it is worth noting that talk of fanaticism is not confined to religious or political contexts. For example, some people are described as fitness fanatics. How does this use of 'fanatic' relate to the use of the label in other contexts? Is there a generic idea of fanaticism, of which there are more specific varieties? If so, what is the content of the generic notion? This chapter aims to provide answers to these questions.

Analysing fanaticism

Analyses of fanaticism in the pejorative tradition face the challenge of explaining why and in what sense fanaticism is problematic. Three different approaches to this challenge can be distinguished. Psychopathological approaches see fanaticism as a *mental disorder*, a malady of the mind that is best understood in psychological terms. Epistemic approaches see it as an *epistemic vice*, a personal quality that gets in the way of knowledge or understanding.[4] Epistemic vices are intellectual failings. Familiar examples are closed-mindedness, gullibility, dogmatism, prejudice and intellectual arrogance. Epistemic approaches add fanaticism to this list. Finally, moral approaches regard fanaticism as *moral vice*, a distinctively moral failing that is harmful to us and our fellow human beings. On this account, a failure to take account of its moral dimension amounts to a failure to understand what fanaticism is. These accounts are not mutually exclusive. In particular, the second and third accounts can easily be combined, and it would be natural to think of Heydrich's fanaticism as both epistemically and morally vicious.

A good example of a psychopathological approach is Hume's account of fanaticism in his 1741 essay 'Of superstition and enthusiasm'. Hume distinguishes 'two species of false religion': superstition and enthusiasm. 'Enthusiasm' was his term for fanaticism. The fanatic sees himself as 'a distinguished favourite of the divinity' (1985: 74) and 'consecrates himself, and bestows on his own person a sacred character' (ibid.: 76). As a result, he rejects human reason and even morality as fallacious. Instead, 'the fanatic madman delivers himself over, blindly and without reserve, to the supposed illapses of the spirit, and to inspiration from above' (ibid.: 74). With its contempt for common rules of reason, morality and prudence, enthusiasm 'naturally begets the most extreme resolutions' and 'produces the most cruel disorders in human society' (ibid.: 77). However, Hume's assessment of fanaticism is not wholly negative. He sees it as conducive to a kind of independence of thought and at odds with priestly power. For example, Quakers are 'the most innocent enthusiasts that have yet been known' (ibid.: 75–6) and do not have priests. Unlike superstition, enthusiasm is 'naturally accompanied with a spirit of liberty' (ibid.: 78) and is a friend to civil liberty. However, these virtues do not deter Hume from representing the fanatic as a madman. For Hume, a person who regards himself as sacred and the distinguished favourite of God is, in a certain sense, deranged.

This theme is taken up by Kant in his 1764 'Essay on the maladies of the head'. The essay was prompted by the presence on the outskirts of Königs-berg of a religious fanatic known as the 'goat prophet'. According to Kant, the fanatic or visionary or enthusiast is 'a deranged person with the pre-sumed immediate inspiration and a great familiarity with the powers of the heavens' (2007b: 73). Enthusiasm 'leads the exalted person to extremes' and 'human nature knows no more dangerous illusion' (ibid.: 73). In a different essay published in 1764, Kant maintains that 'fanaticism must always be distinguished from enthusiasm' in that 'the former believes itself to feel an immediate and extraordinary communion with a higher nature' while the latter 'signifies the state of mind which is inflamed beyond the appropriate degree by some principle, whether it be by the maxim of patriotic virtue, or of friendship, or of religion, without involving the illusion of a supernatural community' (2007a: 58n). Both enthusiasm and fanaticism are 'maladies of the head' but the implication of Kant's account is that the fanatic is much more deranged and dangerous than the enthusiast.

These forays into armchair psychology have a bearing on what would today be called 'religious fanaticism', and it is not difficult to think of fanatics who fit the psychopathological accounts of fanaticism. Osama bin Laden is an excellent example of a fanatic who bestowed on his own person a sacred character and was all the more dangerous for being reli-giously inspired. Joseph Kony, the leader of the Lord's Resistance Army, is another fanatic who claims divine authority for his campaign of torture and mass murder in Uganda and other places in Africa.[5] Kony gives every impression of being dangerously deranged but his type of fanaticism is no basis for a general account of fanaticism. As Heydrich demonstrates, it is quite possible to be a fanatic without being religiously inspired. Ideology rather than religion was the source of his fanaticism, even if there was something quasi-religious about his attitude to Hitler. To describe Hey-drich's fanaticism as a mental disorder is to medicalize it in a way that obscures its political, ethical and intellectual dimensions. A more subtle and multi-dimensional approach is needed if we are to come anywhere close to the heart of the matter.

In his 'Lectures on the Philosophy of History', Hegel avoids the crude pathologizing of fanaticism that one finds in the work of his historical pre-decessors. For Hegel, fanaticism is 'an enthusiasm for something abstract' (2001: 375). This surprising characterization appears in the chapter on Islam. Whereas the West shelters in a 'political edifice of chance, entanglement and particularity', what Hegel calls the 'Revolution of the East' 'destroyed all particularity' and made 'the abstract One the absolute object of attention and devotion' (ibid.: 372). The object of worship in Islam is 'purely intellec-tual' since 'no image, no representation of Allah is tolerated' (ibid.: 373). Muslims struggle for 'an abstract worship' with 'the greatest enthusiasm' (ibid.: 374), and this enthusiasm for something abstract is fanaticism. Hegel goes on to compare the fanaticism of Islam with that of Robespierre. For the former, the guiding principles were religion and terror. For the fanatics of the French Revolution, the principles were liberty and terror. Hegel concedes, however, that 'individuals may be enthusiastic for what is noble and exalted in various particular forms' (ibid.: 376). The enthusiasm that he finds prob-lematic is 'abstract and therefore all-comprehensive enthusiasm' (ibid.: 376).

Whatever one makes of Hegel's account of Islam, there is something right about the idea that fanaticism is enthusiasm for the abstract. Hegel is draw-ing attention to the way that the excesses of the French Revolution were the result of the enthusiasm of Robespierre and others for the ideals of lib-erty, equality and fraternity. These abstractions became ideals in the name of which people could be denounced and sent to the guillotine in large numbers. In the same way, the Khmer Rouge in Cambodia sent millions of people to concentration camps in the name of their Marxist ideals. How-ever, while Hegel was right to draw attention to the role of abstract ideals, fanaticism does not simply consist in a commitment to such ideals. The mere fact that a person idealizes Liberty or Equality does not explain their willingness to send large numbers of people, including former friends, to the guillotine. Still less is Heydrich's violent conduct towards Jews explained by abstract ideals. Hatred of Jews is not an abstract ideal. In Heydrich's case, and that of other senior Nazis, it was visceral and concrete, an expression of pure racial hatred rather than anything recognizable as an ideal. At best, Hegel only tells part of the story about fanaticism.

Is his approach to fanaticism psychopathological? Enthusiasm for the abstract is not a recognized mental disorder. If it is a pathology, it is a highly unusual one. Hegel's account is *sui generis*. Evans' description of Heydrich's mindless and total assimilation of Nazi ideology is the description of failings that are much more straightforward than those identified in Hegel's account of fanaticism. Writing in 1981, R. M. Hare claimed that the roots of fanaticism lie 'in the refusal or inability to think critically' (1981: 172), and it is clear from Evans' account that Heydrich was either unwilling or unable to think critically about Nazism. An inability to think critically is an epistemic vice, and the idea that intellectual failings are at the root of fanaticism is the central claim of what has been called the 'Enlightenment Account of Fanaticism' (Katsafanas 2019: 1). A concern about this account is that it does not make enough of the *moral* failings of fanatics like Heydrich, and fails to explain the connection between their fanaticism and their violence and intolerance. However, before examining these objections in greater detail, it is important to be clear what the Enlightenment Account's diagnosis of fanaticism comes to.

In a useful discussion, Paul Katsafanas notes that several Enlightenment thinkers offer philosophical diagnoses of fanaticism. They see it as arising from 'a defect of rationality' (ibid.: 5) rather than as a haphazard series of disconnected states. For present purposes, defects of rationality are equivalent to epistemic vices. Among the thinkers that Katsafanas cites are Locke, Hume, Shaftesbury, and Kant. These thinkers take the fanatic to be characterized by three traits:

1. Unwavering commitment to an ideal.
2. Unwillingness to subject the ideal to doubt or rational critique.
3. The presumption of a non-rational sanction for the ideal.

As Katsafanas notes, conditions (2) and (3) require some clarification. Unwillingness to doubt is not always irrational. For example, it is not irrational to refuse to doubt that triangles have three sides. What distinguishes the fanatic, the Enlightenment Account says, is 'not simply the refusal to entertain doubts (condition 2) but the *ground* for this refusal (condition 3). The Enlightenment thinkers 'emphasize that the fanatic refuses to entertain doubts *for a particular reason*: He takes himself to be in possession of a distinctive type of ground for his belief … a ground that the Enlightenment thinkers judge to be non-rational' (ibid.: 8). The Enlightenment Account 'treats claims about direct experiences of divinity as paradigmatic examples of non-rational sanction' (ibid.: 8), though non-rational sanctions or justifications can also take other forms. For the purposes of condition (3), the key point is that there *is* a distinction between non-rational and rational justifications for beliefs, however this distinction is understood.

Understood in the way that Katsafanas understands them, (1), (2) and (3) are epistemic vices, that is, intellectual failings. Why should unwavering commitment to an ideal be viewed as an intellectual failing? Because it is closely related to closed-mindedness and dogmatism. To be unwaveringly committed to an ideal is to be unwilling to even consider the possibility that it might be problematic. This explains the fanatic's unwillingness to subject the ideal to critical scrutiny. Is such an unwillingness epistemically vicious? Is it always an intellectual failing to take one's ideals to have a non-rational sanction? These are difficult questions which need not detain us here. For present purposes it can be assumed that (1)–(3) are epistemic vices and that, on the Enlightenment Account, these epistemic vices are at the heart of fanaticism. However, this is barely an adequate account of Heydrich's fanaticism since it omits its moral dimension. Heydrich's fanaticism was a moral as well as an intellectual failing, and an account of fanaticism that fails to do justice to that fact is plainly incomplete.

The ideals to which Heydrich was unwaveringly committed included the 'ideal' of a Europe without Jews. He was certainly unwilling to subject Nazi ideals to rational critique. If the reason he was unwilling to question these ideals is that they were sanctioned by Hitler, then this would be a paradigm case of an ideal with a non-rational sanction. These are all respects in which Heydrich's fanaticism was an intellectual failing. The sense in which it was a *moral* failing cannot be understood without taking account of the nature of his ideals. It was not just his irrational commitment to his ideals that made Heydrich a fanatic but also the fact these were morally *perverted* ideals. The Enlightenment Account says nothing about the nature of the fanatic's ideals, and focuses instead on how the fanatic *explains* or *justifies* them. However, *what* the fanatic believes is as important as *why* he or she believes what he or she believes. The underlying question, similar to one raised about extremism, is whether fanaticism depends on the content of one's ideals or only on the form or nature of one's commitment to them, regardless of their content. The former is what Frank Chouraqui calls the '*content view* of fanaticism' (2019: 10). The latter can be called the *formal view* of fanaticism.

Katsafanas' problem with the Enlightenment Account is that it is insufficient. A 'crucial feature of fanaticism is *intolerance*, which is often manifest in violent behavior' (2019: 9). Yet the 'rational defects' that Enlightenment thinkers focus on – features (1)–(3) 'have no direct connection to intolerance' (ibid.: 9). What these features characterize, Katsafanas argues, is the *true believer*. True believers are strongly committed to some ideal and unwilling to accept any criticism of the ideal, which is justified non-rationally. However, one can be a true believer without being a fanatic, that is, without being violently intolerant. For Katsafanas, fanaticism is not just a rational failure. Rather, it is a peculiar kind of vice or practical defect that 'blends a purely rational failure with a distinctively moral failing' (ibid.: 1–2).

The key to Katsafanas's blended account of fanaticism is the notion of a *sacred value*. Final values are things that are valued for their own sake. Sacred values are final values that are:

1. Inviolable: not to be compromised or attenuated.
2. Unquestionable: not to be doubted, critiqued, or weighed against other values.
3. Associated with characteristic emotions: love, hatred, veneration, contempt, dread, awe, etc.

Thus, in addition to the three features of true believers, there is the following additional condition on fanaticism: (4) *Fanatics adopt one or more sacred values*. A further condition is suggested by Nietzsche. He suggested that fanatics need to commit to something incontestable in order to preserve a unified self. In other words: (5) *A fanatic needs to treat a value as sacred in order to preserve the unity of the self*. Katsafanas calls this the 'fragility of the self' condition. For fanatics, it is not just the self that is fragile but also their own sacred values. Accordingly: (6) *Fanatics take their sacred value's status to be threatened when it is not widely accepted*. The fanatic 'typically wants his values to be accepted by everyone; he is not content to acknowledge alternative sets of values as acceptable for other individuals' (ibid.: 15). Finally, fanaticism has a group orientation that is captured by the following condition: (7) *The fanatic identifies himself with a group defined by a shared commitment to a sacred value*. The fanatic sees outsiders as a threat to his or her group, his or her values and his or her own identity.

According to Katsafanas, features (4)–(7) generate a '*propensity* or *disposition* toward violence' (ibid.: 17) even though they do not necessitate violence. By explaining the link with violence, Katsafanas' account closes a major gap in the Enlightenment Account of fanaticism. If a propensity to violence is a moral failing, then conditions (4)–(7) also explain the sense in which fanaticism is a distinctively moral failing. However, the plausibility of these conditions is open to question. It is doubtful, for example, that a fanatic has to see his scared values as ones that can never be compromised or weighed against other values. During the Second World War, fanatics like Heydrich had to contend on an almost daily basis with the conflict between their anti-Semitic ideals and economic considerations, since many companies in Germany saw Jewish workers as indispensable. Heydrich complained bitterly about this and other constraints on his policy of deporting Jews from Germany but had to compromise on the numbers to be deported in line with his ideals. Compromise in wartime was essential, not least because the ideal of a Germany without Jews conflicted in practice with other Nazi objectives, such as military victory and economic dominance. Yet Heydrich was a fanatic. This raises a question about the extent to which fanatics must view their ideals as ones that could not conceivably be outweighed by other considerations. Fanaticism is compatible with the making of tactical compromises for the sake for the ultimate strategic goal.

The 'fragility of self' condition on fanaticism looks like a piece of armchair psychology that fits some fanatics but not others. There is no evidence that Heydrich needed to treat Nazi values as sacred in order to preserve the unity of his self. Indeed, it is not entirely clear what such evidence would look like. Heydrich was a unified self before he became a Nazi and the denazification of other Nazis after the war did not lead to their crumbling and disintegration as unitary selves. As for whether the sacred status of Nazi values was regarded as threatened by their not being widely accepted, this is hard to say. The Nazis certainly killed people who did not accept their values, but was that because such people were seen as a threat to the sacred status of the values themselves or because it was in the nature of these values not to tolerate dissent? The fact that the fanatic typically wants his or her values to be accepted by everyone *might* have something to do with concerns about their fragility but it is difficult to believe that such concerns are *essential* to fanaticism.

To sum up: Katsafanas is right to criticize the Enlightenment Account of fanaticism for representing it as a purely rational failure rather than a blend of a rational failure with a moral failing. He is right, also, to link fanaticism with intolerance and violence and not to insist that fanaticism *necessarily* leads to violence. However, there are doubts about some of the features that he builds into his account of fanaticism as a way to distinguish fanatics from true believers. As he acknowledges, questions also remain about the relationship between fanaticism as he defines it and the content of a person's values. Are some values more likely than others to generate fanaticism? More generally, is it how a fanatic views his or her ideals that makes him or her a fanatic or also the nature of these ideals? To make progress with these issues, it is necessary to move on from Katsafanas and consider a different approach.

Fanaticism and morality

In his 1963 monograph, *Freedom and Reason*, Hare develops an account of fanaticism that is still of interest. According to Hare:

> [I]t is when people step from the selfish pursuit of their own interests to the propagation of perverted ideals that they become really dangerous. We shall never understand the phenomenon called Fascism, and other similar political movements, until we realize that this is what is happening. The extreme sort of Fascist is a fanatic who not merely wants something for himself, but thinks that it ought to be brought into existence universally, whether or not anybody else, or even he himself if his tastes change, wants it.
>
> (ibid.: 114)

A key distinction for Hare is between ideals and interests. To have an *ideal* 'is to think of some kind of thing as pre-eminently good within some larger class' (ibid.: 159). To have a *moral* ideal is 'to think of some type of man, or, possibly, of some type of society as a pre-eminently good one' (ibid.: 159). To have an *interest* is 'for there to be something which one wants (or may want), or which is (or may be) a means, necessary or sufficient, for the attainment of something which one wants (or may want)' (ibid.: 157). Ideals can conflict with other ideals and with interests, just as interests can conflict. Your ideals can conflict with mine, and my interests can conflict with yours. In these terms, 'morality includes the pursuit of ideals as well as the reconciliation of interests' (ibid.: 157).

A fanatic, for Hare, is someone who is willing to trample on other people's ideals and interests, and even sacrifice his or her own interests, in order to realize his ideals. For example, the Nazis thought that a certain kind of society and a certain kind of person were pre-eminently good. In this sense, they had ideals. What differentiates them from liberals is that 'they not only pursued a certain ideal, but pursued it because of the sort of ideal that it was, in contempt and defiance of both the interests and ideals of others' (ibid.: 160). They 'trampled ruthlessly on other people's interests, including that interest which consists in the freedom to pursue varying ideals' (ibid: 157). In contrast, the liberal '*respects* the ideals of others as he does his own' (ibid.: 178). He is 'in favour of allowing anybody to pursue his own ideals and interests except in so far as their pursuit interferes with other people's pursuit of theirs' (ibid.: 178). Crucially, the liberal is forbidden 'to force his own ideals down the throats of other people by legal or other compulsion' (ibid.: 178).

Hare imagines a conversation between a liberal and a Nazi in which the liberal asks the Nazi the following question: suppose you discover that you are a Jew. Would you still be in favour of the extermination of Jews? The fanatical Nazi will presumably say: if I were a Jew, then I would deserve to be killed. Is this what Heydrich would have said if the rumours that he was a Jew had turned out to be correct? If not, then he was not a fanatic. To suppose that he *was* a fanatic is to suppose that he would have favoured his own extermination if he had turned out to be Jewish. As Hare puts it, the fanatical Nazi 'sticks to his judgements even when they conflict with his own interest in hypothetical cases' (ibid.: 162). Indeed, the fanatic is prepared to sacrifice the interests of his or her nearest and dearest, as well as his or her own interests, in order to realize his or her ideal. For a Nazi, to imagine that he has Jewish blood is to imagine that his children have Jewish blood. If he favours his own extermination in a possible world in which he is a Jew, then he must also favour the extermination of his children in that world. Hare takes this to show that 'really intractable Nazis are perhaps rarer than might be thought' (ibid.: 171). Perhaps not even Heydrich would have been in favour of sending his children to a concentration camp if they turned out to be Jewish.

This may well be wishful thinking on Hare's part. For all he knows, perhaps Heydrich *would* have been willing to sacrifice himself and his children for the sake of his ideals, and true fanatics are less rare than Hare thinks. For present purposes, however, the important question is not whether Hare is right about the rarity of fanaticism but whether his account of fanaticism is along the right lines. His characterization can be broken down into two parts:

i. A fanatic is willing to trample on the interests and ideals of other people in pursuit of his or her own ideals.

ii. A fanatic is willing to sacrifice his or her own interests in order to realize his or her ideals.

The fanatic's willingness to trample the ideals and interests of other people
is an expression of his or her contempt for those ideals and interests. There
are many ways of trampling on other people's interests and ideals, but the
fanatic is prepared to use violence or the threat of violence to do so, and
to compel others to accept his or her own ideals. It might be objected that
people cannot be forced to share the fanatic's *beliefs* and, in this sense,
cannot be forced to accept the fanatic's ideals. However, they can be forced
to *live* by these ideals. This is how ISIS operates in the territories it controls.
On pain of death, everybody in their territory has to live by their rules and
their idea of Islam. Another way for fanatics to force other people to 'accept'
their ideals is to foist on them political and social structures that are based
on those ideals. When Hare talks about the fanatic forcing his own ideals
down the throats of other people, he is talking about something that can and
does happen.

The second condition of Hare's two conditions refers to the fanatic's willingness to sacrifice his or her own life and interests, and the lives and interests of friends, family and other members of his or her in-group in pursuit
of these ideals. The true fanatic is so single-minded in pursuit of his or her
ideals that he or she is willing to do whatever it takes to realize them. The
fanatic would quite literally rather die than abandon his or her ideals. As
noted above, this is not to say that fanatics are unwilling to make tactical
compromises. This should not be allowed to obscure the deeper sense in
which fanatics are uncompromising. However, there is a tension between
their willingness to do whatever it takes to realize their ideals and the invi-
olability of those ideals. What if what it takes to realize their ideals in the
longer term is compromise in the short term? In practice, fanatics vary in
their willingness to compromise, but a willingness to sacrifice oneself for the
sake of an ideal is a core component of fanaticism.

These glosses on (i) and (ii) go somewhat beyond anything that Hare
explicitly says but they are in the spirit of his account. His account of fanaticism raises many questions but the three most important are these:

a. Are Hare's conditions, interpreted as they have been interpreted here,
    necessary and sufficient for fanaticism? Are they too demanding or not
    demanding enough?

b. Is Hare's account a formal or a content view of fanaticism? Or could it be that his account calls into question the distinction between form and content?

c. On Hare's account, is fanaticism an epistemic vice, a moral vice, or a mixture of the two? Is fanaticism *primarily* a moral failing, primarily an epistemic failing, or one that is equally moral and epistemic?

Starting with (a), the case for the first of Hare's conditions on fanaticism is that it makes sense of the distinction between a fanatic and a true believer. A true believer has an unwavering commitment to an ideal but need have no interest in forcing other people to accept it. True believers might or might not be prepared to trample on other people's ideals and interests when they conflict with their own. It is only when they are prepared to do this, and impose their ideals on everyone else, that true believers become fanatics. To put it another way, condition (i) is indeed a necessary condition on fanaticism. Indirectly, this also explains the link between fanaticism and violence. If there are non-violent ways of forcing others to accept one's ideals, then the fanatic need not be violent. However, in cases where there is no alternative, fanatics can be expected to turn to violence to get their way. It is in this sense that, as Katsafanas points out, fanaticism has an in-built propensity or disposition toward violence but doesn't necessitate it.

Condition (ii) is a strange requirement on fanaticism since it makes the fanatic look in some ways like an almost heroic figure, and certainly more attractive than someone who is simply determined to get his or her own way without being willing to give up anything in exchange. However, a person who satisfies condition (i) but not (ii) is a bully rather than a fanatic. Only a person who satisfies both conditions is a fanatic. Accordingly, it now appears that conditions (i) and (ii) are individually necessary and jointly sufficient for fanaticism.[6] An extremist who recruits others to act as suicide bombers and sacrifice their lives for the cause is not a fanatic if he or she is unwilling to put his or her own neck on the line. In these terms, those who carried out the 9/11 attacks were fanatics as well as extremists, whereas those who ordered the attacks while keeping themselves out of harm's way were extremists but not fanatics. Condition (ii) allows the fanatic to claim moral superiority over other extremists as well as his or her ideological opponents. As Hare points out, the fanatic 'might even claim to be morally superior to his opponent, in that the latter abandons his principles when they conflict with his own interest in hypothetical cases' (1963: 162).

Such claims of moral superiority, are of course, cancelled out by the harms caused by self-sacrificing fanatics.

Turning to (b), is Hare's a formal or a content account of fanaticism? More generally, is it better to think of people as fanatics by virtue of the content of their ideals or by virtue of their attitude to their ideals? In a monograph published 18 years after *Freedom and Reason* Hare endorses the latter view. He claims that 'one may be fanatical about moral opinions even when they are sound ones' and that 'it is not the content of a person's intuitive principles that makes him a fanatic, but his attitude to them' (1981: 175). This makes sense of the description of the radical abolitionists as fanatics: they were fanatical in regard to sound moral opinions about slavery. However, in *Freedom and Reason*, the emphasis is on the transition from the selfish pursuit of one's own interests to the propagation of *perverted* ideals. It is when people make this transition that they become fanatics and 'really dangerous' (Hare 1963: 114). Furthermore, the Nazis not only pursued a certain ideal in a certain way but pursued it '*because of the sort of ideal that it was*, in contempt and defiance both of the interests and ideals of others' (ibid.: 160. emphasis added).

The latter formulation is helpful because it draws attention to the problematic nature of the form/content distinction. In the case of the Nazis, their attitude to their ideals was not, as it were, 'external' to the ideals themselves. It was in the nature of their ideals to require their imposition on others. One cannot be a Nazi but against the trampling of other people's interests and ideals. In the same way, one is not a liberal if one is in favour of forcing one's ideals down the throats of other people, even if these are liberal ideals. As Hare points out, 'the liberal is not forbidden by his principle of toleration to propagate his own ideals; but he is restricted as to the means' (ibid.: 178). In other words, what qualifies as an acceptable means of promoting one's ideals is dictated by the ideals themselves. Fanatical liberalism is a contradiction in terms. In this case, as in many others, there is no neat way to separate the form and content of one's ideals.

Abolitionism is an interesting case because what is at issue here is not the imposition of alien ideals on other people. Their argument was that slavery was flatly inconsistent with the American ideal of liberty and justice for all. Far from trampling on the ideals of Americans who did not object to slavery, the point of radical abolitionism was that *respect* for these ideals required the abolition of slavery. This argues against the classification of radical abolitionists as fanatics. It is true that they were happy to trample on the *interests* of slave owners. However, this also does not make abolitionists fanatics since the practice of slave-owning was inhuman and unjust and there is therefore no moral requirement to respect the interests of slave owners. A fanatic is not only willing to trample on the interests and ideals of other people in pursuit of his or her own ideals but is willing to do this even when there is no moral justification for acting in this way. To put it another way, the fanatic's contempt for other people's ideals and interests is *unwarranted*. There is more about the significance of this in relation to radical abolitionism in Chapter 6.

The remaining question is (c): is fanaticism primarily a moral or an epistemic vice? On the Enlightenment Account, it is an epistemic vice. On Hare's account, it looks more like a moral vice. In what sense? Trampling on the ideals and interests of other people in pursuit of one's own ideals might be regarded as morally problematic even if one's ideals are not themselves objectionable. When one's ideals *are* objectionable or, as Hare describes them, 'perverted', then trampling on other people in pursuit of them is doubly problematic. Hare is aware that a person with perverted ideals will not recognize them as perverted. Presumably, the Nazis didn't think their ideals were perverted but this doesn't alter the fact that this is precisely what they were. To give an account of what counts as a perverted ideal is beyond the scope of the present discussion. There are also questions about the relativity or subjectivity of judgements about the moral quality of a person's ideals. However, as the case of the Nazis shows, it is sometimes possible to say with a high degree of confidence that a given ideal is morally objectionable.

The question this raises is whether condition (i) on fanaticism is too weak after all. As it stands, this condition says that to be a fanatic one must be willing to trample on other people's interests and ideals in pursuit of one's own ideals. This says nothing about the nature of the fanatic's own ideals. It might be suggested, therefore, that something stronger is required, and that (i) should be replaced by:

(i)* A fanatic is willing to trample on the interests and ideals of other people in pursuit of his or her own *perverted* ideals.

Here, 'perverted' means morally objectionable. The intuition behind (i)* is that being willing to trample on other people's interests and ideals in pursuit of one's own ideals is not relevant to the question whether one is a fanatic unless there is also something wrong with one's ideals. Another possibility is to draw a distinction between *weak* and *strong* fanaticism. A person who only satisfies (i) might be described as a fanatic in the weak sense. A fanatic in the strong sense, or what one might call a *full-blown* fanatic, is a person who meets condition (i)*. Does it still make sense to describe the abolitionists as radicals rather than fanatics? Given the distinction between strong and weak fanaticism, would it not be better, and more in keeping with how they thought of themselves, to classify them as fanatics in the weak sense? We will return to this question in Chapter 6. In the present chapter, 'fanaticism' means fanaticism in the strong sense. If a fanatic in this sense meets condition (i)*, then it follows straightforwardly that fanaticism is a moral vice. For if one's ideals are morally vicious, then forcing them onto other people *must* be morally vicious.

Is fanaticism also epistemically vicious? It is if, as Hare claims, fanatics are unwilling or unable to think critically about their ideals. However, it isn't clear in what sense Heydrich was *incapable* of critical thinking about his Nazi ideals. Rather, he *refused* to engage in critical thinking about his ideals. Since there is no mention of such a refusal in (i) or (ii), this suggests that these conditions on fanaticism are insufficient. The refusal of fanatics to think critically about their ideals is related to another epistemic failing: being excessively certain about their ideals, or what Katsafanas calls the fanatic's 'unwillingness to doubt' (2019: 8). Some truths, like the truth that triangles have three sides, *are* immune to doubt. However, the propositions the fanatic regards as immune to doubt – like those of Nazi race theory – are not only dubious but demonstrably false. This means that the fanatic's certainty about his or her ideals is *spurious*. At the same time, his or her certainty explains his or her willingness to sacrifice himself or herself and others in pursuit of these ideals. Spurious certainty is a core element of the fanatic's mindset: there is no such thing as a doubtful or uncertain fanatic. This is a claim about the *epistemology* of fanaticism as well as its psychology. It is an *epistemic* failing to regard as unquestionable propositions that are not immune to doubt.

Fanaticism's attitude to doubt and certainty is a respect in which it is anti-modern or, if one prefers, pre-modern. The sociologist Anthony Giddens argues that doubt is a pervasive feature of modernity and 'forms a general existential dimension of the contemporary social world' (1991: 3). 'Modernity' refers to 'the institutions and modes of behaviour established first of all in post-feudal Europe' (ibid.: 14–15). According to Giddens, modernity in his sense 'institutionalises the principle of radical doubt and insists that all knowledge takes the form of hypotheses: claims which … are in principle always open to revision and may have at some point to be abandoned' (ibid.: 3). This is precisely what the fanatic does *not* think. Fanatics regard doubts that question their ideals and objectives as corrosive and immoral. Fanaticism is the rejection of doubt and a return to the certainty that characterizes the pre-modern world. If Giddens is right about the role of doubt in modernity, then fanaticism is diametrically opposed to modernity.

It might be objected that liberals are as certain about their ideals as fanatics are about theirs. Is this not at least one respect in which liberalism is indistinguishable from fanaticism? There is a seeming tension within liberalism between its conviction that 'the ends of men are many' (Berlin 2013a: 239) and its certainty about the ultimate validity of its pluralist ideals. One thing that liberals do not question is that human beings can have fundamentally different ends and still be fully rational. Yet this idea is not immune to doubt in the way that the claim that triangles have three sides is immune to doubt. This is something that a consistent liberal should accept. Liberalism requires epistemic humility, including humility about the standing of liberalism itself. This does not prevent the liberal from arguing for and promoting pluralism. It is possible to be convinced by pluralism without regarding it as immune to doubt. This, then, is one important difference between the liberal and the fanatic: the liberal does not see his or her ideals as unquestionable.

The discussion so far has made no reference to perhaps the best-known definition of a fanatic, one that is usually attributed (possibly mistakenly) to Churchill: 'the fanatic is one who can't change his mind and won't change the subject'. It does not appear to be the case that fanatics can't change their mind. Fanatics who shift from one end of the ideological spectrum to the other *have* changed their minds, though not their mindsets. It is one of the paradoxes of fanaticism that unwavering certainty about their ideals does not prevent fanatics from giving up those ideals and adopting different ideals with which their original ideals are incompatible. Perhaps there is more to the notion of the fanatic being unwilling to change the subject, if this is understood as a picturesque way of describing the *monomania* of many fanatics. Monomania consists in an obsessive preoccupation with just one thing. The single issue with which the monomaniacal fanatic is obsessed is likely to be connected to his or her ideals: multiple ideals can underpin a single obsession.

On a mindset analysis, extremists have preoccupations (plural) that may or may not amount to obsessions. In contrast, monomaniacal fanatics are preoccupied with one thing and their preoccupation is obsessive. As Pierre Salmon puts it, monomania implies a 'distorted and generally ominous perception of one dimension of the world's state, evolution, or future' (2002: 72). To describe a person as a monomaniac is therefore to do two things: it is to identify the *range* of their concerns and the *nature* of their concerns. However, while many fanatics do display monomania, it is doubtful that monomania is a strictly necessary condition for being a fanatic. Heydrich was a fanatic but not a monomaniac. He was preoccupied with, among other things, maintaining the dominance of the Nazi Party in Germany, winning the war, and dealing with the Jews. Are these different preoccupations or different parts of a single preoccupation? It is hard to say, but insisting on describing Heydrich as a monomaniac would be a case of twisting the facts to fit a theory.

We are now in a position to say what makes a person a fanatic and, in this sense, to say what fanaticism is. The idea of a fanatic is a highly complex one that is not amenable to a simple definition but the following characterization captures its main elements:

> (F) Fanatics have unwarranted contempt for other people's ideals and interests, are willing to trample on those ideals and interests in pursuit of their own perverted ideals, and impose their ideals on others, by force if necessary. Fanatics are unwilling to think critically about their ideals because they regard them as indubitable. However, they are willing to sacrifice themselves and others in pursuit of their ideals.

This is an account of fanaticism in the strong sense. It builds on the Enlightenment Account and Hare's insights. It makes no mention of the fanatic's supposed psychological fragility or of the fragility of his or her values or ideals. If these are as certain as fanatics suppose, then they will not be threatened by not being widely accepted. Finally, fanatics may or may not have a group orientation. Isolated fanatics are rare but not unknown, and there is nothing in (F) that rules out the possibility of fanatics who do not identify themselves with a group.

Before moving on, it would be worth asking whether the account of fanaticism given here makes sense of non-political uses of the label 'fanatic', as in the colloquial description of certain individuals as 'fitness fanatics'. In the novel, *The Motion of the Body through Space*, Lionel Shriver introduces the character of Remington Alabaster who, having been sedentary all his life, decides in late middle age to run a marathon and then takes up triathlon. His gruelling and obsessive training regime damages his relationship with his wife Serenata and ultimately damages his own body. The book ends with Remington barely surviving a massive heart attack during a triathlon. Serenata, a former runner, is mystified by her husband's transformation from couch potato to triathlete. She accuses him of fanaticism and wonders whether her own athletic career had 'tracked the seeds of fitness fundamentalism into the house' (2020: 149).

In one sense, talk of fanaticism in this context is plainly inapt since there is no question of the fitness fanatic trying to impose his or her ideals on other people. On the other hand, Shriver's character trains with a group of people with a shared contempt for those who value other things over fitness. They see moderation as a failing and are driven in their conduct by an ideal, not a political one but the ideal of a physically transformed self. In pursuit of this unquestioned ideal, Remington is prepared to trample on Serenata's interests and to sacrifice many of his own interests. The physical damage he inflicts on his body is a form of self-sacrifice in pursuit of a higher ideal. Remington's personal trainer insists that the body thrives from being stressed and that there is no such thing as overdoing it. This sounds like fanaticism, and the vogue for extreme sports might be characterized as a form of 'extremism'. These uses of 'extremism' and 'fanaticism' are metaphorical but they do have a point.

Fanaticism and extremism

How are these things related? Even if extremism were one thing, this would not be an easy question to answer. However, extremism is not one thing. The preceding chapters were organized around the distinction between extremism in three forms: methods, ideological, and psychological. Given this taxonomy, one might begin by exploring the relationship between fanaticism and methods extremism. One issue is: are fanatics necessarily methods extremists? Another is: are methods extremists necessarily fanatics? In Chapter 1, the methods extremist was defined as an individual, organization or group that uses extreme methods in pursuit of its objectives. Extreme methods can be, but need not be, violent. It emerged in Chapter 3 that it is possible to use violence for political ends without being an extremist. The methods extremist uses violence unnecessarily, disproportionately or against innocents. On this account, even the fact that one uses violence in a *just* cause leaves it open that one is still a methods extremist, though the charge of extremism undoubtedly carries greater weight when extreme methods are used to advance *unjust* causes.

Fanatics need not be methods extremists if there are non-extreme methods for getting their way. Fanatics are *prepared* to trample on other people's interests and ideals in pursuit of their own ideals, but what if there is no need to trample on anyone else's interests or ideals in order to realize one's own ideals? This is a theoretical possibility but of little practical relevance since the fanatic's ideals will typically require their acceptance by people who do not already share them. The real question is whether there is any realistic prospect of the fanatic being able to force his or her ideals down other people's throats without using extreme methods. The more outlandish the ideal, the more likely it is that violent methods will be necessary. If a methods extremist is someone who uses *unnecessary* violence, then doesn't this let the fanatic off the hook? Imagine a fanatic who argues that he or she only uses extreme methods because there is no way to get what he or she wants without using them. Can this argument be used to rebut the charge that the fanatic is a methods extremist?

The answer to this question flows from the discussion in Chapter 3. It was noted there that it matters to the identification of someone as a methods extremist *why* they need to use extreme methods in order to achieve their objectives. If the necessity of such methods is simply a reflection of the unpopularity of their cause, then they are still methods extremists. This will typically be the situation of fanatics who use extreme methods to realize their perverted ideals. On the assumption that such ideals are unlikely to be popular, violence may well be the only way for fanatics to get their way. This means that such fanatics are still methods extremists even though there is a sense in which, from their perspective, violence is the only way. So, for example, the reason that ISIS fanatics have to use savagery to compel people to live by their ideals is that their ideals would have few takers otherwise. The implication is that while there is a theoretical possibility of fanaticism without methods extremism, in reality, fanatics are almost always methods extremists. The nature of their ideals makes the use of extreme methods virtually inevitable.

It is less obvious that all methods extremists are fanatics. Take the case of the ANC, whose armed struggle against apartheid included the use of disproportionate violence against civilian targets. This was a respect in which they were methods extremists, but they were not fanatics. Their contempt for the ideals and interests of supporters of apartheid was not unwarranted and the ANC's own ideals weren't perverted. The idea that the right to vote should not be determined by a person's race is hardly perverted, and the ANC did not use violence to force this ideal down the throats of an unwilling public. The vast majority of South Africans strongly supported the principle of one person one vote, and wanted it implemented. The self-sacrifice of members of the ANC who served long sentences in South African prisons did not make them fanatics because their sacrifices were in pursuit of freedom and justice for all South Africans. This is another illustration of the point that one cannot simply read off from people's conduct whether they are fanatics without taking any account of the nature or content of their ideals.

The next question concerns the relationship between fanaticism and ideological extremism. If ideologies are viewed as occupying positions in ideological space, then an ideology counts as extremist because of its position in ideological space. By the same token, a person is an ideological extremist just if they subscribe to an extremist ideology. Since, as noted in Chapter 2, ideological space has multiple dimensions, ideological extremism is relative to a dimension. One way to organize positions in ideological space is by reference to their views of violence. At one end of the Pro-Violence spectrum is pacifism. The pacifist thinks that political violence is never justified. A pacifist in this sense need not be contemptuous of other people's ideals and interests and will certainly not be prepared to use force to impose their own ideals on others. The implication is that it is not just *possible* to be an extremist without being a fanatic but that there are forms of extremism, like pacifism, that are *incompatible* with fanaticism.

In response, it might be argued that a pacifist who is willing to stick to pacifist principles even in the face of, say, Nazi aggression really is a type of fanatic. They say they have no desire to force other people to accept their principles, but they are willing to sacrifice themselves and other people for the sake of their principles. This is the practical implication of not using force to stand up to naked aggression. Apart from that, some may find the classification of pacifism as a form of extremism deeply counterintuitive. For such people, the fact that pacifists need not be fanatics is not much of an argument for the claim that it is possible to be a non-fanatical extremist. A more pertinent question is whether it is possible to be an extremist in the *usual* sense without being a fanatic. For example, is it possible to occupy a position on the extreme right or extreme left of ideological space and not be a fanatic? Isn't fanaticism built into the fascist or communist world-view? Isn't a fascist someone who, by definition, wants to trample on the ideals and interests of other people in favour of his or her own perverted ideals?

This attempt to relate extremism to fanaticism presupposes that extremist ideologies have perverted ideals. If this assumption is incorrect, then extremism does not entail fanaticism as defined by (F). Another consideration is brought into focus by A. J P. Taylor's joke, quoted in Chapter 1, about having 'extreme views, weakly held' (1977: 8). One way for views to be weakly held is for them to be held without a great deal of conviction. However, there is another possibility: one might have conviction in one's views but be unwilling to act on them. This is the position of the *armchair* extremist. The armchair extremist has extreme views but is unwilling to impose them on others, least of all to impose them on others by force. The armchair extremist's extremism is purely theoretical. In contrast, fanaticism cannot be purely theoretical. Fanaticism has a necessary connection to action, or at least to a willingness to act, as well as to a willingness to sacrifice one's own interests. As Taylor's comment illustrates, extremism's connection to action is not as strong.

Extremism without fanaticism is one thing but what about fanaticism without extremism? A fanatic who is not an ideological extremist would need to be someone whose ideological outlook is 'middle of the road' but satisfies the conditions of fanaticism, as set out in (F). This might seem an impossible position for a person to occupy. For example, how can a person who is willing to trample on other people's ideals and interests be anything other than an ideological extremist? On a psychological reading, an extremist is a person with an extremist mindset. How is extremism in this sense related to fanaticism? It is relatively easy to conceive of a fanatic who is not a mindset extremist. One only has to imagine a fanatic who does not have the standard preoccupations of the mindset extremist. For example, (F) does not entail a preoccupation with purity or conspiracy theories. As for mindset extremism without fanaticism, it was suggested in Chapter 4 that mindset extremism is tied to *impositionism*, the conviction that it is legitimate and even essential to impose one's vision of the ideal form of life on other people. This is close to the definition of fanaticism, especially if the extremist's impositionism is based on contempt for other visions of life and sanctions the use of violence to trample on other ideals and interests. To avoid the result that the mindset extremist must also be a fanatic, one would have to break the link between mindset extremism and impositionism. Yet this link is a strong one, except in the case of what was described in Chapter 4 as 'single issue' extremism.

The result of this complex discussion can be summarized as follows: although the labels 'fanatic' and 'extremist' are often used interchangeably, there is a case for not regarding the two concepts as identical. The idea of being far from the centre of ideological space along a given dimension is different from the idea of fanaticism, as defined by (F). Not only are the two ideas or concepts different, it is also possible to be an extremist in the armchair sense but not a fanatic, or a fanatic but not an extremist. The case for extremism without fanaticism is stronger than that for fanaticism without extremism. The possibility of extremism without fanaticism is not purely theoretical, since the armchair extremist is more than a purely theoretical possibility. There are such people. However, none of this is to deny the existence of a substantial overlap in practice between extremism and fanaticism. It would be surprising if most extremists were not fanatics or most fanatics were not extremists. The reason for this substantial overlap is really no mystery: after all, it is in the nature of many extremist ideologies to promote fanaticism, and the fanatic's perverted ideals are typically grounded in an extremist ideology.

Fundamentalism

So far in this chapter, religion has only been mentioned in passing. There are religious extremists but not all extremists are religious. There are religious fanatics but not all fanatics are religious. The link between fundamentalism and religion is much tighter. In one important study of fundamentalism, the concept of fundamentalism is used to refer to 'specific religious phenomena that have emerged in the twentieth century, particularly in the last several decades, in the wake of the success of modernization and secularization' (Almond, Sivan and Appleby 2004: 403). In a similar vein, Malise Ruthven writes that fundamentalism at its broadest may be described as 'a religious way of being that manifests itself in a strategy by which beleaguered believers attempt to preserve their distinctive identities as individuals or groups in the face of modernity and secularization' (2007: 5–6). This raises the question whether non-religious uses of the word are legitimate.

Ruthven provides a succinct account of the history of term 'fundamentalism'.[7] The term goes back to the early twentieth century and a series of tracts called *The Fundamentals: A Testimony of Truth*. These were written by conservative American and British theologians and were aimed at stopping what they considered to be the erosion of the fundamental beliefs of Protestantism, such as the inerrancy of the Bible, the virgin birth and Christ's imminent return to rule over the world. A fundamenta*list* was a defender and proponent of *The Fundamentals*. Thus, as Ruthven emphasizes, fundamentalism originated in the specific theological context of early twentieth-century America. Today the term 'fundamentalist' is used more broadly to label 'ideological purists who stick to the fundamentals of their cause without compromising their principles' (ibid.: 21). Ruthven questions non-religious uses of the term, which collapse the distinction between fundamentalism and extremism. He insists that fundamentalism is 'sharper and more distinctive than extremism' (ibid.: 22).

One sense in which fundamentalism is distinctive concerns the role of texts in genuine fundamentalism. Fundamentalism is what Ruthven calls the 'cult of the text' (ibid.: 45). For fundamentalists, there is always a revered text or canonical statement of their core doctrines ('the fundamentals'). Fundamentalists 'tend towards a literalist interpretation of the texts they revere' (ibid.: 40), although there are also Islamic fundamentalist commentators who 'shy away from strict literalism in their interpretation of the Koran' (ibid.: 44). Two other core elements of fundamentalism are anti-modernism and anti-pluralism. These themes are related since religious pluralism is integral to modernity. Fundamentalism's anti-modernism also comes out in the endorsement by many fundamentalists of patriarchal values and homophobia. More generally, fundamentalists see diversity as threatening, and their own activities as essentially defensive.

Almond, Sivan and Appleby identify five ideological and four organizational characteristics of fundamentalism. The ideological characteristics are:

1. *Reactivity to the marginalization of a religion*: fundamentalism is 'reactive to and defensive toward the processes and consequences of secularization and modernization, as they have penetrated the larger religious community itself' (2004: 405).
2. *Selectivity*: fundamentalism selects and reshapes aspects of the tradition that clearly distinguish it from the mainstream. They also select aspects of modernity to affirm and embrace (for example, the internet) and other aspects for focused opposition.

3. *Moral Manicheanism*: fundamentalists see reality as sharply divided into light and dark, good and evil.
4. *Absolutism and inerrancy*: fundamentalists are committed to 'the absolute validity of the "fundamentals" of the tradition' (ibid.: 407). They reject modern methods of interpretation as having no application to sacred methods and traditions.
5. *Millennialism and Messianism*: fundamentalists believe that good will triumph over evil and that the end of days will be ushered in by the Messiah.

The organizational characteristics of fundamentalist movements are: (1) they tend to have an elect membership and separate themselves from the mainstream; (2) their organizational structure is authoritarian and elitist, based on a leader-follower model; (3) in addition, membership of the movement imposes 'elaborate behavioral requirements' (ibid.: 408), pertaining to such things as facial hair and style of dress; and (4) they insist on a sharp separation between the saved and the sinful.

What do these observations reveal about the relationship between fundamentalism, extremism and fanaticism? The answer to this question depends, in part, on how closely the label 'fundamentalist' is tied to its original religious use. Fundamentalists in a narrow religious sense can be extremists or fanatics but the *concept* of a fundamentalist is not the concept of an extremist or fanatic, and it is easy to be an extremist or a fanatic without being a fundamentalist. Heydrich was an extremist in every sense and also a fanatic but not a religious fundamentalist. Tying fundamentalism more closely to extremism or fanaticism requires one to be prepared to use the 'fundamentalist' label in a looser way, that is, without tying it to religion. This would leave greater scope for the investigation of similarities between fundamentalism and the other two 'isms'. The most striking similarities are between fundamentalism and mindset extremism and, though to a somewhat lesser extent, between fundamentalism and fanaticism.

However, before getting to these similarities, there are some important dissimilarities to take into account. Whereas fundamentalism is essentially a cult of the text, the same is not true of extremism or fanaticism. Clearly, there are extremists who revere certain texts. One only has to think of the reverence of twentieth-century Marxists for the texts of Marx, Engels, Lenin, and Mao. Many engaged in quasi-theological disputes about the correct interpretation of canonical Marxist texts and also appeared to be committed to some version of the doctrine of inerrancy: if Marx or Lenin said it, it must be right. However, it is possible to be an extremist or fanatic without revering a text. For example, the cult of the text plays no significant role in fascism, and one would be hard pushed to identify the canonical texts of fascist ideology. There is, for example, no fascist equivalent of the *Communist Manifesto* or *Das Kapital*, unless one is prepared to treat Hitler's ramblings in *Mein Kampf* as an ideological manifesto. Furthermore, it is questionable whether leading extreme left theoreticians are literalists about their revered texts. In general, it is hard to be a literalist if one is also committed to the idea that one's revered texts cannot be mistaken in any important respect: apparent errors are best explained away by non-literal textual interpretations.

At an organizational level, ideological extremists see themselves as leaders of, or at least participants in, mass movements. They think of themselves as defending the interests of 'the people' rather than those of a chosen few. To this extent they have no interest in separating themselves from the mainstream, though the Marxist ideal of being in the 'vanguard' of the struggle against capitalism can all too easily replicate the elitist leader-follower model that is an organizational characteristic of fundamentalist movements. Whereas fanatics trample on the ideals and interests of other people, this is not a necessary feature of fundamentalism. It is quite possible to revere a text and live by its rules in a community of 'the elect' without having any interest in going mainstream or compelling others to accept one's ideals. Fundamentalists can be fanatics, and fundamentalism might be a risk factor for fanaticism. However, there is no necessary connection between the two.

The similarities between the fundamentalist mindset and the extremist mindset are not hard to spot. The fundamentalist's preoccupation with staying true to the fundamentals can be seen as a version of extremism's preoccupation with purity and virtue, in this case religious purity and virtue. The defensive posture of fundamentalism, and its sense that true religion is being eroded and displaced by secular modernization, are related to the extremist preoccupation with victimhood. Also, like other extremists, fundamentalists regard themselves as victims of persecution. Their perception of themselves as increasingly marginalized gives rise to feelings of resentment and anger. The tendency to see all compromises as rotten is another characteristic that is shared by extremism, fanaticism and fundamentalism. However, just like some fanatics, fundamentalists are not averse to tactical compromises for long-term gains. Anti-pluralism is something else the three 'isms' have in common. So, for that matter, is Manicheanism. Finally, both fundamentalists and extremists are prone to apocalyptic thinking.

These overlaps and similarities between the mindset of the extremist and the religious fundamentalist are so striking as to make the two virtually indistinguishable. It is certainly hard to think of features of the extremist mindset that are not also features of the fundamentalist cast of mind. In this sense, fundamentalists are mindset extremists. If the reverse is not true that is because not all extremists have the religious preoccupations of religious fundamentalists. There is still the question of the relationship between fundamentalism and other forms of extremism. This can be dealt with relatively quickly: fundamentalism is hard to locate on the left-right spectrum, even though some fundamentalist values and preoccupations are shared by some far-right ideologies. With regard to methods extremism, fundamentalism as such is not committed to the use of extreme methods to promote or defend its values, but the use of such methods will undoubtedly appeal to some fundamentalists.

The last point is significant in its own right and also draws attention to another aspect of the discussion so far. It is one thing to be interested in the relationship between two concepts, say, the concepts of fundamentalism and extremism, or the relationship between two properties, like the property of being a fundamentalist and the property of being a fanatic. In these contexts, the tests are conceivability or possibility: is fundamentalism conceivable or possible apart from extremism? Is it possible for a person to be a fundamentalist without being a fanatic, or vice versa? However, even if two properties are not identical, they can still be causally related. As already noted, fundamentalism is a risk factor for fanaticism, in the sense that being a fundamentalist raises to a significant degree the probability of also being a fanatic. Such causal relations might be of considerable practical interest, but can only be known by empirical research rather than philosophical analysis. The latter is of value to the extent that it helps to clarify the relevant concepts and individuate the relevant properties. In this sense, an empirical investigation of the relationship between fundamentalism, extremism and fanaticism needs to begin with a philosophical investigation of these three phenomena. If there is one thing that the discussion in this chapter has made clear, it is that the relations between the three 'isms' are highly complex. To the extent that the popular use of the three terms reveals a degree of confusion about how they are related, this is perfectly understandable.

Notes

1 This account of Heydrich's assassination is based on Chapter 1 of Gerwarth (2011) and Evans (2008: 275).

2 Quoted in Gerwarth (2011: 279).

3 These rumours are discussed in Chapter 2 of Gerwarth (2011).

4 This conception of an epistemic vice is explained and defended in Cassam (2019a).

5 On Kony, see Green (2008).

6 But see below for a possible qualification.

7 Ruthven (2007: Chapter 1).

6 Why not extremism?

Merry's challenge

'Sometimes you have to fucking go to the extreme' (Roth 1997: 105). These words, spoken by Merry Levov in Philip Roth's *American Pastoral*, came up in Chapter 4. The time has come to face up to Merry's challenge. In her eyes, the carpet bombing of Vietnam in the 1960s was something to which only an extreme response was appropriate, both ethically and tactically. For all the supposed virtues of moderation, sometimes it is necessary to be an extremist, especially when confronted by a great evil. In what the political scientist Joel Olson calls the 'pejorative tradition', extremism, fanaticism and zealotry invariably have a negative connotation, but the clear lesson of history is that these supposed political vices 'can advance democracy while moderation and compromise can actually undermine it' (2007: 692).

On the possible benefits of extremism, right and left are united. The far-right American politician Senator Barry Goldwater argued in a speech that 'extremism in defense of liberty is no vice' and 'moderation in the pursuit of justice is no virtue'.[1] In a similar vein, Martin Luther King Jnr wrote as follows in his *Letter from Birmingham Jail*:

> But though I was initially disappointed at being categorized as an extremist, as I continued to think about the matter, I gradually gained a measure of satisfaction from the label … the question is not whether we will be extremists, but what kind of extremists we will be. Will we be extremists for hate or for love? Will we be extremists for the preservation of injustice or for the extension of justice?
>
> (2018: 19–20)

DOI: 10.4324/9780429325472-6

Noting that Jesus was an 'extremist for love', Dr King suggests that perhaps 'the nation and the world are in dire need of creative extremists' (ibid.: 20).

In his account of the virtues of fanaticism, Olson discusses the campaign against slavery in the United States in the mid-nineteenth century.[2] He notes that the Garrisonian wing of the abolitionist movement, led by William Lloyd Garrison, 'was a movement of self-defined fanatics with an unyielding commitment to the immediate and unconditional emancipation of the enslaved' (2007: 686). Garrisonians brimmed with zealotry but zealotry, which Olson sees as equivalent to fanaticism and extremism, is not inherently problematic. Far from being a psychological or moral defect, zealotry is 'a strategy rather than a temperament' (ibid.: 695). Specifically, it is a 'political activity, driven by an ardent devotion to a cause' (ibid.: 688). It was the only effective means of overturning the institution of slavery, and Garrison embraced the description of his wing of the abolitionist movement as fanatics. When it comes to slavery, there is no middle way and no room for compromise. Slavery does not call for a moderate response, and is precisely one of those cases in which, as Merry would have put it, you have to fucking go to the extreme.

In the pejorative tradition, zealots are irrational and intolerant fundamentalists and terrorists. Labelling someone a zealot or a fanatic or an extremist is not so much an attempt to describe them as to call into question the legitimacy of their methods or objectives or both. As Alberto Toscano remarks in his study of the concept, fanaticism 'is rarely, if ever, an object of political affirmation, serving almost invariably as a foil against which to define the proper path of politics' (2017: xxv). The fanatic is always the enemy, 'an inscrutable, intransigent and alien enemy' (ibid.: 1). Yet the fact that people like Garrison were described as fanatics should give us pause. In effect, the charge of fanaticism was used to defend slavery 'against the threat of an uncompromising egalitarianism' (ibid.: 8). Yet it is clear in retrospect that if Garrison was a zealot, he was a 'reasonable zealot' (ibid.: 10). If he was an extremist, his extremism was justified in the context of his fight against slavery.

But is it actually *true* that Garrisonian abolitionists were fanatics or extremists? This question brings out a fundamental lack of clarity in attempts by writers like Olson and Toscano to rehabilitate fanaticism. There are two ways of reading their arguments. On the one hand, all they are doing is pointing out that 'fanatic' is a pejorative label that has been applied to people whom we now regard not just as admirable but as positively heroic.

This leaves it open whether fanaticism, *properly so-called*, can be admirable because it leaves it open whether people like Garrison were *in fact* fanatics or, if they were, whether their fanaticism was what made them admirable. On this interpretation, it is possible to deplore the misuse of labels like 'fanatic' or 'extremist' without endorsing either fanaticism or extremism. Indeed, challenging the misuse of these labels might make it easier to see what is *actually* wrong with fanaticism.

On a stronger reading, the argument is that Garrison and his followers were *actually* extremists and were admirable by virtue of their extreme or fanatical opposition to slavery. This would then be a compelling illustration of Olson's point that fanaticism can advance the cause of democracy. However, for this argument to be compelling, one would need to be sure that the labelling of people like Garrison as fanatics or extremists is not anachronistic. According to Toscano, 'the epithet "fanatic" was worn as a badge of pride among the radical wing of the abolitionist movement' (ibid.: 9). However, this does not settle the question whether these radicals were right to think of themselves as fanatics or to regard their tactics and methods as fanatical or extremist. Like Olson, Toscano tends to take radical abolitionists at their word but if this is a mistake, then the case for fanaticism is considerably weakened. It is perfectly possible to see the abolitionists in a positive light without seeing fanaticism or extremism in a positive light.

The next section will go into these issues in greater depth since radical abolitionism is one of the most cited and appealing examples of the upside of extremism. As will become apparent, the imagined virtues of extremism are the actual virtues of something with which it is too easily confused: radicalism. The following section will leave behind the discussion of abolitionism and consider whether there is a more general case for extremism in any of the three forms – ideological, methods and psychological – distinguished in the preceding chapters. Apologists for extremism do not argue that it is intrinsically good. They argue, rather, that it is, or can be, an effective means of achieving worthwhile political ends. The implication is that its consequences are, in many cases, better than those of the primary alternative to extremism, namely, moderation. The consequences that are at issue here are the consequences for human rights, justice, democracy, and freedom. The question, then, is this: to the extent that one cares about these things, is it better to be an extremist than a moderate? This is the question that will inform much of the following discussion.

Moderation has been described as 'the quintessential political virtue' (Craiutu 2012: 1). To decide the relative virtues of extremism and moderation, it is important to be clear about the notion of moderation, and what is involved in being a 'moderate'. An influential critic of extremism and defender of moderation was the eighteenth-century woman of letters, Germaine de Staël, otherwise known as Madame de Staël.[3] Her reputation and opposition to Napoleon once led someone to observe that 'there are three great powers struggling for the soul of Europe: England, Russia and Madame de Staël'.[4] Published posthumously in 1818, her *Considerations on the Principal Events of the French Revolution* has been described as a 'true manifesto of moderation' (ibid.: 190). Her criticisms of extremism and defence of moderation will be taken up in the final part of this chapter. If moderation is the quintessential political virtue, then extremism is the quintessential political vice.

Extremism and emancipation

Olson begins his defence of fanaticism with an anecdote about Stephen Foster, who is described as belonging to the Garrisonian wing of the abolitionist movement. At a meeting in 1842, Foster rose, unannounced and uninvited, and began to lecture against slavery. He was rewarded by being thrown down a flight of stairs. He dusted himself off and continued his lecture at several other venues, including a Quaker meeting. On each occasion he was subjected to physical violence. Yet he remained undeterred. The conclusion Olson draws from this is that 'Stephen Foster was a zealot' who, despite his unpopularity, 'never shrank from his fanatical approach to abolitionism' (2007: 685). In the pejorative tradition, the fanatic is against reason and tolerance, a religious fundamentalist, and 'often but a terrorist in waiting' (ibid.: 688). However, since Foster was none of these things, why call him a fanatic? He was principled, determined, and courageous to the point of foolhardiness, but these traits do not add up to fanaticism in the pejorative sense. Olson's insistence on labelling Foster a fanatic is therefore based on a rejection of the pejorative definition of fanaticism.

For Olson, the fundamental error of pejorative accounts is to suppose that fanaticism or zealotry is a matter of character or temperament. What this

147

approach fails to see is that zealotry is a political strategy, and that fanaticism is first and foremost a type of political activity, a means to an end:

> Zealotry is an activity practiced not so much by disturbed temperaments as by collectivities working to transform relations of power by creating an "us" in struggling against a "them", and by pressuring those in between to choose sides. Accordingly, zealotry is *political activity, driven by ardent devotion to a cause, which seeks to draw clear lines along a friends/enemies dichotomy in order to mobilize friends in the service of that cause.*
>
> (ibid.: 688; original emphasis)

In reading this definition, it needs to be kept in mind that zealotry, for Olson, is equivalent to fanaticism and extremism. The essence of all three is encapsulated in President George W. Bush's statement in the aftermath of 9/11 that 'either you are with us, or you are with the terrorists'. The implied rejection of a middle way and commitment to the politics of us and them are the essence of zealotry, as Olson understands it. For the radical wing of the abolitionist movement, there could be no compromise on its fundamental demand: the immediate and unconditional emancipation of slaves. Its strategy was to flatly reject any notion of gradual emancipation and force so-called 'gradualists' to choose between standing with the slaves and supporting their masters. Even if it came to a choice between the Union and emancipation of the slaves, the former was to be sacrificed to the latter. In Garrison's words, 'A repeal of the Union between northern liberty and southern slavery is essential to the abolition of one, and preservation of the other.'[5]

If Garrisonian abolitionists were indeed zealots, and their zealotry did indeed lead to the emancipation of the slaves, then this would both support Olson's contention that 'fanaticism can advance democracy' (ibid.: 692) and Merry's contention that that sometimes you have to be an extremist. Unfortunately, both premises of this argument are dubious. It is for historians to decide on the contribution of radical abolitionism to the emancipation of American slaves in 1865, the year in which the 13th Amendment to the Constitution was ratified. This amendment abolishes slavery and involuntary servitude in America, except as punishment for a crime. However, slavery came to be replaced by the incarceration of African Americans on a massive scale, to the extent that, according to one authority, there are more African American men in prison or on parole today than were slaves at the end of the Civil War.[6] In this sense, it is not clear that true black emancipation, as this would have been understood by Garrison, has been achieved to this day. However, even if Garrison *was* successful on his own terms, Olson is wrong to classify him as a fanatic. This classification says more about the defects of Olson's conception of fanaticism than about Garrison's politics. There is a sense in which Garrison was an *extremist*, but this only goes to show that fanaticism and extremism should not be equated. Furthermore, the sense in which Garrison was an extremist was far removed from extremism as this would be understood today.

It is instructive to compare Olson's account of zealotry with the account of fanaticism given in Chapter 5:

(F) Fanatics have unwarranted contempt for other people's ideals and interests, are willing to trample on those ideals and interests in pursuit of their own perverted ideals, and impose their ideals on others, by force if necessary. Fanatics are unwilling to think critically about their ideals because they regard them as indubitable. However, they are willing to sacrifice themselves and others in pursuit of their ideals.

Garrisonians like Stephen Foster were willing to sacrifice themselves in pursuit of their ideals, but this is the only respect they look like fanatics according to (F). In demanding an immediate end to slavery without compensation for slave owners, radical abolitionists showed contempt for the interests and ideals of slave owners, but this contempt was *warranted*. Since Garrison was a pacificist, he was against the use of force in the cause of black emancipation, and it would be perverse to classify his ideals as perverted. He was uncompromising but the compromises he rejected were rotten in Margalit's (2010) sense.[7]

These are not the only respects in which the classification of Garrison as a fanatic seems bizarre. In her study of Garrison, Aileen Kraditor notes that, in his writings, Garrison 'frankly expressed uncertainty about his opinions on given issues' and invited further discussion that 'might change his mind' (1989: ix). There is no trace here of the fanatic's immunity to self-doubt. In addition, Garrison was no dogmatic ideologue. He insisted that an antislavery society should be broad enough to 'include members with all religious, social, and political views, united only by their devotion to abolitionist principles' (ibid.: 8). His radical pacifism took the form of a commitment to the doctrine of nonresistance, the rejection of all government based on force. Far from favouring abolition by force, Garrison saw persuasion and propaganda as the key to bringing people over to his side of the argument. He supposed that 'the conscience of even the most unregenerate slave-holder could be awakened by the redeeming truth if only the channels of communication were kept open and flooded by unremitting propaganda that permitted the guilty soul no hiding place' (ibid.: 255). On this basis, Garrison might reasonably be accused of naïveté but not fanaticism.

Even on the issue of compromise, his position was more nuanced than one would expect a fanatic's stance to be. Kraditor represents Garrison's uncom-promising commitment to immediate and unconditional emancipation as at least partly tactical, and as ultimately making favourable compromises possible. The more extreme the abolitionists' demands, the greater the con-cessions required of politicians prepared to meet them halfway. Garrison's refusal to water down his demands was 'eminently practical' (ibid.: 28), and he did not display the true fanatic's tendency to see all compromises as rotten. Garrisonians 'repeatedly explained that they were not averse to prac-tical alliances with those who disagreed with them, provided such alliances did not entail sacrifice of principle' (ibid.: 213).

This account of Garrison makes it plain that the description of him and his followers as zealots or fanatics is anachronistic. Indeed, it is difficult to imagine a less fanatical campaigner than Garrison. In the final analysis, Olson's only real argument for classifying Garrison as a zealot is that his pol-itics were the politics of us and them. It is true that genuine fanatics have a Manichean view of the world, that is, a strong sense of dualism 'between the realm of light and goodness (us) and the realm of darkness and evil (them)' (Margalit 2010: 153–4). However, for Garrison, the drawing of a clear line between friends and enemies was not Manichean but strategic. It was a way to mobilize moderates in the cause of radical abolitionism by promoting the idea that a commitment to anything less than unconditional and immediate emancipation amounted to being on the side of slave-owners. Yet Garrison plainly didn't think that moderates were evil or the forces of darkness. For that matter, he didn't even think that people who kept slaves were irredeem-ably evil. As noted above, he assumed that they had consciences to which it was possible to appeal. The is not the perspective of a zealot.

There is more to be said for classifying Garrison and his followers as extremists rather than fanatics, but their brand of extremism was a form of what was described in Chapter 2 as *ideological* extremism. For slavery is an issue concerning which, in Garrison's day, there was a spectrum of views, ranging from the undiluted pro-slavery stance of some in the South to the passionate abolitionism of the Garrisonians. In between were gradualists who argued for the gradual abolition of slavery with compensation for slave owners. Garrison was at one end of this spectrum and, in this sense, an 'extremist', but few today would see the uncompromising rejection of slavery as the standpoint of an extremist.

What Olson describes is not zealotry or fanaticism but radicalism, defined as contention 'outside the common routines of politics present within a society, oriented towards substantial change in social, cultural, economic, and/or political structures, and undertaken by any actor using extra-institutional means' (Beck 2015: 18). Radical abolitionists 'were often willing to defy decorum' (Olson 2007: 690) and showed no respect for 'the boundaries of "respectable" politics' (ibid.: 689) but these are the tactics of the radical as well as the Olsonian zealot. Radicals embrace the philosophy of 'you are either with us or against us', but this does not make them zealots. The latter believe in compulsion or the use of force to tackle those who are 'against us' whereas the Garrisonian radical believes in winning people over by appeal to their reason or emotions. Whereas radicalism is compatible with self-doubt, zealotry is not. Zealotry and dogmatism are inseparable but the radical need not be dogmatic. In these and several other respects, there is a clear dividing line between radicalism and zealotry, and Garrison was no zealot.

If one is looking for a more convincing example of a fanatical abolitionist one might consider a figure like John Brown. In 1856, he responded to slave-holder aggression by killing eight pro-slavery settlers at Pottawatomie. Five were hacked to death with broadswords by men in Brown's party in a summary execution. Three years later Brown led a disastrous raid on a federal armory at Harper's Ferry. He and his fellow raiders were tried for treason and executed. Brown's methods were very different from Garrison's and might justify the judgement that he was a fanatic and an extremist in a way that Garrison was not. In the terminology of Chapter 3, Brown was a methods extremist. Extreme methods needn't be violent and using violence for political ends does not necessarily make one a methods extremist. Nevertheless, the nature and circumstances of Brown's violence suggest that it would not be eccentric to classify him as an extremist in the methods sense.

The argument that extremism is sometimes necessary is the argument that extreme methods are sometimes the only effective means of combatting cruelty and injustice. So, if one cares about these things, then one should be a methods extremist. The raid on Harper's Ferry may have contributed little to combatting the cruelty and injustice of slavery but this is not to say that extreme methods are *generally* ineffective. This is the crux of Merry's challenge. Moderates who criticize extremists for their use of extreme methods can be seen as wittingly or unwittingly conniving in cruelty and injustice when they reject the use of the only effective means of righting these wrongs. However, moderates can reply that violence or other extreme methods are rarely effective in advancing the cause of freedom and democracy and cause injustices that are at least as serious as the ones they are supposed to combat.[8] Thus, the crux of the matter is whether extremism in one form or another is in fact an effective means of fighting for good political causes.

Does extremism work?

The extreme methods used by methods extremists do not need to be violent but frequently are. One such method is terrorism, which can be used for a variety of goals. One question is whether terrorism is an effective means of achieving its goals, whatever those goals happen to be. As Richard English notes, 'terrorism is an instrumental business: people become involved in the terrorist process in order to achieve something else' (2016: 3). If terrorism succeeds in bringing about the political changes that terrorists typically seek, then that is one sense in which it works, and if terrorism works, then that is one central type of extremism that works. If terrorism doesn't work, it doesn't follow that extreme methods don't work since there are extreme methods other than terrorism. However, terrorism is the method of choice for most methods extremists, and is certainly what Merry has in mind when she talks about having to go to the extreme.

It isn't enough for the purposes of Merry's defence of extremism that terrorism works. It also matters whether it is the *only* way, or whether the ends of terrorism could also have been achieved by less extreme methods. Like the extremists described in Chapter 3, apologists for extremism too easily assume that there is no viable alternative to the use of extreme methods. Furthermore, given the variety of goals that terrorism might be a means of achieving, there is also the issue of whether terrorism is better at achieving some goals than others. Apologists for extremism see it as a way of achieving goals like democracy, freedom, justice, and human rights but what if it turns out that these are the unlikeliest outcomes of terrorism? If terrorism causes injustices that are at least as great as the ones that it supposedly combats, then it doesn't 'work' in the sense that apologists have in mind.

Terrorism can be defined as 'the intentional use or threat of violence against individuals or groups who are victimized for the purpose of intimidating or frightening a broader audience' (Jackson 2011: 123). In his account of the effectiveness of terrorism, English distinguishes four senses of terrorism 'working': (1) strategic victory (the achievement of its primary goal or goals); (2) partial strategic victory (such as the partial achievement of the primary goal); (3) tactical success (such as the securing of interim concessions or publicity for one's cause); and (4) 'the inherent rewards of struggle as such, independent of central goals' (2016: 30). To this list a fifth sense of 'working' should be added: an act of terrorism can be a political gesture whose purpose is to give expression to a sense of outrage, injustice or resentment about the status quo, or a desire for political change, but without any serious expectation of bringing about political change as a result of the act. On this interpretation, terrorism 'works' just if it succeeds in expressing the feelings or desires that motivate it.

The conclusion of English's painstaking investigation is that 'the terrible human costs of terrorism have been far more certain than have any benevolent outcomes brought about politically by it' (ibid.: 220). Commenting on John Brown's 'terroristic methods' (ibid.: 225), English observes that 'slavery was brought to an end through a very different set of dynamics from the small-scale violence used to pursue it by this American terrorist' (ibid.: 225). In the case of the ANC's campaign against apartheid, terrorism was at best a minor element in its success. The ANC took power not because of the activities of its military wing but despite them. Indeed, Audrey Cronin's (2009) study of 450 terrorist campaigns suggests that 87 per cent achieved none of their strategic aims, with only 4 per cent fully achieving their primary objectives.[9]

The only sense in which terrorism is virtually guaranteed to 'work' is in expressing the feelings and desires of those responsible but this sense of 'working' is at odds with the idea that terrorism, properly so-called, is 'focused on the pursuit of political change' (English 2016: 1). Expressing oneself is one thing, bringing about political change is another. Moreover, the satisfaction extremists derive from expressing their feelings by means of acts of violence needs to be weighed against the near certainty that 'terrible human suffering will ensue from terrorist violence' (ibid.: 265). If there is one thing that is worse than achieving worthwhile political change by causing terrible suffering, it is *failing* to bring about any such change as a result of terrorism.

Even in those rare cases in which terrorism works, there is the question whether other methods would have been just as effective. In the case of the ANC, this question is not difficult to answer. Non-violent methods would have been as effective, indeed more effective, because they *were* more effective. Politics and economics, rather than terrorism, were responsible for the ANC's ultimate victory. An example of a successful terrorist campaign was the Irgun's in Palestine.[10] The Irgun achieved its central strategic goal, which was British withdrawal from the region and the establishment of the state of Israel. However, 'other factors too pushed in the same direction' (ibid.: 221). In this type of case, it is an open question whether the other factors pushing in the same direction might have produced the same outcome, albeit more slowly, without the help of terrorism.

Even if terrorism is capable of delivering strategic victory, there is a potential mismatch between its means and ends. When extremists resort to terrorism to advance the cause of human rights, they ignore the human rights of the victims of their terrorism. In cases where their victims bear no responsibility for the injustices to which terrorism is supposedly a response, those victims have themselves suffered the injustice of being killed or maimed for wrongs that are not their fault. This is the basis of the intuition that justice and human rights are not among the likeliest outcomes of terrorism. The standard extremist response to this concern is to argue that while terrorism might treat its victims unjustly and violate their human rights, this is in the interests of greater justice and human rights overall. However, this assumes that the rights of the victims of terrorism can be traded against the rights of its supposed beneficiaries. There are arguments against the legitimacy of this kind of trade-off, and these arguments are strengthened by the observation that those who come into power through terrorism have a poor track record of respecting human rights and treating people justly.

The lesson of studies of the effectiveness of terrorism is that it doesn't work more often than it does. When it does, it is only in a tactical or expressive sense, or by delivering a partial strategic victory. Terrorism rarely achieves its primary objectives, and those objectives are not necessarily benign. Even when the objectives are benign, they can be undermined by the use of terror to achieve them. Even to the limited extent that terrorism 'works', it is rarely the case that it was genuinely the only possible method for achieving its objectives. In most cases, the alternatives include the use of extreme methods that are non-violent, and political methods that are not extreme.

As noted in Chapter 3, the 1981 hunger strikes at the Maze Prison transformed the political fortunes of the IRA. The hunger strikes were effective because they changed hearts and minds. The same goes for the ANC's successful political campaign against apartheid.

So far, then, Merry's challenge has proved somewhat less compelling than apologists for extremism like to think. If one really cares about freedom, justice, democracy and human rights, it is generally (though perhaps not always) better not to resort to terrorism and often also better not to use extreme methods at all. This was Garrison's view and there is every reason to think that he was right. As Garrison saw, the most effective way to bring about political change is to change hearts and minds. Methods extremism rarely does that. That leaves ideological and psychological extremism. Are these forms of extremism any better at advancing the cause of freedom, justice, democracy, and human rights than methods extremism?

In the case of ideological extremism, the answer depends on the nature of ideologically extremist ideologies. If one considers the left-right spectrum, there is little reason to think that ideologies on the far left or far right are politically benign or beneficial. Far from advancing democracy and human rights, these ideologies are anti-democratic and no respecters of human rights or freedom. In contrast, if ideologies are placed on what was referred to in Chapter 2 as the authoritarianism spectrum, then matters are less clear-cut. Most authoritarian ideologies are hostile to freedom and democracy but what about ideologies at the opposite end of the spectrum? Anarchism is one such ideology, and arguably also a friend of democracy and human rights, but not a realistic objective for a serious political movement. The idea that the best way to advance the cause of democracy and human rights is to be an anarchist, or for that matter any other kind of ideological extremist, is too far-fetched to be worthy of serious discussion.

The same goes for the idea that psychological extremism is the key to positive political change. Effective campaigners for radical political change need almost bottomless supplies of resilience, courage, and political intelligence but these virtues have very little to do with the preoccupations, attitudes, emotions and thinking styles that constitute the extremist mindset. Unlike archetypal psychological extremists, change-makers like Garrison and Mandela *display* political virtues but aren't *preoccupied* with virtue. They have no preoccupation with purity and do not see all compromises as rotten. They are moved by anger and resentment but anger and resentment at genuine cruelty and injustice. They cannot properly be described as suffering from *fantasies* of victimhood since the people they represent *are* victims. They are radicals rather than extremists.

The remaining question for this chapter concerns the supposed quint-essential political virtue of moderation. The discussion so far suggests a straightforward answer to the question 'Why not extremism?'. The case against extremism in any of its forms is that it generally does more harm than good. However, the case against extremism is not a case against radi-calism. Indeed, if one looks at historical struggles for freedom, democracy, justice, and human rights, one might draw the conclusion that radicalism rather than moderation is the quintessential political virtue. This assumes, however, that radicals cannot be moderates. Is this assumption correct? If it is, then is it correct that radicalism is preferable to moderation? To answer these questions, one would require a better understanding of what it is to be a moderate and why writers inspired by Madame de Staël are so convinced of the benefits of moderation. Do they have an answer to the accusation that moderation is really a bastion of the status quo and stands in the way of progress? The time has come to turn our attention to these important questions.

Moderates and radicals

In a book on moderation, which he describes as a 'virtue for courageous minds', Aurelian Craiutu comments that Madame de Staël's works and personal trajectory constitute 'a particularly interesting case study for the student of moderation' (2012: 158). He quotes her observations about the Terror that followed the French Revolution, including her identification of fanaticism as its main cause. The antidote to fanaticism is moderation, and the lesson of the Terror was that justice and humanity depend on modera-tion. This is how Craiutu describes de Staël's view of fanaticism:

> As the opposite of moderation, fanaticism is the outcome of an extreme partisan spirit and, though pretending to speak on behalf of virtue, equality and morality, is instead one of the most dangerous of political passions … The fanatic mind, Mme de Staël argued, is dan-gerous because it knows no limits, is incapable of self-restraint, and admits of no guilt. Fanatics demand unconditional obedience and uniformity of thought, and they have no scruples about sacrificing

the fate of current generations to the hypothetical happiness of future ones. They tend to reduce every political and moral issue to one single problem (or dimension) on which they focus blindly. Fanaticism is a malady of the spirit, more dangerous than the passion for vengeance or domination, because it so easily masks its true face under a veil of generosity and humanity.

(ibid.: 168)

In this striking passage, Craiutu represents Madame de Staël as responding directly and with considerable force to the main assertion of apologists for fanaticism and extremism: that the wholehearted and effective pursuit of freedom and justice *requires* these attributes and that we would not have many of the liberties we take for granted today were it not for the fanaticism of figures from the past. Madame de Staël sees clearly that fanatics view themselves as friends of liberty and justice, but she argues that these claims to political virtue are a fraud. As the post-revolutionary Terror illustrates, the consequences of fanaticism are the exact opposite of those claimed by its apologists.

Madame de Staël is careful to distinguish between fanaticism and enthusiasm. She has no qualms about praising the latter while criticizing the former. Enthusiasm is an 'elevated and powerful passion' that is qualitatively different from fanaticism (ibid.: 167). It is enthusiasm rather than fanaticism that enables us to 'pursue the truth disinterestedly' and to contemplate 'the good, and the noble things of life as ends in themselves, without being distracted by their practical aspects' (ibid.: 167). Surprisingly, de Staël concedes that 'a small dose of fanaticism *sui generis* might be a good thing in pursuit of worthy political causes' (ibid.: 5). This is not very different from Olson's view, but it is difficult to see how it can be correct if fanaticism is understood as de Staël understands it. How can 'the most dangerous of political passions' and a 'malady of the spirit' be a genuine force for good? Mme de Staël's considered view is that the fanatic's claim to be speaking on behalf of virtue is both baseless and dishonest. The fanatic is no friend of justice and lacks humanity.

What is 'moderation' and what do moderates stand for? There is no better place to look for answers to these questions than Craiutu's study. He admits that it is virtually impossible to offer a single definition of moderation, and that it might be easier to define it by reference to what it opposes. Moderation is opposed to extremism, radicalism, zealotry and fanaticism. It can also be interpreted as an antonym for rigidity, stubbornness, dogmatism, perfectionism, and utopianism. Moderation can be interpreted as a state of mind and a 'distinct political style' (ibid.: 15). Its essence is 'trimming', that is, 'the art of compromise needed for maintaining equipoise between different interests, groups and powers' (ibid.: 30). Trimmers avoid 'one of the greatest sins in politics – single-mindedness – being sometimes of several minds and uncertain which way to go' (ibid.: 245).

This makes it sound as though moderates don't stand for anything in politics apart from splitting the difference between contrary standpoints or ideologies but Craiutu is keen to correct this impression. On his account, moderates affirm three basic attitudes:

> First, they defend pluralism – of ideas, interests, and social forces – and seek to achieve a balance between them in order to temper political and social conflicts. Second, moderates prefer gradual reforms to revolutionary breakthroughs, and they are temperamentally inclined to making compromises and concessions on both prudential and normative grounds … Third, moderation presupposes a tolerant approach which refuses to see the world in Manichean terms that divide it into forces of good (or light) and agents of evil (or darkness).
>
> (ibid.: 14–15)

However, moderation is not the same as centrism since moderates can be found 'on the left, at the center, and on the right of the political spectrum' (ibid.: 15). Craiutu stresses that being a moderate can be hard since 'searching for the mean is always a demanding task, arguably more difficult than making one's journey along paths that are more extreme' (ibid.: 19). Contrary to what is often supposed, moderation is 'a *difficult* virtue for courageous minds' (ibid.: 19).

Viewed in one way, this account of moderation makes it sound like a political style to which no reasonable person could possibly object. Rigidity, stubbornness, and dogmatism sound like intellectual and political vices, so if moderation is the opposite of these things, then how can it fail to be a virtue? Again, toleration might be seen as essential for a civilized society so if moderation promotes toleration, then that is surely a good thing. By the same token, linking fanaticism to intolerance and Manicheanism and representing it as a malady of the spirit make it look like a disease for which moderation is the antidote. However, viewed in another way, Craiutu's characterization of moderation confirms the worst fears of radicals who see it as an obstacle to the pursuit of social justice and as promoting complacency and political apathy.

There are several illustrations of these defects, or potential defects, in Craiutu's account. It cannot be right, for example, that single-mindedness is one of the greatest sins in politics or that being uncertain which way to go is preferable. Without the single-mindedness of reformers like Garrison, the fight against slavery would have been much less effective, and this is just one of countless examples of the value of single-mindedness. When it comes to cruelty and injustice, it is no good being of several minds. A tendency to engage in trimming is another potentially problematic feature of the moderate mindset. Trimming might be the art of compromise but in Craiutu's account there are no safeguards against rotten compromises, that is, compromises that 'establish or maintain an inhuman regime, a regime of cruelty and humiliation' (Margalit 2010: 2). Indeed, moderation, as Craiutu construes it, might even be regarded as *promoting* rotten compromises. Rotten compromises will be unavoidable if maintaining equipoise between different interests, groups and powers is a priority. For example, how would it have been possible for radical abolitionists to balance the interests of slaves and slave-owners without making rotten compromises? More to the point, why should any concessions be made to the interests of slave-owners? Equipoise or a balance of interests cannot be a worthy objective in this case. Moderates prefer gradual reforms but what if such reforms are not feasible or prolong the suffering of victims of cruelty and injustice? In such cases, a preference for reform over revolution is not necessarily commendable.

Underlying these concerns is a deeper question about the moderation. A presupposition of Craiutu's defence of this supposed virtue is that compromise is possible and stark choices can be avoided. While this might be true in some cases, there are many cases in which there is no middle way and no possibility of reconciling diametrically opposed interests. This is one lesson of what Jonathan Israel calls the Radical Enlightenment. In these cases, radicalism and moderation are logically incompatible, and it is the radical rather than the moderate who is on the side of progress. Radical Enlightenment is a set of principles

> that can be summed up concisely as: democracy, racial and sexual equality; individual liberty of lifestyle; full freedom of thought, expression, and the press; eradication of religious authority from

the legislative process and education; and full separation of church and state.

(Israel 2009: vii–viii)

The contrast is with the Moderate Enlightenment, which was not opposed to reform as such but much more gradualist in its approach and opposed to sweeping programs of reform. Between Radical and Moderate Enlightenment principles, 'no compromise or half way position was ever possible, either theoretically or practically' (ibid.: 17–18). To put it another way, there is no possibility of trimming.

The contrast between Radical and Moderate Enlightenment is illustrated by the different approaches of Tom Paine, on the one hand, and, on the other, by thinkers like Hume, Burke and Ferguson. For Paine, 'progress was inseparable from transforming attitudes as well as overturning the prevailing monarchical-aristocratic-ecclesiastical order, and not only in one country but universally' (ibid.: 11). Radical Enlightenment 'emerged in opposition to mainstream thinking' (ibid.: xii) and required a revolution of the mind. For moderates, reform had to take place 'within the framework of monarchy, aristocracy and the existing order' (ibid.: 7). The ideal, according to Ferguson, was the mixed British system that was democratic but not too democratic. More radical reformers 'betrayed a considerable lack of respect for the divinely fashioned order of things' (ibid.: 17).

On this account, it is clear why trimming between Radical and Moderate Enlightenment ideals was not an option either theoretically or practically. This is how Israel makes the point:

> Either history is infused by divine providence or it is not, either one endorses a society of ranks or embraces equality, one approves representative democracy or opposes it. On these questions it was the polarization, the division of opinion, that shaped developments. Beyond a certain level there were and could only be two Enlightenments – moderate … Enlightenment, on the one hand, postulating a balance between reason and tradition and broadly supporting the status quo and, on the other Radical … Enlightenment.
>
> (ibid.: 18–19)

In a way, this takes us back to Merry's challenge: sometimes one has to choose, and moderation is not a way to avoid choosing. Moderation is itself a choice and, in many instances, the wrong choice. It is not just that, as Craiutu admits, moderation is not a virtue for all seasons and can be a 'political liability' (2012: 18). The point is stronger than that: in the history of the Enlightenment, pleas for moderation have been anti-democratic, anti-egalitarian, and used to limit criticism of the established order.

It is important to note, however, that these criticisms of moderation are not arguments for extremism or fanaticism. The criticisms of the latter still stand even if moderation has been an obstacle to progress at various stages in human history. Furthermore, it is easy to criticize moderation when the alternative is Radical Enlightenment but not when the alternative is an extremist, totalitarian dictatorship. From the perspective of the twentieth century, in which such dictatorships held sway in Europe and elsewhere, it is difficult not to think that greater moderation would have alleviated the suffering of millions. A balanced or, as one might call it, a moderate perspective on moderation needs to acknowledge its benefits as well as the ways in which it can be problematic. Moderation *per se* is neither a virtue nor a vice; it can be harmful or beneficial, depending on the circumstances.

In this respect, at least, there is more to be said for moderation than for fanaticism. The circumstances in which moderation is beneficial are somewhat easier to envisage than those in which fanaticism is beneficial, especially in view of the failure of apologists for fanaticism to demonstrate that admirable figures like Garrison were fanatics. They were radicals not fanatics and it would be appropriate to bring this chapter to a close by taking a closer look at the notion of a radical. So far in this chapter, the characterization of radicalism has not gone beyond the one proposed by Colin Beck: radicalism is contention outside the common routines of politics present within a society, oriented towards substantial change in social, cultural, economic, and/ or political structures, and undertaken by any actor using extra-institutional means.[11] Is that all there is to it? If so, does radicalism have a better claim than moderation to be regarded as the quintessential political virtue?

Several features of radicalism stand out in Beck's analysis. The first is that radicalism is both transgressive and innovative. One sense in which this is so is that radicals use extra-institutional means in pursuit of their objectives. Extra-institutional means 'are those things that are not part of institutional governance, such as protests, boycotts, sit-ins, arson, violence, and so on. When institutional actors, like politicians, begin to use extra-institutional means, they approach radicalism' (Beck 2015: 19). Furthermore, 'radical goals and ideas must involve changing society or social trends' (ibid.: 19).

This change can be progressive or reactionary, so radicalism can be a feature of the political right as well as the political left.

Extremists and fanatics tend to be radicals but not all extremists are radicals and radicals need not be extremists or fanatics. Armchair extremists aren't radicals because they do not use extra-institutional means in pursuit of their objectives; in a practical sense, they do nothing to advance their political agenda. Not even methods extremists are necessarily radicals. They use extra-institutional means but may lack radical goals; the use of extreme and extra-institutional methods in defence of the established order is not radicalism. Military dictators who use para-military death squads to eliminate opposition to their rule are not radicals despite their use of extra-institutional means. The likelihood that, like other fanatics, such dictators are willing to trample on other people's ideals and interests also shows that fanatics needn't be radicals. This is not to deny that many extremists and fanatics *are* radicals. The point is that extremism and fanaticism do not *entail* radicalism.

Nor is it the case that radicalism entails fanaticism or extremism. Radicalism does not entail unwarranted contempt for other people's ideals and interests or an unwillingness to think critically about one's own ideals. Radicals whose methods include violence might be methods extremists, but protests, boycotts, and sit-ins are hardly extreme methods. Unless all extra-institutional methods are, by definition, extreme, it is possible to be a radical without being a methods extremist. Furthermore, radicals needn't have the typical preoccupations and attitudes of psychological extremists, and so needn't be extremists in this sense. The relationship between radicalism and ideological extremism is less clear. On the one hand, a commitment to radical social change might place one at the far end of an ideological spectrum. On the other hand, if the social change the radical seeks is the implementation of the basic principles of the Radical Enlightenment, then this would not be extremism by our lights, though in other historical contexts it would be extremism.

Turning, finally, to the relationship between radicalism and moderation, the changes to the social order that radicals seek might be ones that moderates also endorse. Radicals who do not use violence in pursuit of their objectives are, at least in this respect, moderate. However, moderates tend to be gradualists whereas radicals tend to be 'immediatists': they seek change now, not at some point in the distant future. Radicals are also disinclined to engage in trimming and see no merit in retaining elements of the established order that are at odds with their radical agenda. From a radical perspective, the rotten compromises that trimming will almost certainly require are totally unacceptable.

All of this might make radicalism seem preferable to moderation, but the truth is more complicated. From a progressive standpoint, reactionary or right-wing radicalism will not be preferable to moderation. From a conservative standpoint, progressive or left-wing radicalism will not be preferable to moderation. Radicalism is a political style rather than a substantial political ideology. The attractions of radicalism in a given context will therefore depend both on the nature of the extra-institutional means employed and the merits of the radicals' political objectives. In and of itself, radicalism is neither a political vice nor a virtue, neither admirable nor deplorable. In this respect, it is no different from moderation.

A good way to capture the sense in which radicalism and moderation are neither virtues nor vices *per se* would be to reflect on something that the philosopher Philippa Foot says about the nature of virtue. For Foot, virtues like courage, temperance and wisdom are in some general way beneficial: 'Human beings do not get on well without them' (1978: 2). The virtues are *corrective*: each one stands at a point at which 'there is some temptation to be resisted or some deficiency of motivation to be made good' (ibid.: 8). There is a virtue of industriousness only because idleness is a temptation, and a virtue of humility only because human beings tend to think too well of themselves. Viewed in this light, one might be reluctant to characterize moderation and radicalism as virtues because they are not in some *general* way beneficial to us. Each can be beneficial but can also be harmful in some circumstances. To be sure, even the benefits of genuine virtues have some degree of context-relativity – for example, courage does not invariably benefit the courageous – but the context-relativity of the benefits of radicalism and moderation goes much deeper than that.

Nevertheless, there is something to be said for the idea that radicalism and moderation can both be corrective. Moderation can be an effective antidote to fanaticism and extremism, and we are more inclined to admire moderation where fanaticism, extremism and radicalism of the wrong sort are the main threats to our well-being. Where extremism is on the rise, or we are in danger from the excesses of fanaticism, moderation has the feel of a corrective virtue. In the same way, radicalism is an antidote to moderation and has the feel of a corrective virtue in circumstances in which moderation is an obstacle to progress. Merry's idea is that extremism is a corrective virtue that counteracts the natural human tendency to side with the status quo even when doing so conflicts with the demands of justice. We are now in a position see why this is not so: the extremist cure that Merry proposes is, in many cases, worse that the ailments for which it is supposed to be a remedy, and less toxic but still radical remedies are usually also available. When they are, there is no justification for extremism.

Notes

1 See Wilkinson (2016) for further discussion of Goldwater's aphorism, which should really be credited to his speechwriter Karl Hess.

2 See, also, Kraditor (1989), Sinha (2016) and Toscano (2017).

3 See Holmes (2017: Chapter 8), for a biographical sketch of Madame de Staël.

4 See (ibid.: 160), for the source of this epigram.

5 Garrison (1973: 3).

6 Alexander (2019).

7 See Chapter 4.

8 See Chenoweth and Stephan (2011). The conclusion of their study is:

> nonviolent civil resistance works, both in terms of achieving campaigns' strategic objectives and in terms of promoting the long-term well-being of the societies in which the campaigns have been waged. Violent insurgency, on the other hand, has a dismal record on both counts.
>
> (ibid: 222)

9 Cronin (2009: Appendix).

10 The Irgun Zvai Leumi was a Zionist terrorist group operating in Palestine in the 1930s. Its ultimate objective was the establishment of an independent Jewish state. See English (2016: 149–51).

11 Beck (2015: 18).

7 Pathways to extremism

The radicalization process

'Who is Timothy McVeigh?'. This is the question with which journalists Lou Michel and Dan Herbeck begin their study of the man whose bombing of the Alfred P. Murrah Federal Office Building in Oklahoma City killed 168 people in the most lethal terrorist attack in the United States apart from 9/11. McVeigh was sentenced to death for the bombing and executed in June 2001. Relying on correspondence and lengthy interviews with McVeigh, Michel and Herbeck try to understand 'his transformation from average American boy to decorated soldier to mass murderer' (2001: xv). At the end of their investigation they announce, optimistically, that they have the answer to their question: they know who McVeigh is, and, by implication, how he could have done what he did in Oklahoma City on 19 April 1995.

McVeigh was an extremist by any reasonable measure. He had extreme political views, employed extreme methods in pursuit of his political objectives, and displayed many elements of the extremist mindset. Yet he wasn't born an extremist, any more than anyone else is. He was not born into an extremist family and was not radicalized by anyone else. Still, he became an extremist, the kind of extremist who would plant a bomb in a government building and time the detonation to maximize the body count. How did he get to this point? The process of becoming an extremist is defined as the 'radicalization process'.[1] With a better understanding of this process, one might hope to arrive at a better understanding of McVeigh's transformation. But what better way is there of understanding the radicalization process than by studying people who have been subject to it?

DOI: 10.4324/9780429325472-7

In this way of thinking, radicalization is a *personal journey*, and understanding the journey in the case of a specific individual is a form of biographical understanding, the type of understanding of their subjects that biographers seek. The hope is that achieving a biographical understanding of McVeigh's transformation from average American boy to violent extremist will not only tell us something about *his* journey but also about the nature of a process that was by no means unique to him. However, it is clear, on reflection, that this conception of how to study radicalization is fraught with difficulties. The most obvious is that it underestimates the extent to which personal journeys are personal and idiosyncratic. One person's journey to extremism may have very little in common with another's, and the assumption that McVeigh's unique personal journey tells us anything about how other people radicalize seems dubious.

Consider McVeigh's personal journey in relation to that of another notorious extremist, Ramzi Yousef.[2] McVeigh was born in Lockport, New York, on 23 April 1968, four days before Yousef was born in Kuwait. Prior to 9/11, Yousef was the most wanted terrorist in the world as a result of his bombing of the World Trade Center in 1993. Yousef was the nephew of Khalid Sheikh Mohammed, who planned the 9/11 attacks. He studied electrical engineering in Wales and, like his uncle, became a terrorist entrepreneur responsible for numerous terrorist plots. Hatred of Israel and America were the driving forces in his radicalization, and his personal journey is utterly different from McVeigh's. The two extremists, whose paths were to cross one day, were born in different parts of the world, into different cultures, and had entirely different lives and world-views. They are the perfect illustration of Andrew Silke's important observation that there is 'no one path into terrorism' (2003: 34). By the same token, there is no one path into extremism, and no such thing as *the* radicalization process. There are many such processes.[3]

However, before drawing the conclusion that pathways to extremism are idiosyncratic and person-specific, it is important to consider the possibility that there are common factors in the radicalization pathways even of individuals as different as McVeigh and Rami Yousef. This is how the influential terrorism scholar Peter Neumann makes the point:

> Most experts agree that *there isn't a simple formula or template that would explain how people radicalize.* Each case is different, and each individual's pathway needs to be examined on its own merits. That doesn't mean, however, that the concept is "unfounded" or that

the whole idea of radicalization is a "myth". Those who are familiar with the academic literature on the subject know that over the past decade, researchers have managed to identify a number of drivers that seem to be common to the majority of radicalization trajectories.

(2011: 15; emphasis added)[4]

Radicalization is 'a progression which plays out over time and involves different factors and dynamics' (Neumann 2013: 874). The study of the individual journeys of people like McVeigh and Yousef might help us to identify these factors and dynamics. There is now an extensive biographical literature on individual extremists, and the greater the range of personal journeys studied, the greater the likelihood of identifying genuine common factors.[5]

Even if such factors can be identified, it is a further question to what extent they *cause* or *explain* any individual's radicalization. Consider Neumann's list of radicalization drivers or risk factors: (1) the perception of grievance; (2) the adoption of an extremist narrative or ideology; and (3) social or group dynamics. However, the adoption of an extremist ideology is common to the majority of radicalization trajectories because becoming an extremist *consists in* the adoption of an extremist ideology. To regard the latter as a cause or risk factor for radicalization amounts to regarding radicalization as cause or risk factor for itself. For two things to be causally related, they must be logically distinct, but being radicalized and adopting an extremist ideology are not logically distinct. To be radicalized *just is* to adopt an extremist ideology.

This assumes the radicalization is *cognitive* rather than *behavioral* radicalization.[6] To be cognitively radicalized is to adopt an extremist ideology. Behavioral radicalization means turning to violence or using other extreme methods to advance one's political objectives. Assuming that cognitive radicalization is a risk factor for behavioral radicalization, the challenge is to identify the risk factors for cognitive radicalization, that is, the factors that increase the chances of a person adopting an extremist ideology. Since the second of the three drivers listed by Neumann describes the end result of radicalization rather than an independent risk factor, it makes sense to focus on the other two. The perception of grievance and group dynamics are plausible candidates, but every proposed risk factor needs to be assessed in the light of what is known about individual extremists.

It also needs to be explained where the extremist mindset fits into this analysis. If a person who adopts an extremist ideology is *cognitively* radicalized, and a person who employs extreme methods is *behaviorally* radicalized, then a person who develops an extremist mindset is *psychologically* radicalized. What are the causes of psychological radicalization and how does psychological radicalization relate to radicalization in the other two senses? These are among questions that will be addressed below. Neumann's reference to group dynamics brings another issue into focus: in representing radicalization as a personal journey, one is in danger of omitting what many experts regard as a key factor in this process, the role of groups. It has been claimed that 'individuals who become extremists do not generally do so in isolation, but in a social context of which groups are an essential component' (Breton and Dalmazzone 2002: 56). To put it another way, extremism is a 'sociological and not merely a psychological matter' (Hardin 2002: 4). If this is right, then the study of radicalization must include the study of group dynamics and social learning.

Socio-dynamic accounts of radicalization come in many different varieties, but one idea is that group dynamics sustain and accentuate extremism and fanaticism via their impact on what group members are able to know. Extremist groups become echo chambers that actively discredit alternative voices. In this way, 'suppressing knowledge is the route to power' (ibid.: 19) for extremist leaders, and the extremism of individual group members is a function of what Hardin calls their 'crippled epistemology' (ibid.: 10). This suggests that extremism has an epistemological as well as a psychological and sociological dimension. It remains to be seen whether this is plausible, especially in view of many examples of extremists who became extremists prior to joining any group and who are not epistemologically defective.

Aside from personal journeys and group dynamics, there is one more factor to consider. Instead of mainly thinking of individuals or small groups as undergoing this process, one might consider the possibility of entire nations or societies becoming radicalized. For example, it is arguable that German society was radicalized during the Nazi era even though not all Germans supported the Nazis. Radicalization in this sense works by making what would once have been unthinkable – the passing of racial purity laws, for example – not only thinkable but politically feasible. When a country's entire political discourse moves to the extreme right or the extreme left, the result is *not* that extremist policies are no longer extremist relative to the 'new normal'. Rather, extremist policies are no longer *regarded* as extremist, and this shift in the Overton Window is itself a form of radicalization.[7] It normalizes extremist policies and makes it possible for people who do not think of themselves as extremists to adopt them. This type of macro-level radicalization of political discourse will be discussed in the final part of this chapter. Before that, there are other matters to discuss in the following order: personal journeys to extremism, group dynamics, and the alleged crippled epistemology of extremism.

Becoming an extremist

McVeigh's personal journey to extremism began with a hobby. He was introduced to guns by his paternal grandfather, and handling weapons was a source of self-esteem for the teenage McVeigh. As he started to read magazines and books for gun enthusiasts, he became an ardent defender of the right to bear arms under the Second Amendment. He also read *The Turner Diaries*, a novel by a former American Nazi Party official.[8] *The Turner Diaries*, known for its racism and advocacy of gun rights, made a big impression on McVeigh, who also became a conspiracy theorist. He believed the theory that the federal government and the UN were part of a New World Order which planned to criminalize gun ownership. Yet, despite his antipathy to the government, he joined the military and fought in the first Gulf War. He received a medal for killing two Iraqi soldiers with one shot but felt guilty about the killing. 'These were human beings', he is reported to have said, 'even though they speak a different language and have different customs. The truth is, we all have the same dreams, the same desires, the same care for our children and our family' (Michel and Herbeck 2001: 76). These do not sound like the words of an extremist.

The turning point for McVeigh was Waco. In 1993, a U.S. law enforcement agency, the Bureau of Alcohol, Tobacco, Firearms, and Explosives (ATF), and the FBI stormed the Waco home of the Branch Davidians, a religious cult led by David Koresh. In the resulting inferno, 76 cult members died, including Koresh and 25 children. McVeigh was obsessed and enraged by Waco. As rumours spread of further gun legislation, he told friends that the time had come to act: 'Whatever form it took, Timothy McVeigh was going to engage in a major act of violence against the government' (ibid.: 161). It did not take long for him to be arrested after the bombing of the Alfred P. Murrah Federal Office Building, which he mistakenly believed to be the source of the order to lay siege to the Branch Davidians. He tried, unsuccessfully, to convince his legal team to mount a 'necessity defence' of his action, on the basis that he and other Americans were in imminent danger from the federal government. A guilty verdict was followed by the death sentence, and he spent some of his last days in a Supermax prison, in the company of two other notorious extremists, the so-called 'Unabomber', Ted Kaczynski, and Ramzi Yousef.

There is no question that McVeigh saw himself as 'motivated by his deep concern for his country' (ibid.: 345) and a defender of the U.S. Constitution. His attorney argued in court that millions of Americans shared McVeigh's views, including his conspiracy theories and attitude to gun control. Indeed, these views and attitudes are still the views and attitudes of millions of Americans, and this raises the question in what sense he was an extremist. Kaczynski addressed this issue in a letter to Michel and Herbeck.[9] According to Kaczynski, McVeigh was like many on the right who 'are attracted to powerful weapons for their own sake ... [and] tend to invent excuses, often far-fetched ones, for acquiring weapons for which they have no real need' (ibid.: 400). However, according to Kaczynski, McVeigh did not fit the stereotype of extreme right-wingers since 'he spoke of respect for other people's cultures, and in doing so he sounded like a liberal' (ibid.: 400).

In what sense, then, *was* he an extremist? He might be described as an extreme anti-government libertarian, whose ideological extremism had more in common with anarchism than classical right-wing extremism. However, it seems doubtful that he had a sufficiently coherent political ideology to merit description in these terms. Libertarians have views about a range of issues, including taxation and the proper role of the state. McVeigh only cared about one thing – the right to bear arms – and this made him a single-issue extremist, located at one end of a spectrum of views about gun control. As a result, he adopted an extremist narrative about the federal government. Furthermore, the perception of grievance played a major role in his adoption of this narrative. These are at least two respects in which Neumann's description of the radicalization process seems apt in relation to McVeigh.

Indeed, it would not be much of an exaggeration to say that McVeigh's radicalization, like that of many other extremists, was *grievance-led*. On what can be called a *grievance model*, the perception of grievance, in the form of injustice, oppression or socio-economic exclusion, is an important factor which makes people 'receptive to extremist ideas' (Neumann 2011: 17). McVeigh's grievances focused on what he saw as threats to his personal freedom emanating from the federal government. In the case of

Ramzi Yousef, the grievances that underpinned his radicalization were more wide-ranging. Nevertheless, as Michel and Herbeck note, the words Yousef spoke at his trial 'might have come from McVeigh's lips' (2001: 360). Yousef accused America of killing innocent people with nuclear weapons in 1945 and of being responsible for the deaths of Iraqi civilians as a result of economic sanctions. Responding to the charge that he was a terrorist, he stated in court: 'I support terrorism as long as it is against the United States government and Israel; you are the ones who invented terrorism and use it every day. You are butchers, liars, and hypocrites.'[10]

One question about the grievance model is whether the grievances it identifies as drivers of radicalization can be genuine. It might be tempting to say that the grievances that underpin political extremism are spurious or lack any basis in reality, but such a stipulation should be avoided. It is relatively easy to make the case that McVeigh's grievances were unfounded. With Yousef, however, matters are perhaps more complicated, especially in relation to his views about American policy in Iraq. However, Yousef was an extremist even if his complaints about American foreign policy were justified. It is worth noting, also, that McVeigh's grievances centered on an issue that affected him personally whereas Yousef's grievances were vicarious. Although he was neither a Palestinian nor an Iraqi, he saw himself as fighting against America on behalf of Iraqis and against Israel on behalf of the Palestinians. Both Yousef and McVeigh saw their hostility to the American government as morally justified, and it comes as no surprise to discover that when they met, they became involved in 'deep political discussions' (ibid.: 361).

McVeigh's views were and are widely shared in the United States. Yousef's views were and are widely shared in the Arab world. Those who share their views might be described as extremists in an ideological sense but few people with the same grievances as McVeigh and Yousef become terrorists. The point at which McVeigh and Yousef committed terrorist acts is the point at which they became methods extremists but how should their behavioural radicalization be explained, given that most people who are cognitively radicalized are *not* radicalized in the behavioural sense? One view is that this question is unanswerable. In an influential critique of conventional accounts of radicalization, Jonathan Githens-Mazer and Robert Lambert point to the 'inherent unpredictability of who becomes violent and who doesn't' (2010: 893). In much the same vein, Arun Kundnani insists that 'the micro-level question of what causes one person rather than another in the same political context to engage in violence is beyond analysis and best seen as unpredictable' (2012: 21).

It is one thing for a person's turn to political violence or terrorism to be unpredictable and another for it to be 'beyond analysis'. Aside from the perception of grievance, there are at least two other factors that play a role in behavioural radicalization in a wide range of cases. One is activation of a martial social identity.[11] In simpler terms, individuals like McVeigh come to think of themselves as soldiers or warriors. Only a small proportion of individuals who share his grievances will self-categorize as soldiers but those who do are more likely to turn violent than those who do not. As Marc Sageman puts it, 'soldiers are supposed to fight; violence is simply what they do' (2017: 145). Hence, 'self-categorization into a martial social identity means that violence is imminent because people with this identity are likely to act out who they believe they are' (ibid.: 145).

There remains the question why one ideological extremist self-categorizes as a soldier while another with the same ideology does not. According to Sageman, 'we must leave this issue of personal predisposition unresolved since it completely lacks any reliable database of detailed violent political perpetrators' personality that could be scientifically analyzed' (ibid.: 38). Perhaps so, but the scientific perspective is not the only one that can deliver valuable insights into the radicalization of individuals. There is also the biographical perspective. It is not hard to understand why a person with McVeigh's interest in weapons and time in the military should be disposed to adopt the persona of a warrior. It only requires a modest degree of biographical knowledge and understanding to see that he was a prime candidate for the martial self-categorization described by Sageman.

The same biographical perspective makes it intelligible that McVeigh not only *thought* of himself as a soldier but also *acted* as he did. The transition from the perception of grievance to political violence is a reflection of another key driver of radicalization. Not only do some people think of themselves as soldiers, they also see themselves as warriors for justice who have *no option* but to act as they do. This is one respect in which they display what was referred to in Chapter 4 as the militant-extremist mindset. Those with this mindset are convinced of the *necessity* of extreme measures, and this was precisely the basis on which McVeigh wanted his legal team to defend him at his trial. Furthermore, the extreme and unconventional measures that militant extremists endorse include terrorism, and the *necessity* of such measures is seen as absolving them from the adverse consequences of the violence they advocate. As McVeigh put it, 'In any kind of military action you try to keep collateral damage to a minimum. But a certain amount of collateral damage is inevitable' (Michel and Herbeck 2001: 331).

In what sense does the militant extremist see extreme measures as 'necessary'? Extremists believe that they are acting for the greater good and that acting as they do is a political and *moral* necessity. In other words, they believe that there is a moral obligation on anyone capable of fighting to do so, by whatever means would be most effective. In Scott Atran's striking formulation, 'terrorists, for the most part, are ... extreme moralists' (2010: x–xi). McVeigh maintained to the last that what he did 'was needed to right a faltering America'. Many other violent extremists make similar claims to the effect that they are only doing what they 'have' to do. In defending their actions on the basis of their supposed moral necessity, methods extremists reveal their preoccupation with their virtue and the purity of their motives. These preoccupations were identified in Chapter 4 as core components of the extremist mindset, and so encourage one to think of radicalization either as *consisting in* the acquisition of an extremist mindset or as a process *facilitated* by possession of an extremist mindset.

On the latter interpretation, the question *why* or *how* individuals develop an extremist mindset is set aside. Instead, the focus is on how, in the presence of other radicalization drivers like the perception of grievance, having an extremist mindset makes it more likely that a person will also become a positional and methods extremist. It is not difficult to reconstruct the thought process of extremists like McVeigh or to see how a preoccupation with virtue can lead them to act violently. A virtuous person, they reason, is someone who does not stand by and do nothing in the face of injustice or oppression. A virtuous person stands up and fights for what is right. Extremists believe that they cannot stand idly by while the people or communities they care about or identify with are being oppressed. In this way, they convince themselves that they are duty-bound to act as they do. Like other extremists, McVeigh thought of himself as a crusader, and even as someone with respect for human life. In his words, quoted by Michel and Herbeck, 'My decision to take human life at the Murrah Building – I did not do it for personal gain. I ease my mind in that ... I did it for the larger good' (2001: 382).

This points to an obvious difficulty for analyses of extremism: people who are *actually* virtuous may well reason in exactly the same way. The idea that virtue requires a willingness to stand up for the right and the good is one that is widely recognized as correct. In that case, how can it be right to condemn McVeigh? One reason is that while extremists *believe* they are fighting for justice, it does not follow that they are. However, this is a matter of ideological or political judgement. A second consideration is that even if an extremist's cause is just, this does not necessarily legitimize his or her methods. In fighting his war against the government, McVeigh used disproportionate violence and targeted individuals who were in no way responsible for the policies to which he objected. Finally, while morally virtuous individuals do the right things for the right reasons, they are not preoccupied with their own virtue. In contrast, the extremist's preoccupation with virtue borders on the pathological.

There are several other components of the extremist mindset that facilitate cognitive and behavioural radicalization. Although it was not one of McVeigh's preoccupations, many examples have been given in previous chapters of the extremist preoccupation with purity and of how this preoccupation can lead to violence against the supposedly 'impure'. Victimhood is another extremist preoccupation that is implicated in cognitive and behavioural radicalization. It was certainly one of McVeigh's preoccupations. He came to believe that being a young white male counted against him, that he was a victim of reverse discrimination, and that 'certain affirmative-action guidelines were blocking his way to civil service jobs with the state and federal governments' (ibid.: 100). In this way, his 'victimology' contributed to his perception of grievance and helped to motivate his violence.

The perception of grievance often leads to resentment and anger, and these are among the emotional components of the extremist mindset. McVeigh's anger directed at the federal government played a key role in his turn to violence, and his indifference to the consequences of bombing a public building made it possible for his to go through with his plan. This type of indifference is one of the attitudes that makes up the extremist mindset. Yousef displayed the same indifference in his actions, which included testing an explosive device by leaving it under a seat on board a Boeing 747. When the device detonated, Yousef had already disembarked but a Japanese passenger was killed. Yousef showed no remorse. Unwillingness to compromise is another extremist attitude that plays a role in cognitive and behavioural radicalization. As far as McVeigh was concerned, there was no possibility of compromise on the issue of gun control and any compromise on this issue would be a rotten compromise. Last but not least, his turn to violence was also underpinned by his conspiracy and apocalyptic thinking. If the government was conspiring against people like him, then, in his mind, he was within his rights to respond with violence. What Michel and Herbeck describe as McVeigh's 'increasingly apocalyptic world view' (ibid.: 154) would have had the same effect.

When describing the ways in which an extremist mindset facilitates and underpins both cognitive and behavioural radicalization, it is helpful to distinguish *causes* of radicalization and *enabling conditions*. Causes either trigger or increase the risk of radicalization. The perception of grievance is a trigger, as is evident from McVeigh's response to Waco. Enabling conditions are the background conditions that make it possible for triggers to function as they do. So, for example, a spark will not cause a fire in the absence of inflammable material in the vicinity. The latter is a background enabling condition for a spark to cause a fire. In the same way, the perception of grievance will not lead a person to resort to violence unless the appropriate background conditions obtain. These conditions include a preoccupation with victimhood and indifference to the consequences of violence. In the absence of these preoccupations and attitudes, it is hard to see how the perception of grievance would, on its own, lead a person to resort to violence. An extremist mindset eases the path from trigger to behavioural outcome.

The difficulty that now arises is this: suppose that, as the grievance model suggests, the perception of grievance triggers the cognitive and behavioural radicalization of a person with an extremist mindset. But a person with an extremist mindset has *already* been radicalized, at least in a psychological sense. Thus, one might think of radicalization not just as *facilitated* by having an extremist mindset but as *consisting in* the acquisition of an extremist mindset. In other words, one becomes an extremist by developing an extremist mindset, which then facilitates cognitive and behavioural radicalization. If this is the picture, then it raises an obvious question: how does psychological radicalization happen? What are *its* triggers, and enabling conditions? Without answers to these questions, the account is incomplete. And if it turns out that psychological radicalization is itself caused by cognitive radicalization, then the account is circular: the psychological properties that facilitate cognitive radicalization are in fact the *result* of cognitive radicalization.

The idea that cognitive radicalization causes psychological radicalization is not at all far-fetched. Cognitive radicalization consists in the adoption of an extremist ideology, and many such ideologies promote precisely the preoccupations, attitudes, and thinking styles that add up to an extremist mindset. For example, extreme right-wing ideologies tend to encourage a preoccupation with purity and victimhood, so that a person who lacks these concerns to begin with might come to have them as a result of adopting an extreme right-wing ideology for other reasons. Extremist ideologies in general promote conspiracy theories as well as an implacable hostility to compromise and pluralism. To the extent that they are Pro-Violence, they may result in behavioural as well as cognitive radicalization. In that case, it might seem natural to press the question: which comes first? Is psychological radicalization prior to radicalization in the other two senses, or are cognitive and behavioural radicalization prior to the development of an extremist mindset?

The answer is: neither. There is no logical or temporal priority to speak of because the relationship between the different forms of radicalization is symbiotic or, to put it another way, a relationship of mutual dependence. This is especially evident in the case of the relationship between cognitive and psychological radicalization, and helps to explain the fact that becoming an extremist in the psychological sense is partly a matter of what one believes and not just of the form of one's ideological commitments. Extremist ideologies might appeal to people who have an extremist mindset, but the extremist mindset is also partly a *product* of ideology. It is virtually inconceivable that a person with no extremist ideological commitments should have, ready-made, all the elements of an extremist mindset. It is far more likely that cognitive and behavioural radicalization develop hand in hand, and might be the result of extraneous events. For example, a study of 42 Taliban fighters found that as many as 12 had lost family members to American air strikes and 6 had joined the insurgency as a direct result.[12] This is a case of an extraneous event leading to radicalization in all three senses.

In such cases, it is easy to imagine the political, psychological and behavioural impact of losing a child or spouse to military action. This was a common occurrence in Iraq following the 2003 U.S. invasion and partly explains the violence of the anti-American insurgency. In L.A. Paul's terminology, the loss of a family member is a potentially 'transformative experience'.[13] Such experiences can radicalize people with no prior radical instincts. It is vacuous in such cases to insist that a person who is radicalized by a transformative experience must have had a psychological disposition to be radicalized. There is no independent evidence of such a disposition, and equally little evidence that an extremist mindset is endemic in certain cultures or religions. Radicalization is a *political* response to political grievances that, as in the case of Taliban air strike victims, also have a personal dimension. It is in many ways a natural response or, at any rate, not one to which many people can be said to be immune.

To sum up: we have seen that there are multifarious individual pathways to extremism but that does not preclude the discovery of common trends or features. The grievance model is of value because it identifies the perception of grievance as a key factor in radicalization. The grievances by which people are radicalized may or may not be genuine and may or may not result in violence. Violence results when aggrieved and ideologically radicalized individuals self-categorize as soldiers and become preoccupied with the need to 'do something' in the face of a perceived injustice. Any number of factors can result in the perception of grievance, and a sense of grievance is further heightened by radicalization. There is a sense in which cognitive radicalization is facilitated by an extremist mindset, and also in which the development of an extremist mindset is in turn promoted by cognitive radicalization. As between cognitive and psychological radicalization, there is no logical or causal priority, but these forms of 'mental' radicalization usually precede and cause behavioural radicalization. People turn to violence because they have been mentally radicalized rather than the other way round.

From a methodological standpoint, the search for common radicalization drivers is best carried out with the help of a biographical understanding of radicalized individuals. The study of a wide range of personal journeys to extremism serves a number of different purposes: as well as highlighting common features, engaging with the idiosyncrasies of personal journeys makes it easier to guard against over-generalization. Not even the perception of grievance plays a role in every radicalization trajectory. The best one can hope for is that it or some other factor is detectable in a wide range of cases. The identification of common factors in radicalization is also helpful for the purposes of deradicalization and counter-radicalization. These are matters for Chapter 8. However, before reflecting on possible responses to radicalization, there is still the issue of group dynamics to consider. The idea that social or group dynamics play a part in radicalization has not yet been given its due, and it is time to fill in this gap.

Group dynamics and epistemology

It has been suggested that 'groups are the natural habitat of extremism' (Breton and Dalmazzone 2002: 55) and that social or group dynamics play a significant role in all forms of radicalization. According to Sunstein, 'when people find themselves in groups of like-minded types, they are especially likely to move to extremes' (2009: 2). That is, they 'usually end up at a more extreme position in the same general direction as their inclinations before deliberating began' (ibid.: 3). This means that 'political extremism is often a product of group polarization' (ibid.: 4). There are many studies that support this conclusion, and the issue is not *whether* extremism can be a product of group dynamics but *how* this can be so. This leads to the question that Sunstein tries to answer in his book: why do like-minded people go to extremes?

The key is the way that groups exchange and filter information. In groups of like-minded people, a mechanism that leads to extremism and polarization is corroboration. That is, people's views become more extreme because 'their initial views have been corroborated and because they have been more confident after learning of the shared views of others' (ibid.: 23). Another mechanism is that low-status group members tend to be excessively deferential to high-status members. There is also evidence that in intra-group discussions, more extreme views enjoy what Sunstein calls a 'rhetorical advantage' (ibid.: 35) over less extreme views. Thus, when juries discuss the appropriate level of punitive awards, jurors arguing for higher awards enjoy a rhetorical advantage over those arguing for lower awards, with the result that awards tend to go up after discussion rather than go down. Another mechanism that leads to greater extremism is that more moderate group members tend to exit groups that become more extreme, leaving behind only group members with more extreme views. This is particularly significant since extremists are especially prone to polarization: 'when people start out at an extreme point and are placed in a group of like-minded people, they are likely to go especially far in the direction toward which they started' (ibid.: 40).

Although this is not Sunstein's own terminology, his is effectively an account of the role of group dynamics in *cognitive* radicalization. Others describe the role of group dynamics in psychological radicalization. On this account, extremism refers to 'the inability to revise a large set of one's beliefs even in the face of contradicting evidence, to the consequent lack of independence in the formation of one's judgements, and to expressions of closed-mindedness and intolerance' (Breton and Dalmazzone 2002: 47). These traits can be accentuated by the social environment and the way it affects the individuals' beliefs. Social mechanisms have the power to weaken individual autonomy, foster homogeneity of beliefs and behaviour within groups, and 'heighten the extremity of opinions' (ibid.: 53). Like other accounts of the social dynamics of radicalization, this one explains why groups are the natural habitat of extremism in partly *epistemic* terms. Groups control the information available to their members and so constrain what members can know. They promote radicalization by promoting their own narratives, attitudes, and ways of thinking, and by systematically excluding alternative voices.

A socio-epistemic approach to radicalization is developed by Russell Hardin (2002) in his influential article 'The Crippled Epistemology of Extremism'. Hardin notes the extent to which our beliefs depend on the larger society's assessments and reinforcements. This means that any belief, but ideological beliefs in particular, 'can be manipulated within small segments of society so long as the larger society and its views are held at bay' (ibid.: 8). Thus, 'if I am in a small community with beliefs that others would think are very odd, I may find those beliefs not at all odd because, after all, they are held by everyone I know' (ibid.: 8), that is, by all other group members. Those with different views are simply excluded from the group. Under this norm of exclusion, 'the less intensely committed members of a group depart while extremists remain' (ibid.: 9).

The consequences of the isolation of people in a group with relatively limited contact with wider society include paranoid cognition and the sinister attribution error. Group members 'suppose the worst from those they do not know or even from those with whom they are not in immediate communication' (ibid.: 11). As a result, their opinions become immune to external correction because outsiders who question the opinions of group members are automatically mistrusted and ascribed nefarious motives. However, the explanation of this is epistemological rather than psychological. Paranoid cognition and the sinister attribution error 'may primarily be simple matters of the skewed epistemology that comes from lack of contact with and, hence, lack of accurate knowledge of relevant others' (ibid.: 11).

In effect, Hardin represents groups of extremists and fanatics as cults, and their crippled epistemology as a reflection of the way that cults operate. Two ideas for representing the epistemology of cults and, by extension, the epistemology of extremist groups, are those of an *echo chamber* and an *epistemic bubble*. C. Thi Nguyen (2018) explains these ideas as follows: an epistemic bubble is an informational network from which relevant voices have been excluded by omission. The omission might be intentional or inadvertent. For example, a person's Facebook friends might be an epistemic bubble from which people who do not share their views are *de facto* excluded, even if there is no policy of excluding people with contrary opinions. An echo chamber is a social structure from which other relevant voices have been actively discredited:

> Where an epistemic bubble merely omits contrary views, an echo chamber brings its members to actively distrust outsiders ... [A]n echo chamber is something like a cult. A cult isolates its members by actively alienating them from any outside sources. Those outside are actively labelled as malignant and untrustworthy. A cult member's trust is narrowed, aimed with laser-like focus on certain insider voices. In epistemic bubbles, other voices are not heard; in echo chambers, other voices are actively undermined.
>
> (ibid.)

If this is how extremist groups operate, then their members will either never hear arguments for moderation or regard those who put forward such arguments as discredited. In the absence of any serious pushback, extremist groups inevitably become more extreme as dissenting voices are excluded and group members are increasingly radicalized by their epistemic isolation.

There is a lot to be said for this approach to radicalization, but it is important to register the limitations of socio-epistemic accounts. Such accounts make little sense of extremists like McVeigh and Yousef, neither of whom was radicalized by membership of a tightly-knit group. Neither was informationally isolated from the larger society or manipulated by others. There may be respects in which McVeigh and Yousef were epistemologically defective, but no more so than millions of ordinary citizens who are not extremists. Their personal journeys to extremism were not cult-like, and focusing on the role of epistemic bubbles and echo chambers in their radicalization risks underestimating far more salient factors. Crucially, socio-epistemic accounts do not make nearly enough of the fact that their radicalization was grievance-led, and their sense of grievance was not the result of a skewed epistemology. None of this would matter if McVeigh and Yousef were unrepresentative extremists but they are not.

McVeigh self-radicalized. He was influenced by things he read but so are we all. *The Turner Diaries* resonated with him because, like the gun magazines he devoured, it was a piece of writing that expressed views he already held. McVeigh was not a 'lone wolf' terrorist since he was assisted by co-conspirators in the Oklahoma bombing but he and his co-conspirators hardly constituted a cult, and they came together because their views were already similar. Their views did not converge as a result of their collaboration. Group dynamics did not play a significant role in their radicalization, any more than in the case of Ramzi Yousef. His anti-Semitism and hostility to America and Israel did not result from isolation from the larger society's assessments and reinforcements since his views *were* those of the larger society – not in the United States but in Kuwait, where he was born, and Pakistan, where his family came from. If anything, epistemic isolation from mainstream opinion in his wider community would have *reduced* the likelihood of his being radicalized.

Sunstein argues that the sense in which a person has a crippled epistemology is that 'they know relatively few things, and what they know is wrong' (2014: 12). Extremists who fall into this category are not irrational. Rather, their extremism stems from the fact that 'they have little relevant information, and their extremist views are supported by what little they know' (ibid.: 12). However, the idea that McVeigh and Yousef knew relatively few things and had little relevant information is implausible. McVeigh avidly followed news coverage of the Waco siege, and his interpretation of events at Waco had more to do with his ideology than with lack of information. McVeigh was well aware of the official story from the FBI and ATF, but he did not believe it. In the same way, Yousef was well aware of the justifications given by successive U.S. administrations of their Middle East policy. The fact that he did not accept these justifications does not show that he was lacking in relevant information. Rather, it was a matter of political judgement. Overall, the evidence suggests that his trajectory had more to do with his background and personality than with a crippled epistemology.

It is easier to make the case that extremists have a crippled epistemology when their political analyses and judgements are totally baseless, and sometimes this is undoubtedly the case. McVeigh's conspiracy theory about the government's plan to disarm Americans and deprive them of the right to bear arms under the Second Amendment was baseless and points to someone who had lost his epistemological bearings, at least to some extent. However, the fact that McVeigh was hostile to gun control and willing to kill innocents for the right to bear arms says more about his perverted values than about his epistemology. In the case of extremists like Yousef, matters are even more complicated since the grievances about America by which they are motivated undoubtedly have some basis in reality, even if they do not justify their actions. It is not a sign of ignorance to claim that since the end of the Second World War American policy in the Middle East and elsewhere has not been, to put it mildly, wholly benign. Extremists who point this out are not disconnected from reality or epistemologically defective. The problem with people like Yousef and McVeigh is not with their *epistemology* but the fact that they resort to terrorism to make their point.

If epistemic bubbles are ones in which other voices are not heard, then few extremists with access to a television or the internet live in epistemic bubbles. Certainly, neither McVeigh nor Yousef resided in an epistemic bubble. There are cults or communities whose members do not have access to the media but few of the extremists discussed in this book are cut off in this way. It is more plausible to place them in echo chambers in which other voices are *discredited* rather than *unheard*, and this brings into focus the issue of trust. McVeigh did not accept the FBI's account of Waco not because his trust in the FBI had been actively undermined but because he never trusted them in the first place. Mistrust of federal agencies was built into his world-view and did not need to be inculcated by someone else in his friendship group. Nor did Yousef's trust in the United States have to be actively undermined. There was never any trust to begin with.

A question this raises concerns the characterization of an echo chamber as a social structure from which relevant voices have been actively discredited. A 'relevant voice' is not simply one that promotes a view that is contrary to one's own. When a climate scientist derides the opinions of climate change deniers, or when historians ridicule Holocaust deniers, they are not guilty of actively discrediting *relevant* voices, even if the views of deniers in these domains are contrary to their own. Relevant voices are not just contrary voices but ones that have a proper claim to be taken seriously. This is always a matter of judgement, and when it comes to politics, the judgements are political. The political judgement of extremists who reject official accounts may or may not be flawed but attributing their errors to a crippled epistemology is usually a mistake, except in the case of actual cults.

The fundamental problem with socio-epistemic theories of radicalization is that they deny epistemic autonomy to extremists. It is reassuring to think that people whose views are diametrically opposed to one's own must have been tricked or manipulated into believing what they believe. Surely those who disagree with us about fundamental questions cannot be fully informed or must be victims of 'information control' (Breton and Dalmazzone 2002: 49). This is wishful thinking on at least two grounds: it assumes that political disagreement must be the result of ignorance of factual matters but there is no reason to think this is so. Sometimes people disagree because their values or ideologies are different. It is also wishful thinking to suppose that radicalization is always something that *happens* to a person, rather than an expression of their own agency. The value of studying people like McVeigh, Yousef and other extremists is that it forces us to confront the reality that their values and objectives are genuinely *theirs*, and no more the result of manipulation or information control than any other person's values and objectives. By the same token, they are responsible for their beliefs and actions. This is not to deny that social or group dynamics have a part to play in the radicalization process, but it is important not to exaggerate their role.

Social media and radicalization

The focus in the discussion so far has been on micro-level radicalization, that is, on the radicalization of individuals or small groups of individuals. However, there is also macro-level radicalization, for example, radicalization at a national level. To take a recent example, both the rise of the alt-right in the United States and the election of President Trump in 2016 can be interpreted as evidence of the radicalization of American politics. Much has been written both in this connection and in connection with micro-level radicalization about the importance of social media. Indeed, it has become something of a cliché to blame radicalization on social media. The epistemic bubbles and echo chambers referred to above are virtual rather than physical, and this suggests that socio-epistemic accounts would be well advised to focus on the radicalizing role of social media if they want to make the case that radicalization is a socio-epistemic phenomenon.

There is an extensive literature on the role of social media in micro-radicalization. The following is a representative passage:

Social media is an effective tool to use to radicalize and recruit members into a cause. It is always there whenever the user is. It lures members with a promise of friendship, acceptance or a sense of purpose ... Al-Qaida and its affiliates understand the Western world's reliance on information sharing and use of technology to communicate. They are increasingly using the grievances of alienated youth to radicalize them, and give them a sense of purpose.

(Thompson 2011: 168)

A 2013 report for RAND Europe paints a more nuanced picture (Von Behr et al. 2013). It confirms that the internet – which includes social media – may enhance opportunities for radicalization and act as an echo chamber for extremist beliefs. On the other hand, it did not find that it accelerates radicalization or allows radicalization to occur without physical contact.[14]

In a 2020 study, Alexander Meleagrou-Hitchens distinguishes between top-down and bottom-up radicalization. Top-down models focus on the role of external radicalizers whereas 'bottom-up theories argue that an individual's radicalization is a grassroots process that comes about because of one's interaction in tight-knit groups with links to wider social networks' (2020: 6). Meleagrou-Hitchens prefers a top-down approach and gives a compelling description of the importance of one external radicalizer: Anwar Al-Awlaki. Born in the United States to Yemeni parents, Awlaki became the 'pied piper of Western jihad' (ibid.: 2) before being killed by a U.S. drone strike in Yemen in 2011. Between 2009 and 2016, a high proportion of individuals charged in America for jihadist-related offences were linked to or inspired by Awlaki, who was a YouTube star among jihadists. He was the archetypal online radicalizer and remains influential several years after his death. Awlaki himself was not radicalized by anyone else, and Meleagrou-Hitchens argues that his embrace of jihadism was barely influenced by external factors. Rather, 'Awlaki's reaction to both global events and personal experiences was fundamentally shaped by his preexisting ideological framework' (ibid.: 262). In other words, he was not externally radicalized, but this did not prevent him from becoming a radicalizer of other people.

It should be noted, however, that a number of those supposedly radicalized by Awlaki were in contact with him by text and email, and it is at best misleading to describe them as having been radicalized by 'social media'. In discussion of these matters much confusion is caused by a lack of clarity about the relationship between social media and the internet. In its report on radicalization in the digital era, RAND Europe defines the internet as including 'all communication, activity or content which takes place or is held on the world wide web (www) and cloud structures' (Von Behr et al.

2013: 2). This includes social media platforms but Marc Sageman draws attention to an important distinction that is missed by the RAND definition. The distinction that Sageman highlights is between the 'passive' and the 'active' internet. The former is simply the collection of all websites that provide information to users. People who access these sites 'passively absorb the information provided' (2008: 113). In contrast, the internet 'is also a vast active system of communication between individuals and between individuals and groups' (ibid.: 114). Such systems of active communication include email, forums and chat rooms.

It is the active internet that plays the key role in radicalization: 'it is the forums, not the images of the passive websites, which are crucial in the process of radicalization. People change their minds through discussion with friends, not by simply reading impersonal stories' (ibid.: 116). Social media platforms enable personal communication through direct messaging, but this is not their main function. On Christmas Day 2009, an Awlaki disciple and UCL student called Umar Farouk Abdulmutallab tried unsuccessfully to bring down an airliner over Detroit. However, when Abdulmutallab first decided to contact Awlaki, he flew to Yemen to meet him and had already been radicalized by his lectures. Social media played a negligible role in Abdulmutallab's radicalization by Awlaki. In November 2009, a U.S. Army psychiatrist called Nidal Hasan shot dead 12 American soldiers in Fort Hood, Texas. However, Hasan had been in contact with Awlaki by email, and his radicalization had more to do with personal factors than with social media.

None of this is to deny that social media can play a role in radicalization. For example, there is evidence of young Muslims being radicalized by YouTube videos of the maltreatment of fellow Muslims in other parts of the world. In these cases, the perception of grievance is a key factor in radicalization, and the effect of social media channels like YouTube is to heighten this perception or, in some cases, to generate it. However, there is an ongoing debate about whether YouTube's recommendation algorithm encourages or discourages extremism. In general, social media is not an autonomous driver of micro-level radicalization, and the focus on social media gives the misleading impression that radicalization is a passive process rather than one that relies on people's active participation and initiative.

It is at the level of macro-radicalization that the effects of social media are most clearly visible. One view is that social media encourages polarization, which in turn causes extremism. Polarization is 'a condition where political officials and ordinary citizens are so deeply divided that there is no basis for compromise or even productive communication among them' (Aikin and Talisse 2020: 31). Social media is thought to contribute to political polarization by creating echo chambers in which opposing views are either unheard or discredited. Yet there is also evidence that exposure to opposing views on social media can actually increase polarization.[15] The extent to which social media contributes to polarization and the mechanisms by which this effect is achieved remain controversial. However, it is also possible that social media causes radicalization more directly, not by fomenting polarization but by shifting the Overton Window so as to make what would previously have been regarded as extremist policies and discourses look mainstream.

Recall that the Overton Window is the idea that at any given time there is a set of ideas and policies that are widely accepted throughout society. As Marantz puts it:

> Ideas in the center of the Overton window are universally acceptable, so mainstream that they are taken for granted. The outer panes of the window represent more controversial opinions; radical opinions are close to the window's edge; outside the window are ideas that are not just unpopular but unthinkable.
>
> (2019: 54)

Marantz gives a compelling account of how the so-called 'alt-right' in America has used social media to shift the Overton Window substantially to the right. By making thinkable what would previously have been unthinkable, the alt-right has succeeded in radicalizing American politics and preparing the way for Trump's election in 2016. This was an example of macro-level radicalization by social media. Marantz sees the rise of right-wing populism in the U.S. as confirmation of Richard Rorty's view that 'what was unacceptable can become acceptable' (ibid.: 59). Sooner or later the electorate will decide that 'the system' has failed them and 'start looking around for a strongman to vote for' (Rorty 1998: 90).

It should be noted, however, that in Rorty's persuasive account of the radicalization of American politics, there is no mention of social media. This is partly a reflection of the fact that Rorty was writing before the heyday of social media but also of his well-grounded conviction that the radicalization he describes has to do with deeper structural factors. His dire warning that the old, industrialized economies are 'heading into a Weimar-like period' (ibid.: 89) is based on an analysis of the impact of globalization on the white working class, a rise in economic inequality, job insecurity, and the political failings of the Left. Compared to the influence of social media, these factors are much more significant. To put it another way, although social media may have contributed to the rightward shift in the Overton Window, the alt-right's media tactics have been so effective because they have been able to exploit the deeper structural changes that Rorty describes.

Why should factors like inequality and job insecurity result in a marked rightward shift in the Overton Window? What have economic factors got to do with radicalization? In Chapter 4, mention was made of the Nietzschean concept of *ressentiment* as a component of the mindset of extremism. Ressentiment is a mixture of resentment and vengefulness whose source is the recognition of one's powerlessness.[16] It is fuelled by the perception of grievance, a sense of injury 'whose collective politics mixes hatred and envy of those who we believe have injured us' (Kimmel 2017: 38). Using social media, the alt-right in the U.S. has succeeded in directing this ressentiment against the so-called 'liberal elite'. However, this methodology would have had little chance of success if it had no basis in socio-economic reality. If it were not for the fact that liberal capitalism and globalization have combined to generate feelings of impotence in middle America, there would be no ressentiment for the alt-right to exploit.[17] The fact that these feelings of impotence have some basis in reality makes them all the more potent as a political force. As more people start to feel that they have no stake in the status quo, they are increasingly attracted by the disruptive tactics of the alt-right.

On this account, the grievance model of radicalization remains in place. According to this model, the perception of grievance, in the form of injustice, oppression or socio-economic exclusion, is an important factor which makes people receptive to extremist ideas. What needs to be explained is *how* the perception of grievance does this. Ressentiment is the missing link or, at any rate, a missing link. Receptivity to extremism results from the ressentiment that flows from the perception of grievance. This is not to underestimate the importance of social media but rather to see its role in radicalization as something that the grievance model can account for. The upshot, once again, is that social media is not an autonomous source of radicalization. It can be exploited by extremists because, and only because, the various *structural* conditions for radicalization are already in place, that is, conditions of the sort that Rorty describes.

Clearly, there is more to the radicalization process than the perception of grievance. For all the attractions of the grievance model, it remains the case that there is not a simple formula or template that would explain how people radicalize. Still, it is legitimate to try to identify key drivers of radicalization, and the account in this chapter has identified the grievance perception as one important driver of cognitive radicalization. Behavioural radicalization results when a small minority of cognitively radicalized individuals start to think of themselves as soldiers. An extremist mindset plays an enabling role in relation to both forms of radicalization. This view of radicalization is of theoretical interest and also has practical implications. If extremism is a vice rather than a virtue, then there is good reason to try to prevent it. However, proposed antidotes must be based on a realistic conception of how radicalization works. Chapter 8 will assess a range of antidotes to extremism in the light of the account of radicalization given in this chapter.

Notes

1 Neumann (2013: 874).

2 For more on Yousef, see Reeve (1999) and McDermott and Meyer (2012).

3 This is the crux of 'particularism' about radicalization, an approach explained and defended in Cassam (2018).

4 This passage is an implicit response to Arun Kundnani's criticisms of the concept of radicalization in Kundnani (2012).

5 This literature includes Reeve (1999) (on Ramzi Yousef), Michel and Herbeck (2001) (on Timothy McVeigh), Malik (2007) (on 7/7 London bomber Mohammad Sidique Khan), McDermott and Meyer (2012) (on Khalid Sheikh Mohammed), Borchgrevink (2013) and Seierstad (2015) (on Anders Behring Breivik), Gessen (2016) (on the Boston Marathon bombers Tamerlan and Dzhokhar Tsarnaev), and Meleagrou-Hitchens (2020) (on Anwar al-Awlaki).

6 See Sageman (2017: 90) for one version of the distinction between cognitive and behavioral radicalization. Some such distinction is widely accepted in the academic literature on radicalization.

7 The Overton Window came up in Chapter 2 and will come up again later in the present chapter.

8 Macdonald (1978). The author was, in fact, William Luther Pierce, a white supremacist and neo-Nazi.

9 Kaczynski's letter, which is well worth reading, is reproduced in Michel and Herbeck (2001: Appendix B).

10 Quoted in Michel and Herbeck (2001: 360).

11 A key discussion of this aspect of behavioral radicalization is Sageman (2017), especially Chapter 4.

12 Sluka (2011).

13 Paul (2014).

14 Von Behr et al. (2013).

15 Bail et al. (2018).

16 See Reginster (1997) for further discussion of ressentiment.

17 This is one of the lessons of Lind (2020).

Countering extremism

Counter-radicalization and deradicalization

Not long before Mohammad Sidique Khan killed himself and five other people by detonating a bomb at London's Edgware Road Underground Station on 7 July 2005, he recorded a so-called 'martyrdom' video in which he explained and justified his action in the following terms:

> Your democratically elected government perpetrates atrocities against my people all over the world. And your support of them makes you directly responsible, just as I am directly responsible for protecting and avenging my Muslim brothers and sisters. Until we feel security, you will be our targets … We are at war and I am a soldier.[1]

Khan was a textbook extremist, driven by a profound sense of grievance, committed to an extremist ideology, and someone who saw himself as a soldier for justice. He was cognitively, behaviourally, and psychologically radicalized, a textbook illustration of the grievance model of radicalization, as well as Sageman's idea that violence results from the activation of a martial social identity.

In a 2007 *Prospect* magazine article, Shiv Malik describes Khan's transformation from 'a softly spoken youth worker, into the mastermind of 7/7', a day of four separate bomb attacks in London.[2] Khan was born in the UK and, like two of his fellow bombers, came from the Beeston area of Leeds, in the North of England. Khan was of Pakistani origin and Malik sees internal frictions within the British Pakistani community as the key to his radicalization. Like many other British Muslims, he may have felt indignant about western

DOI: 10.4324/9780429325472-8

foreign policy but Malik insists, not wholly convincingly, 'that wasn't the reason he led a cell of young men to kill themselves and 52 London commuters' (Malik 2007). At the heart of the tragedy, according to Malik, was a conflict between different generations of British Pakistanis, 'with many young people using Islamism as a kind of liberation theology to assert their right to choose how they live' rather than have important life decisions dictated by community elders. However, Khan's video suggests that his motives were political as well as personal.

As with other accounts of radicalization, Malik's leaves key questions unanswered. We learn that at some point in the 1990s Khan became interested in Wahhabi fundamentalism and that this pitted him against his family's more traditional approach to religion. What we do not discover is why or how Khan became interested in Wahhabi fundamentalism. We learn that while his family was aware of Khan's extremism, 'no one had expected him to become a suicide bomber' (ibid.). Why would he blow himself up just a year after his wife had given birth to a baby girl on whom he doted? Not surprisingly, no answer to this question is forthcoming. The only things that are certain are that Khan became radicalized, that he self-categorized as a soldier, and turned to violence. What triggered his turn to violence is unknown and now unknowable.

Nevertheless, from the perspective of those who lost loved ones on 7/7, it is natural to wonder whether Khan's radicalization could have been prevented or reversed. This question, which can be asked about any actual or potential extremist, is about the prospects of counter-radicalization or deradicalization. Effective counter-radicalization would have prevented Khan from becoming an extremist and effective deradicalization would have convinced him to 'permanently repent and abandon violence' (El-Said 2013: 6). The question whether extremism is harmful was addressed in Chapter 6, where it was argued that its supposed benefits are the benefits of something with which it is all too easily confused, namely, political radicalism. If, like 9/11, 7/7 is viewed as an illustration of where extremism can lead then it is understandable that policy-makers and others should have prioritized the search for antidotes. The question for this chapter is whether counter-radicalization and deradicalization are effective antidotes to extremism.

What is the difference between counter-radicalization and deradicalization, and how do these two notions relate to another notion that is often mentioned in these contexts, that of disengagement? As Peter Neumann observes, counter-radicalization 'seeks to prevent non-radicalized populations from being radicalized' (2011: 16). More controversially, Neumann also argues that the objective of counter-radicalization is 'to create individual and communal resilience against cognitive and/ or violent radicalization through a variety of non-coercive means' (ibid.: 16). This talk of 'resilience' is much more contentious than it might seem and deserves to be carefully scrutinized. As for deradicalization and disengagement, these two terms:

> describe processes whereby radicalized individuals (or groups) cease their involvement in political violence and/or terrorism. While deradicalization aims for substantive changes in individuals' (or groups') ideology and attitudes, disengagement concentrates on facilitating behavioral change, that is, the rejection of violent means.
>
> (ibid.: 16)

Not all extremists are violent extremists. Some employ non-violent means while others are armchair extremists. Nevertheless, it is understandable that the focus of most discussions of counter-radicalization, deradicalization and disengagement is violent extremism. The terrible human consequences of terrorism, combined with its ineffectiveness as a method for bringing about political change, make it imperative to walk people back from the brink of committing acts of terrorism, or to prevent them from moving in this direction in the first place. In this way, the theory and practice of counter-radicalization and deradicalization are closely related to the theory and practice of counter-terrorism.

The 7/7 bombings happened two years after the publication of the UK's CONTEST counter-terrorism strategy. CONTEST has undergone numerous revisions but at its heart is the *Prevent* strand, whose aim is to prevent people from becoming terrorists or supporting terrorism. However, preventing terrorism goes hand in hand with preventing people from becoming radicalized. As the 2011 *Prevent Strategy* puts it, 'the line between extremism and terrorism is not always precise' and 'preventing people becoming terrorists will require a challenge to extremist ideas where they are used to legitimise terrorism' (HM Government 2011: 24). To put it another way, counter-terrorism involves counter-radicalization. The latter involves, among other things, challenging extremist ideas and protecting 'vulnerable people' (ibid.: 56), that is, people who are 'at risk of radicalisation' (ibid.: 56).[3]

The *Prevent* model of counter-radicalization will be the focus of the *'Prevent'* section of this chapter. Why focus on a British government document when radicalization and terrorism are by no means uniquely British phenomena? Because *Prevent* is representative of how many Western governments conceive of counter-radicalization and counter-terrorism. *Prevent* is built on a series of foundational myths about radicalization that prevent it from telling a convincing story. Each myth is based on the idea that becoming radicalized is analogous to catching a disease to which some people are more vulnerable than others. The notion of extremism as a contagion that is spread by so-called 'radicalizers' is the ultimate foundational myth. The contagion model overlooks the key point that, unlike diseases, ideologies are supported by *reasons* and *narratives*. They persuade rather than infect, and it is important to recognize the extent to which people are radicalized by *arguments* in favour of the views they adopt and by stories that convey their ideology, values and core concerns. These arguments and narratives might be flawed but they need to be addressed. Unfortunately, counter-radicalization requires a type of engagement with extremism that is politically difficult. There is always the concern that those who engage with extremist narratives and the grievances they express will be seen as soft on extremism. However, without such engagement, there is no hope of effective counter-radicalization.

At least in this respect, the deradicalization programmes that have been developed in several Muslim majority states are more to the point since they tackle extremists on their own terms and challenge their theological arguments and narratives. Much has been made of the success of Saudi Arabia's deradicalization programme, which has been described as the 'de facto model' (Boucek 2008: 65) for all such programmes. However, as has also been noted, 'it would be quite impossible to transplant or emulate the Saudi strategy anywhere else in the world, particularly in Western Muslim-minority countries' (El-Said and Barrett 2013: 220). When it comes to deradicalizing individuals whose extremism has nothing to do with Islam, the relevance of the Saudi model is even more doubtful. These issues will be addressed in the section 'Deradicalization'.

The final section will develop a perspective on counter-radicalization and deradicalization that avoids the foundational myths of the former and the limitations of country-specific accounts of the latter. A key idea in this connection is that of a *strategic narrative*. Strategic narratives are 'compelling story lines which can explain events convincingly and from which inferences can be drawn' (Freedman 2006: 22). Given the role of such narratives in radicalization, it is natural to suppose that counter-radicalization requires strategic *counter*-narratives. The need for such narratives has been recognized but the weakness of the counter-narratives that have been proposed is an indication of the inherent difficulty of coming up with plausible counter-narratives and a failure to grasp the full force of extremist narratives. Furthermore, counter-narratives are not enough since they run up against the extremist *mindset* as well as extremist ideologies. Neither minds nor mindsets are easy to change.

Prevent

According to *Prevent*, 'radicalisation is driven by an ideology which sanctions the use of violence; by propagandists for that ideology … and by personal vulnerabilities and specific local factors which, for a range of reasons, make that ideology seem both attractive and compelling' (HM Government 2011: 5). Accordingly, 'preventing terrorism will mean challenging extremist (and non-violent) ideas that are also part of a terrorist ideology' (ibid.: 6). Objective One of *Prevent* is therefore to 'respond to the ideological challenge of terrorism' (ibid.: 7). Objective Two is to 'prevent people from being drawn into terrorism and ensure that they are given the appropriate advice and support'. Objective Three is to 'work with sectors and institutions where there are risks of radicalisation' (ibid.: 7).

One might quibble about the idea that radicalization is *driven* by an ideology which sanctions the use of violence, since radicalization, at least in the cognitive sense, *consists in* the adoption of an extremist ideology. The factors that drive radicalization include those that make these ideologies attractive, such as their own nature and the narratives by which they are sustained. There is much talk in *Prevent* about the need to challenge extremist ideologies but no explanation of what makes them attractive to some people in the first place. One of the myths of *Prevent*, which underpins much of its thinking without ever being made explicit, is that extremist ideologies can be challenged without any serious engagement with their substance or with the grievances to which they give expression.

Consider *Prevent*'s account of the context of Objective One. It lists among the drivers of radicalization 'grievances, some real and some imagined' that are 'exploited by apologists for violence and made a reason for engaging with it' (ibid.: 18). Yet it matters whether the grievances referred to are real or imagined, since responding to an imagined grievance is one thing while responding to genuine grievance is another. In principle, imagined grievances can be tackled by showing that they have no basis in reality. This will not work with grievances that *do* have a basis in reality. In the case of imagined grievances, the challenge is to alter the perceptions that account for them. Genuine grievances call for a quite different response and one that, for reasons of practical politics, documents like *Prevent* simply cannot contemplate. Instead, they make recommendations that essentially bypass the important issues.

To illustrate the point, consider *Prevent*'s account of how to challenge the ideologies that play a crucial role in the radicalization process:

> Ideology depends on ideologues, people who promote that ideology and encourage others to subscribe to it … Challenging ideology also means identifying these ideologues, ensuring that they cannot take advantage of the freedoms in this country to peddle their messages without debate or rebuttal, prosecuting them where they have broken the law and restricting their access to this country where we judge it appropriate to do so.
>
> (ibid.: 44)

It is striking that the focus in this passage is on the messenger rather than the message, on the importance of disrupting the activities of *ideologues* rather than tackling their *ideologies*. In keeping with its eccentric definition of extremism as involving 'vocal or active opposition to fundamental British values' (ibid.: 107), *Prevent* asserts that challenging extremism is 'also about being confident in our own values' (ibid.: 44). However, it remains obscure how such confidence contributes to the rebuttal of extremist narratives and arguments.

The authors of *Prevent* are, of course, well aware of the narratives that underpin the actions of people like Khan, who believe that the 'West is at war with Islam, and that it is deliberately mistreating Muslims around the world' (ibid.: 47). Faced with this narrative, *Prevent* has nothing better to offer than the bland assertion that 'far from being at war with Islam', Western governments are 'making great efforts to address deprivation, human rights issues and governance in Muslim majority countries' (ibid.: 48). Unfortunately, the force of these assertions is considerably weakened by political reality. While there is no war against Islam, there is a history of bloody Western military intervention in Muslim majority countries like Iraq. At least to this extent, the extremist narrative cannot be said to be to be completely disconnected from reality even if it contains a number of falsehoods. Rather, it is grounded in a particular interpretation of real events.

In addition, the West's supposed concern with democracy and human rights has to be weighed against a record of political and military alliances with regimes in the Middle East with poor human rights records and no interest in democracy. This places documents like *Prevent* in a tricky position when it comes to constructing a compelling counter-narrative to the extremists' narrative. The difficulty is to rebut the charge that it is *Prevent's* own account of the West's supposed interest in democracy and human rights in Muslim majority countries that is disconnected from reality. This is not to justify the extremist narrative but simply to make the point that it is no use trying to counter this narrative with assertions that won't ring true to people who are drawn to extremism.

Another core myth in *Prevent* concerns the extent to which people are 'drawn into terrorism' and can be prevented from doing so by being given the appropriate advice and support. *Prevent* is full of 'drawing in' talk, as is the 2015 Counter-Terrorism and Security Act, which imposes on public bodies a duty – the so-called Prevent duty – 'to have due regard to the need to prevent people from being drawn into terrorism'.[4] It is worth pausing to reflect on the implications of this terminology, which is also at the heart of another *Prevent* document, *Individuals at Risk of Being Drawn into Serious and Organised Crime – a Prevent Guide*.[5] To describe a person as having been *drawn into* something is to imply that their involvement is to a significant degree unwitting or reluctant or against their own better judgement. There is an implication of passivity here that bears on questions of responsibility. A person might be responsible for placing themselves in a position to be drawn into an activity but their being drawn into it is not something for which they are fully responsible. It is possible to be drawn into something to which one is not drawn. A person might not be *drawn to* a life of serious crime – that is, find it appealing – but still be *drawn into* it by, say, the influence of others. In such cases, it might be appropriate to speak of manipulation or the absence of agency.

These ways of talking are a poor fit for the radicalization of Mohammad Sidique Khan and many others like him. These individuals were radicalized but cannot be regarded as having being 'drawn into' extremism or terrorism.

To describe their radicalization in this way is to underestimate the extent to which their political journeys were an expression of their own agency. Khan chose to attend lectures by Anwar Al-Awlaki, who came up in Chapter 7, watched his videos and even transcribed them. Awlaki presented *arguments*, albeit arguments with a strong emotional appeal, and Khan was evidently convinced by them. Being convinced by an argument is not the same as being 'drawn into' acceptance of its conclusion, even if the argument is flawed. When one is led by acceptance of the premises of an argument to accept its conclusion, there might be an element of rational compulsion – hence the description of some arguments as compelling – but there is no question in such cases of one's acceptance being unwitting or against one's better judgement. One's acceptance of a conclusion *is* one's judgement and following an argument to a conclusion can be both a rational process and an expression of one's own agency.

As well as presenting arguments for extremism, online radicalizers also play on the emotions of their targets, for example, by displaying graphic images of Muslims being humiliated or mistreated. However, these are images in support of an argument, and their capacity to elicit emotions like anger and resentment does not entail that their impact is non-rational. Emotions can be rational. Radicalizers use graphic images as evidence in support of their extremist narratives. They understand that the best way of convincing audiences is to combine an emotional appeal with an appeal to their reason. A person who is drawn into something might be helped by being given 'appropriate advice and support'. A person who is convinced by an argument needs something different: a counter-argument or an explanation of where the argument goes wrong. That requires precisely the kind of engagement with the substance of the argument described above.

This is not to deny that the *Prevent* terminology is sometimes appropriate. In the case of adolescents or younger children who are groomed by online extremists, it might be wholly appropriate to describe them as having been drawn into extremism or terrorism. What makes this terminology appropriate is the assumption that online grooming victims lack the maturity to make up their own minds about the merits of the causes they are induced to support. They are assumed to lack the agency of adults, and to be vulnerable to manipulation or exploitation in ways that normal adults are not. In these cases, some of the interventions recommended by *Prevent* make sense, and young people might indeed be helped by being given appropriate advice and support. The problem with *Prevent* is that it treats adults in the same way. Yet the sense in which a mature adult is 'vulnerable' to or 'at risk' of radicalization is quite different from the sense in which a 12-year-old is vulnerable or at risk.

This raises a more general question about *Prevent*'s notions of risk and vulnerability. It is in this context that the influence of the contagion model of radicalization is most clearly visible. The sense in which a disease is contagious is that it is easily spread from one person to another, usually by close contact. Diseases aren't spread by arguments, and vulnerability to infection is a phenomenon that is open to investigation by epidemiologists. When a section of the population is identified as being at special risk of catching a particular disease, there is a scientific basis for this identification. By the same token, epidemiologists have a well-grounded conception of resilience to infection, and the factors that contribute to or detract from such resilience.

These are implicitly the terms in which *Prevent* conceives of the spread of extremism. Its conception of vulnerability to radicalization parallels the epidemiological conception of vulnerability to infection. Furthermore, as Charlotte Heath-Kelly points out, the language of resilience as resistance to extremist ideologies 'directly parallels the language of contagions and the fostering of immunity' (2017: 305). However, these supposed parallels are misplaced. It is true that individuals or groups might be *susceptible* to certain arguments or ideas but there is no meaningful parallel between susceptibility to an argument and vulnerability to a disease. Lack of resistance or resilience might make one especially vulnerable to infection but susceptibility to *cogent* arguments, even arguments for unwelcome conclusions, is hardly a personal vulnerability or a sign of a lack of intellectual resistance or resilience. Quite the opposite. By the same token, if there are strong arguments for extremism, then the idea of countering extremism by increasing people's resistance to such arguments makes little sense. In these circumstances, the only way to inoculate people against radicalization is to develop even stronger and more compelling arguments against extremism.

Prevent assumes that the arguments put forward by extremists are not cogent and that people vary in their susceptibility to these arguments. This is not an unreasonable assumption. Even fallacious arguments can be seductive, and it is possible to think of people like Awlaki as especially dangerous by virtue of their ability to make bad arguments for highly dangerous conclusions look perfectly reasonable and, indeed, inescapable. It might be appropriate, in such cases, to describe certain groups or individuals as especially 'vulnerable' to fallacious arguments but increasing their resilience will be a matter of equipping them with the means to see through these arguments and identify their defects. For a variety of different reasons, this might be beyond some converts to extremism, and the fact that an argument is recognized as flawed will not automatically deprive it of persuasive force. Talk of personal vulnerability and lack of resilience gives entirely the wrong impression about the nature of radicalization. It encourages the idea that radicalization is something that happens to a person, like an illness, rather than an expression of their own agency and values. The failure of *Prevent* to provide a convincing model of counter-radicalization is a consequence of this idea. Since both radicalization and counter-radicalization involve the exercise of reason, the myths of the contagion model have little to offer.

Deradicalization

These defects of the contagion model of counter-radicalization are in stark contrast to influential models of deradicalization. While radicalization has generated a vast scholarly literature, deradicalization is a relatively neglected subject. Writing in 2009, Omar Ashour noted that there was at that time not a single book on this subject despite the peaceful deradicalization of thousands of Islamist movements which used to engage in terrorist acts. Ashour's book *The De-Radicalisation of Jihadists* started the process of closing this gap in the literature. Ashour's question is: 'why do radical Islamist militants revise their ideologies, strategies and objectives and initiate a de-radicalization process?' (2009: 3). This process can be ideological, behavioural or both. The former happens when 'a radical group reverses its ideology and de-legitimizes the use of violent methods to achieve political goals, while also moving towards an acceptance of gradual social, political and economic changes within a pluralist context' (ibid.: 5–6). Behavioural deradicalization means abandoning the use of violence to achieve political goals. This can happen with or without ideological deradicalization. Lastly, there is also organizational deradicalization, that is, the dismantling of armed units of an extremist organization and the demobilization of its fighters.

Based on his study of deradicalization in several Muslim majority countries, Ashour identifies four factors that are necessary for deradicalization: (1) state repression; (2) selective inducements; (3) social interaction; and (4) charismatic leadership. The first of these is self-explanatory. The second refers to socio-economic incentives offered to Islamist movements 'in return for behavioral, ideological and/or organizational changes' (ibid.: 15). The social interactions that contribute to deradicalization are social interactions between members of an extremist group and others who do not share their ideology. Finally, leadership is important as a source of legitimacy for deradicalization. Without leadership support, deradicalization is too easily represented as a form of betrayal.

This account raises a number of questions. One might wonder, for example, whether all four conditions are necessary for deradicalization. Ashour is correct that state repression alone will not only *not* lead to deradicalization but is a common cause of radicalization. Why, in that case, would state repression be necessary for deradicalization? Why would the other three factors be incapable of bringing about deradicalization even in the absence of state repression? One might also ask how ideological deradicalization, as distinct from behavioural or organizational deradicalization, can be bought by socio-economic incentives. One can be paid to change one's behaviour, but not one's ideological commitments unless the beliefs that underpin these commitments are voluntary. One cannot simply decide not to believe what one previously believed, however great the financial reward.

There are many other aspects of Ashour's account that are worth pondering but the main point to note is that this account is primarily an account of deradicalization at the level of groups or organizations. What is missing is an account of deradicalization at the level of individual extremists, who may or may not be members of an organization. Organizational deradicalization without some individual deradicalization is hard to envisage but the reverse is not true. It is quite conceivable that some individual members of extremist organizations deradicalize even though their organizations do not. How does this happen? Furthermore, Ashour is only concerned with the deradicalization of Jihadists rather than deradicalization of extremists more generally. If one were to ask how Timothy McVeigh could have been deradicalized prior to the Oklahoma bombing, then Ashour's account has little to offer. The question of how to deradicalize individual extremists more generally will be tackled in the next section. Before then, there is something to say about the methods for deradicalizing individual Islamist extremists. These methods, which have been developed and perfected by the government of Saudi Arabia, deserve a closer look, especially in relation to the *Prevent* perspective on counter-radicalization.

One might begin by asking a question that has not received the attention it deserves: why do individuals decide to *leave* terrorist and extremist organizations? Michael Jacobson calls such individuals 'terrorist dropouts' and stresses the importance of understanding this phenomenon.[6] Individual dropouts have been a serious problem for a number of high-profile extremist organizations, including Al-Qaeda. Jacobson identified a range of factors that have resulted in individuals dropping out, including petty grievances, unmet expectations, the role of family, and a change in the personal circumstances of dropouts. Another factor is growing disillusionment with the group's hypocrisy, as when its leadership is seen as advancing its own interests in ways that are at odds with its ideology. However, of all the factors listed by Jacobson, the one that is most relevant for present purposes is theological. He notes that senior defectors from Al-Qaeda always cite its 'inaccurate interpretation of Islam as a major factor' (2010: 8). It is when defectors come to see the *theological* flaws in the programmes of groups like Al-Qaeda and ISIS that they pull out.

This insight is the starting point for Saudi Arabia's deradicalization programme. It has been noted by Christopher Boucek that the Saudis see the struggle against violent extremism as 'part of a "war of ideas" centred upon issues of legitimacy, authority and what is permitted in Islam' (2008: 61). According to Boucek:

> This strategy has perhaps become best known for its counseling programme which seeks to encourage Saudi security detainees to repent and repudiate extremist ideologies. Through intensive religious debate and psychological counseling, religious scholars work to demonstrate that they have been following corrupted interpretations of Islam.
>
> (ibid.: 60)

More recent research has confirmed Boucek's account. Hamed El-Said and Richard Barrett agree that 'one of the most notable features of the Saudi deradicalization programme is the participation of distinguished scholars, scientists, and clerics' (2013: 211). Saudi authorities encourage respected religious figures to visit extremists in prison to engage them in dialogue. The aim is to undermine the extremists' narrative and expose the defects in their religious understanding. There is special emphasis on the point that 'only credible and knowledgeable scholars can issue fatwas to justify jihad' (ibid.: 209), and that extremists like Osama bin Laden lack the necessary scholarly and religious credentials. At the end of a course in Islamic jurisprudence, detainees sit an exam which they need to pass to move to the next stage of the deradicalization programme.

There is much more to the Saudi programme than religious instruction but, for present purposes, this is the key aspect. Like Western counter-radicalization programmes, the Saudi programme is based on the idea that the key to victory against violent extremism is 'the defeat of the ideological infra-structure that supports and nurtures political violence' (Boucek 2008: 61). However, in sharp contrast to *Prevent*, the Saudi programme accepts the need for a detailed *intellectual* engagement with the ideology and narratives of Islamist extremists. In a battle of ideas, it is essential that one has the intel-lectual ammunition needed to prevail. In the Saudi case, it is religious schol-ars who provide the necessary ammunition, and great care is taken to ensure that scholars who are sent to engage in a dialogue with extremists are seen as credible and not simply as government agents. The assumption is that many extremists are attracted to extremism by arguments and narratives, and that the remedy is a barrage of counter-arguments and counter-narratives that are designed to satisfy extremists that they have been misled by those who were responsible for their initial radicalization. In place of the plati-tudes of *Prevent* is a serious programme of education that engages extremists on their own terms, that is, in terms of what is and is not genuinely permissi-ble or obligatory in Islam. Educating and persuading are a serious and time-consuming task that cannot be accomplished with platitudes.

There are few traces of the contagion model in the Saudi programme. The emphasis on the need to *convince* extremists and prevail in a battle of ideas presupposes a rationalistic conception of deradicalization: convincing extremists to repudiate their extremist ideologies is a matter of giving them *reasons*, relative to their own religious framework, to change their views. The assumption is that, at some level, they were reasoned into extremism and they can be reasoned out of it. The extremists' so-called 'vulnerability to radicalization' is intellectual. Those responsible for deradicalization in the Saudi context work on the basis that because the individuals for whom they are responsible 'did not correctly learn the tenets of their faith origi-nally, they were susceptible to extremist propaganda' (ibid.: 63). In place of the somewhat nebulous notion of 'resilience' to radicalization in *Prevent* is a much more precise model of resilience as grounded in knowledge and understanding.

One might be sceptical of the idea of reasoning extremists out of their extremism, but the results of the Saudi programme are impressive, with apparently low rates of recidivism. Questions have been raised about the basis on which the success of the Saudi programme has been measured but nothing to suggest that it is unsuccessful. This would be encouraging if it were not for the fact that, as Boucek has cautioned, the Saudi programme is a Saudi solution to a Saudi problem and may not have application elsewhere. The programme relies for its success not just on the factors described so far but also on a cultural tradition that makes Saudi extremists receptive to the Saudi government's approach. In other Muslim majority countries, the same methods will not necessarily deliver the same impressive results.

Even more to the point, there is also the question of how Saudi-style deradicalization is supposed to work in non-Muslim or non-religious contexts. The Saudi approach works, to the extent that it does, because there is a canonical text and set of traditions to which scholars can appeal in their dialogues with extremists. As has often been pointed out, many extremists who claim to be fighting for Islam have, at best, a shaky grasp of its fundamental tenets and rituals. They attack other Muslims for not being true to their religion but their own lack of knowledge and understanding makes them ripe for scholarly deradicalization by experts with an indisputably higher level of religious knowledge. However, where extremists do not rely on a canonical text, they cannot be educated out of their extremism in the Saudi manner. To take Timothy McVeigh as an example, his reading of *The Turner Diaries* might have played a role in his radicalization but, even for him, the *Diaries* did not have the authority of a canonical religious text. In that case, what would a deradicalization programme look like for someone like him?

Another way to ask this question is to return to the contrast drawn above between extremism and fundamentalism. Unlike extremism more generally, fundamentalism is the 'cult of the text' (Ruthven 2007: 45). The subjects of the Saudi deradicalization programme might be described as failed fundamentalists. They purport to revere a canonical text whose prescriptions they claim to follow, but it turns out in many cases that they barely know this text and rely instead on the simplifications and distortions of extremist ideologues who know little more than they do. A fundamentalist who misunderstands the fundamentals of his or her creed can, in certain circumstances, be deradicalized by having the fundamentals explained to him or her by someone whose credentials are demonstrably superior to those of the individuals responsible for his or her initial radicalization. However, this won't work for extremists like McVeigh because this type of extremist is not a fundamentalist. There are no texts which they are failing to understand. In their case an alternative approach is needed. What might such an alternative look like?

While non-fundamentalist extremists might not revere a specific text, they do rely on a narrative. In many ways, talk of a narrative is much more useful than talk of an ideology. McVeigh had an ideology, a way of making sense of the world, but his ideology took the form of a narrative. Narratives are sometimes described as stories, and McVeigh's narrative was literally a story, based on a piece of fiction: *The Turner Diaries*. This points to a potential deradicalization and counter-radicalization strategy that might be effective both with fundamentalist and non-fundamentalist extremists. Extremism is always underpinned by a narrative, a narrative of purity, humiliation, virtue, or any number of other preoccupations that figure in the extremist mindset. Is it possible, then, that extremism can be countered through the construction of compelling counter-narratives? The next task, therefore, is to develop a better understanding of the nature and potential of counter-narratives as a weapon in the fight against extremism.

Counter-narratives

Narratives have been defined here as compelling story lines which can explain events convincingly and from which inferences can be drawn.[7] This is Lawrence Freedman's conception of a *strategic narrative*, which he elaborates as follows:

> Narratives are designed or nurtured with the intention of structuring the responses of others to developing events. They are strategic because they do not arise spontaneously but are deliberately constructed or reinforced out of the ideas and thoughts that are already current … Narratives are about the ways that issues are framed and responses suggested. They are not necessarily analytical and, when not grounded in evidence or experience, may rely on appeals to emotion, or on suspect metaphors and dubious historical analogies.
>
> (2006: 22–3)

On a grievance model of radicalization, one would expect extremist narratives to highlight the grievances by which extremists are motivated. As well as highlighting the grievances themselves, extremist strategic narratives identify those responsible for their problems and potential solutions, including violence. Strategic narratives see the world in terms of good and evil and portray the people the extremists claim to represent as victims.

Strategic narratives are exercises in what Karl Weick calls *sensemaking*, 'the making of sense' (1995: 4). Sensemaking is 'about such things as placement of items into frameworks, comprehending, redressing surprise, constructing meaning, interacting in pursuit of mutual understanding, and patterning' (ibid.: 6). Stories are particularly effective in sensemaking because they can help to create the illusion of understanding, if not genuine understanding. Effective sensemaking yields *cognitive satisfaction*: it provides those to whom the sensemaking narrative is directed with the clear sense that what was previously opaque is now comprehensible. It provides them with a framework for understanding their predicament in a way that meshes with their experiences, interests and values.

The best way for a narrative to achieve this is to be grounded in reality. When narratives misrepresent the facts, they create an illusion of understanding rather than the real thing. Narratives are unlikely to deliver cognitive satisfaction if they are disconnected from reality. As Freedman points out, 'although some stories can be sustained as matters of faith, in many cases if they are not grounded in some sort of reality, they are likely to fail eventually' (2006: 24). It is important to note that even narratives that are inaccurate in many respects can still be grounded in *some* sort of reality. For example, they can be grounded in the lived experience of sections of the population.

To the extent that extremism is sustained by strategic narratives, it stands to reason that one potentially effective way to counter extremist ideologies is to develop compelling strategic counter-narratives. Counter-narratives are 'counter' in at least two senses: first, they are narratives that directly challenge the extremist narrative by highlighting its inherent flaws. However, it is important that counter-narratives are not purely negative. They also require a positive vision that is both cognitively satisfying in its own right and represents an alternative to the extremist's vision. An effective counter-narrative must tell its own story that represents its own contribution to sensemaking. The test for a counter-narrative is whether it is an effective piece of sensemaking that can convince radicalized individuals to abandon their support for extremism. Counter-narratives that do not resonate with, or speak to, their target audience have no chance of success.

Are there rules or general guidelines for the construction of counter-narratives that are designed to counter extremist narratives? Kurt Braddock and John Horgan believe that there are.[8] Counter-narratives are an attempt to beat extremists at their own game. According to Braddock and Horgan, the first step is to identify the themes that extremist narratives try to communicate. Once the themes that comprise the extremist narrative have been identified, it should then be possible to develop effective counter-narratives based on them. The following is a set of guidelines, derived from the work of Braddock and Horgan, for the development of effective counter-narratives:

- avoid reinforcing the extremists' own narrative;
- reveal incongruities and contradictions in the extremist narrative;
- challenge false analogies in the extremist narrative;
- disrupt the binary themes of extremist ideology;
- advocate an alternative view of the extremist narrative's target.

Braddock and Horgan argue that 'the effectiveness of any counter-narrative will be partially contingent on the degree to which it contradicts themes intrinsic to a terrorist narrative' (2016: 391). They also stress the importance of masking. For counter-narratives to be effective, both their persuasive intent and their source must be concealed. Concealing of sources requires duplicity: in online forums, for example, 'officials seeking to distribute counternarratives must cultivate the impression that they are genuine members of the forums' (ibid.: 392).

The limitations of this account can be brought out by considering two examples from Braddock and Horgan's account. In the case of the Animal Liberation Front (ALF), which is taken to have an extremist narrative about animal rights, effective counter-narratives 'may emphasize the kind-hearted nature of humans in relation to animals – a notion that contradicts many of the themes that pervade the ALF narratives' (ibid.: 386). Another example is *The Turner Diaries*, in which the United States is represented as a police state whose government is intent on depriving citizens of their right to bear arms under the Constitution. In this case, the remedy is to point out that 'this comparison represents a false analogy' and to develop a counter-narrative in which neither the Second Amendment to the Constitution nor gun rights 'are in danger of being repealed' (ibid.: 390).

It is difficult to imagine such counter-narratives achieving anything other than the reinforcing of extremist narratives. Animal rights activists who are moved by graphic images of the cruelty of factory farming are unlikely to be impressed by appeals to the 'kind-hearted nature of humans in relation to animals'. Faced with evidence of cruelty to animals on an industrial scale, a counter-narrative is going to have to do better than to assert that humans are generally nice to animals. Such an assertion will strike animal rights extremists as utterly lacking in credibility. The same goes for the second example. The narrative of *The Turner Diaries* resonates with extremists like Timothy McVeigh because they see gun control laws as a threat to their right to bear arms. Simply denying that this is the case is hardly going to lead such people to agree to give up their extremist views. *The Turner Diaries* are effective because, from an extremist perspective, its story of a group of militants battling the tyranny of 'the System' rings true.

The limitations of Braddock and Horgan's conception of a counter-narrative are partly a reflection of the limitations of their conception of a narrative as 'any cohesive and coherent account of events with an identifiable beginning, middle, and end about characters engaged in actions that result in questions or conflicts for which answers or resolutions are provided' (ibid.: 382–3). What is missing from this characterization is a proper acknowledgement of the sensemaking role of narratives. Narratives are stories and a story 'recounts events in a way that renders them intelligible, thus conveying not just information but also understanding' (Velleman 2003: 1). A narrative can be coherent, cohesive, and have a beginning, middle and end and yet fail as an exercise in sensemaking, that is, fail to convey an understanding of events. Such a narrative will not deliver cognitive satisfaction and will have little persuasive force.

A more realistic account of what it takes to produce an effective counter-narrative will be grounded in a deeper understanding of what makes (some) extremist narratives as forceful as they are. Here are five core features of compelling extremist narratives and, by extension, compelling counter-narratives:

1. *Resonance*: effective narratives resonate with their audiences. Many factors are involved in achieving such resonance, but two key factors are *narrative fidelity* and *narrative coherence*.[9] Effective narratives and counter-narratives ring true and are internally and externally coherent. Internal coherence is internal consistency. External coherence is consistency with the audience's lived experience and other narratives.[10] Narratives and counter-narratives that display fidelity and coherence will

strike a chord with their audiences by providing, or at least seeming to provide, them with an understanding of their situation. In the example of animal rights extremists, a counter-narrative that emphasizes the kind-hearted nature of humans in relation to animals will fail, since it lacks narrative fidelity.

2. *Credibility*: effective counter-narratives are credible not just in the sense that they have the ring of truth but also in the sense that they have credible sources. Ashour notes that counter-narratives have to be 'conveyed, promoted, and supported by credible messengers' (2010: 16) if they are to be effective. This is one of the key lessons of the Saudi programme, with its reliance on religious authorities who would easily be recognized as such by extremists. Attempts to mask or disguise the identity of those responsible for counter-narratives will almost certainly result in a total loss of credibility if uncovered.

3. *Narrative depth*: narratives can be more or less deep, more or less superficial, and the same goes for counter-narratives. While extremist narratives are designed to resonate with their consumers and may have some basis in reality, many are shallow and oversimplified. As Nagel notes, many extremist organizations have 'little understanding' of 'the balance of forces, the motives of their opponents and the political context in which they are operating' (2016: 19). Counter-narratives must avoid oversimplification and shallowness and offer realistic alternatives to extremists who claim that violence is the only option. In cases where extremist grievances have deep historical roots, counter-narratives must engage in a serious and well-informed manner with such considerations.

4. *Relevance*: a relevant counter-narrative will, among other things, address the grievances by which extremists are motivated. Counter-narratives that ignore, downplay or misrepresent these grievances will be seen as irrelevant and almost certainly be ineffective. Relevant counter-narratives are *targeted* and *tailored*. They target extremist grievances and other factors that make extremist narratives effective. They use their understanding of extremist preoccupations, attitudes and ways of thinking to build effective narratives that speak to extremist concerns. It is also essential to 'tailor the message to different audiences' and take account of 'the specifics of the group(s) in question, the peculiarities of their ideology and ontology, and the nuances of the context(s) in which it operates' (Ashour 2010: 17). There is no one-size-fits-all counter-narrative that would work for both Mohammad Sidique Khan and Timothy McVeigh. This is not to

deny that there are similarities between different extremist ideologies, but these similarities are no excuse for overlooking the specifics of an extremist ideology against which a given counter-narrative is directed.

5. *Accessibility*: one sense in which extremist counter-narratives must be accessible concerns relatively mundane aspects of the way that they are circulated. So, for example, if the target audience consists of native Arabic speakers, then counter-narratives in Arabic are going to be accessible to a larger number of people than counter-narratives in English. Equally, where the target audience has no internet access, there is not much point relying on the internet to get one's message across. There is also a deeper dimension of accessibility that has to do with narrative style. Bernard Lewis points to the importance of 'historical allusions' (2003: xvii) in Osama bin Laden's anti-Western narrative.[11] Elisabeth Kendall draws attention to the role of poetry in bin Laden's pronouncements. Counter-narratives that take no account of this are in danger of approaching the Jihadist narrative 'through a skewed prism that is out of synch with that of its primary Arab audience' (Kendall 2016: 225).

The narrative fidelity requirement raises an obvious question about fictional narratives like *The Turner Diaries*. Stories with narrative fidelity 'represent accurate assertions about social reality' (Fischer 1987: 105), and that is hardly something that *The Turner Diaries* and other such narratives can be accused of doing. The obvious lesson of such examples is that the power of a narrative is at least as much a function of what Fischer calls its 'felt fidelity' (ibid.: 146) as its literal fidelity. Narratives with felt fidelity are ones that have the ring of truth from the perspective of their target audiences. They seem truthful even if not factually correct. Truthfulness in this sense is a matter of expressing what is perceived as a deeper truth about social reality, one that identifies deeper trends and connects with a given audience's lived experience and pre-existing narratives. Narrative fidelity in this sense is really a form of narrative coherence, though the most effective counter-narratives will be ones that manage to combine literal with felt fidelity.

The construction of counter-narratives with all five of these features is no easy task, and one should not be surprised that governments and their agencies are so bad at producing effective counter-narratives. They lack the necessary skills and, in many cases, the necessary understanding. For all the talk in *Prevent* of the importance of countering extremist narratives, one would be hard pushed to find any evidence in this or other official documents of any real understanding of what it would take to do this. Simply pointing out that extremist claims are false does not constitute a counter-narrative. When Jihadists claim that the West is at war with Islam, it is no use just asserting that the West is not at war with Islam. The challenge is to figure out why the Jihadist claim resonates with its target audience and develop a counter-narrative that has a greater ring of truth. This means facing up to the political realities that the Jihadist narrative is so good at exploiting, and demonstrating, in a compelling and accessible manner, that these realities do not mean what the Jihadist narrative says they mean.

Even if one were to succeed in developing a counter-narrative along these lines, there is a further concern that has yet to be addressed. In previous chapters much was made of the so-called 'extremist mindset' and the ways in which this mindset makes a person receptive to extremist ideologies and narratives. This presents those trying to devise an effective counter-narrative with the following difficulty: however impressive the counter-narrative in terms of its credibility, narrative depth, relevance and accessibility, resonance is always going to be a problem. Counter-extremist narratives are unlikely to resonate with extremist audiences to the extent that such audiences have an extremist mindset. Extremist narratives are much easier to sell than counter-extremist narratives to audiences whose mindset is extremist. Counter-extremist narratives attempt to change minds but in this domain it is hard to change *minds* without also changing *mindsets*. Unless counter-narratives can counter the extremist mindset, they are surely going to struggle to counter extremist narratives. Can counter-narratives change mindsets as well as minds? This is the final question for this chapter.

Changing minds, changing mindsets

It was suggested in Chapter 7 that ideological and psychological radicalization are in a symbiotic relationship. Extremist ideologies appeal to people with an extremist mindset, but a person's extremist mindset is typically at least partly a product of their extremist ideology. Neither ideological nor mindset extremism is logically or temporally prior. Possession of an extremist mindset facilitates ideological radicalization, but extremist ideologies reinforce and promote the preoccupations, attitudes, emotions, and ways of thinking that constitute mindset extremism. To the extent that an extremist mindset facilitates ideological radicalization, does it also obstruct ideological deradicalization? To the extent that this mindset is Pro-Violence, does it not also obstruct behavioural deradicalization? If so, then ideological and behavioural deradicalization depend on psychological deradicalization. At the same time, why rule out the possibility that ideological deradicalization can change a person's mindset?[12]

The malleability of mindsets has been extensively studied by researchers who accept Dweck's conception of mindsets as beliefs.[13] Since a person's beliefs are not generally fixed and unalterable, there is no reason in principle why mindsets should be fixed and unalterable. The same is true if mindsets are understood as they have been in this book. After all, people's preoccupations, attitudes and emotions can change, so why not the preoccupations, attitudes and emotions that are part and parcel of the extremist mindset? The question whether people's *thinking* can change might strike some as more controversial, but it shouldn't. It would be surprising if extremist thinking could not be modified given the existence and widespread use of therapies like CBT that are predicated on the possibility of changing one's thinking.[14] Furthermore, extremist thinking is influenced by extremist beliefs, so if the latter can change, then so can the former. For example, people who engage in conspiracy thinking have a conspiracist world-view, so one would expect changes in their world-view, including their beliefs, to have an impact on how they think.

Given the relationship of mutual dependence between a person's mindset and their ideology, one would expect effective anti-extremist counter-narratives to have an impact on a person's extremist mindset. One cannot rule out the possibility that some extremists are impervious to counter-narratives because their extremist mindset is something like a fixed personality trait. Whether this is so or not is a question for psychologists but the significant number of people who have been deradicalized suggests that claims about the fixity of mindset extremism should be treated with caution. Apart from concerns about the empirical basis of such claims, treating extremism as a personality trait risks downplaying the role of politics in radicalization. Extremism is, by and large, a response to political realities, and if these realities had been different, the extent of radicalization would have been very different. Can it seriously be denied that organizations like Al-Qaeda would have been less influential if the history of Western involvement in the Middle East had been different?

This question takes us back to Mohammad Sidique Khan, the person with whom this chapter began. What could have been done to counter his extremism? One possible answer to this question is 'nothing'. It is at least conceivable that the attractions of a violent extremist ideology for someone with his extremist mindset were so great that there was no possibility of talking him down. However, there is another possibility: depending on who was doing the talking and what they said, it might have been feasible effectively to counter his extremism by challenging his ideology and changing his mindset and his mind. Interlocutors who are capable of achieving these results would need to have credibility in the eyes of people like Khan. They would need to be both authoritative and willing and able to engage with Khan by addressing his concerns, his narrative and his reasons.

In terms of his mindset, one would need to tackle his preoccupation with virtue, with standing up and defending 'his people'. This would involve convincing him that the truly virtuous do not regard the killing of innocents as an acceptable means of advancing their cause, however just. In keeping with the Saudi model of deradicalization, the theological basis of his preoccupations would also need to be challenged and corrected, as well as his attitude to violence more generally. The difficulty is that Khan had a political narrative that made violence look both necessary and legitimate in his eyes. In his narrative, 'his people' were under attack and he had both the right and a duty to fight back. One would need to develop an alternative narrative that not only delegitimizes terrorism but also resonates with him. What would such a narrative look like?

It would not consist of homilies about British values or Western foreign policy, but then what would it consist of? It was suggested above that an extremist mindset might make a person like Khan unreceptive to an anti-extremist counter-narrative, but the real problem is more straightforward: regardless of Khan's mindset, attempts to counter his extremism by means of counter-narratives will not succeed if they don't ring true, don't make sense, or do not deliver cognitive satisfaction. Any attempt to develop a counter-narrative that avoids these pitfalls will come up against the political reality of the government policies to which Khan objected. Yet changing these policies will not be an option for a government that is not only committed to them but also has no desire to be seen to be making political concessions to extremists. Extremists want to change the facts on the ground and will continue with their campaigns as long as governments do not give in to their demands. How can governments be expected to do that?

In fact, it is not true that governments are never willing to alter their policies in response to violent extremism. Nor is it true that making concessions to extremists is always wrong. It depends on whether extremists have genuine grievances. It was not wrong for the government of South Africa to make concessions to the ANC because, in the final analysis, the ANC had a point. In this and in many other similar cases, the extremist narrative is undermined by policy changes and not just by counter-narratives. It is how governments act that gives counter-narratives the ring of truth. The cases in which extremist narratives are impervious to counter-narratives are those in which there are no practical measures that are both politically possible and capable of satisfying the extremists' demands. There is nothing that can or should be done to placate ISIS, and it is naïve to suppose that a change in American and British policy in the Middle East would bring its campaign of terror to an end. Some extremists are too far gone and must be defeated rather than deradicalized.

Seen in this light, programmes of counter-radicalization and deradicalization still have a point since not all extremists are like ISIS in being beyond the reach of such programmes. The mistake is to think that promoting 'our values' and 'our narrative' is the way to speak to them. At best, this method will only be effective at the margins. Perhaps it would have worked with Khan, or perhaps not. There are few certainties in this area, except that myths about radicalization and deradicalization make the challenge of countering extremism even more difficult than it already is, and that governments are especially prone to the wishful thinking that underpins these myths. If the identification of these myths makes it easier for governments to avoid them, then it is worth the effort. Perhaps extremism will always be with us but that is no reason not to be more intelligent about how we deal with it.

Notes

1 Quoted in Sageman (2019: 141). Sageman's is the most detailed analysis of the 7/7 London bombings and Khan's role in what happened that day.

2 Malik (2007).

3 There are also later versions of *Prevent* but the 2011 version is cited here since it better illustrates some of this chapter's key themes. Later versions of *Prevent* subscribe to some of the same myths as the 2011 version, but in a less stark form.

4 Counter-Terrorism and Security Act 2015, Part 5, Chapter 1, Section 26, Clause 1.

5 HM Government (2015).

6 Jacobson (2010).

7 The importance of narratives in radicalization reflects a deeper point about the role of storytelling in our lives. In the words of Alasdair MacIntyre, 'man is in his actions and practice, as well as in his fictions, essentially a story-telling animal' (1981: 201).

8 Braddock and Horgan (2016).

9 Fischer (1987: 47). See, also, Goodall (2016: 31). Fischer also refers to narrative coherence as 'narrative probability'. His work on narratives, which draws on MacIntyre (1981), is highly illuminating. See, especially, Chapter 3 of Fischer (1987). One of Fischer's insights is that reasons, including reasons for acting, can take the form of stories. It is in this sense that a story like *The Turner Diaries* provides far-right extremists with reasons for acting as they do.

10 This account of narrative coherence is mine rather than Fischer's.

11 Soon after 9/11, bin Laden talked about 'the humiliation and disgrace' that Islam has suffered for 'more than eighty years'. The allusion is to the abolition of the Ottoman sultanate in 1922 and the caliphate in 1924. As Lewis notes, such allusions would have seemed abstruse to Western audiences but bin Laden's Muslim listeners – the people he was addressing – would have 'picked up the allusion immediately and appreciated its significance' (2003: xv).

12 Ideological and behavioural deradicalization are the deradicalization analogues of what terrorism scholars like Marc Sageman refer to as 'cognitive' and 'behavioural' radicalization. The former refers to 'the acquisition of extreme ideas' and the latter to 'the turn to violence' (Sageman 2017: 90).

13 Dweck (2012: 16).

14 Edelman (2006).

Conclusion
The new extremism

It is hard to think or write about extremism without having in one's mind a mental image of the archetypal extremist. This image is not an abstract idea but the picture of a specific extremist group or individual that serves as a standard or pattern for extremism more generally. The identity of this archetypal extremist is largely a matter of context. In the aftermath of the 9/11 attacks, Osama bin Laden would have been, at least for many in Europe and America, the standard-setting extremist, the individual against whom all other putative extremists were to be measured. At other times, and in different political and cultural contexts, other figures would have come to mind.

It can be helpful to have a specific figure in mind when thinking about something as seemingly abstract as extremism. Individual extremists can be a source of insights about the nature of extremism and can be used to test accounts of extremism. However, there are dangers with this approach. The biggest danger is that the chosen figure is not in fact representative of extremists and extremism more generally and has idiosyncratic features that are far from universal. For example, from the fact that one's representative extremist is a religious extremist, it does not follow that all extremists are religious. At one point in the early 2000s, extremism became so closely associated in the minds of many people with Al-Qaeda that there seemed little room for the thought of other varieties of extremism. Yet many other varieties exist.

One way to guard against over-generalizing from a single instance is to have a range of archetypes available. The extremism of, say, the Khmer Rouge, is not as salient today as other forms of extremism, but familiarizing oneself with the Khmer Rouge and other extremists who are now a distant

DOI: 10.4324/9780429325472

memory helps to emphasize the sheer variety of extremism and the need to think about the phenomenon in sufficiently general terms to allow for this variety. However, there is one form of extremism that barely figured in the preceding chapters but that came to the fore in the aftermath of the 2020 U.S. Presidential election, in which the Republican President Trump was defeated by the Democratic candidate Joseph R. Biden. Trump claimed – falsely – that the election had been stolen and that Biden's victory was fraudulent. Trump urged his supporters to march on the Capitol on 6 January 2021, the day on which Biden's victory was due to be ratified by the Electoral College. What followed was one of the most shameful episodes in recent American history.

Trump's supporters took him at his word and launched a vicious assault on the police who had been tasked with protecting the Capitol. Rioters entered the building, and some were intent on capturing and executing senior Democrats as well as Vice-President Pence, who had incurred Trump's wrath. The sight of the President's supporters storming the U.S. Capitol and killing a police officer in the process gave extremism a new and, to some, unfamiliar face. Like other extremists, the rioters had been radicalized but what made their extremism unusual was that they were radicalized, at least to some extent, by the President of the United States. This was a new type of extremism, not the extremism of a terrorist organization or a fringe party, but of a group of insurgents who correctly regarded their violence as sanctioned by the leader of an establishment political party.

The concept of a 'new' extremism is not new. According to Roger Eatwell and Matthew Goodwin, postwar European governments faced the nationalist-separatist extremism of groups like the IRA as well as the extremism of some animal rights, ecological and anti-globalization groups. However, 'while these forms of extremism have posed varying threats to life, property and public order they have not threatened a radical de-stabilization of Western democratic politics and society' (2010: 2). In contrast, the 'new' extremism does pose a serious threat to the liberal democratic order. Writing in 2010, Eatwell and Goodwin identified 'Islamism and the organized and electorally resurgent extreme right-wing' (ibid.: 232) as the two main forms of this extremism in Britain. Islamist extremism was represented by Al-Qaeda and associated groups while far-right extremism was represented by the British National Party (BNP). These groups posed 'a significant threat to the liberal democratic polity' (ibid.: 3). They created the prospect of 'interactive violence' (ibid.: 6) between them and a 'cumulative extremism' (ibid.: 7) resulting from a spiral of violence and communal polarization.

Reading Eatwell and Goodwin more than a decade after they published their analysis, it is hard not to conclude that they overstated their case. While the organizations they discuss might *aspire* to destabilize liberal democracy, they are far from posing an actual threat. The BNP is hardly a force to be reckoned in Britain today and terrorist attacks by individuals who claim to be affiliated with Al-Qaeda have not undermined parliamentary democracy. However, the concept of a new type of extremism that *effectively* targets the liberal democratic order is a valuable one. Far-right parties are a major political force on the European continent, and some are even in power. These parties *do* pose a threat to liberal democracy and are more deserving of being labelled as 'new' extremists. However, it is one thing for avowedly far-right parties to come to power. It is another for their extremism to be shared by establishment political parties with a long history of winning elections. Unlike more traditional forms of extremism, this is a type of extremism that seeks to undermine democratic norms *from within* the liberal democratic polity rather than from without.

The archetype of the new extremism is Donald Trump's Republican Party, the so-called 'Grand Old Party' (GOP). The GOP's long-standing reluctance to act against extremists at its fringes has been noted by others.[1] However, the radicalization of the Republican Party under Trump went much deeper. Extremism was no longer something that only existed at the fringes of the party. It was now front and centre. If the test of the 'new' extremism is posing a threat to the liberal democratic order, then the GOP under Trump passed this test with ease. There is no greater threat to liberal democracy than when the leader of a major political party not only refuses to abide by the result of a fair election but encourages his supporters to resort to violence in support of his cause. Given polling evidence of substantial support among Republican voters for the storming of the Capitol, it is difficult not to draw the conclusion that democratic norms are not deeply entrenched in American politics.[2] As noted in Chapter 2, ideological extremism is matter of where a party, group, or individual stands on an ideological spectrum, and there is more than one such spectrum. The ideological extremism of the Republican Party under Trump is evidenced both by its position on the far right of the left-right spectrum and at the Pro-Violence end of the Pro-Violence spectrum.

A methods extremist is someone who uses extreme methods in pursuit of a political objective. The violent methods employed by many of those who stormed the Capitol on 6 January can certainly be described as extreme. Consider this report from the *New York Times*:

> The Capitol assault resulted in one of the worst days for injuries for law enforcement in the United States since the Sept. 11th 2001, terrorist attacks. At least 130 officers – 73 from the Capitol police and 65 from the Metropolitan Police Department – were injured, the departments have said. They ranged from bruises and lacerations to more serious damage such as concussions, rib fractures, burns and even a mild heart attack.[3]

Officers were smashed in the head with baseball bats, flag poles and pipes. Given that Trump encouraged the use of such extreme violence by his supporters and refused to intervene even when the lives of Members of Congress were under threat, his method of trying to hold on to power can reasonably be described as extreme. Furthermore, when he was impeached for his actions on 6 January 2021, a large majority of GOP senators voted for his acquittal and thereby endorsed, or at least refused to condemn, a violent insurrection that fulfilled all the criteria for methods extremism. Their complicity made them methods extremists at one remove.

Among the Republican Members of Congress who stood by President Trump was one who, according to *CNN*, repeatedly indicated support for executing senior Democrats.[4] She also 'trafficked in a slew of conspiracy theories, many of which are rooted in antisemitism, Islamophobia and white nationalism'.[5] In this and in several other respects, the mindset of such senior Republicans and their supporters is recognizably extremist. Yet the Republican Party is also the party of Lincoln and other towering figures in the history of American democracy. The fact that such a party can be so effectively radicalized is highly significant. Furthermore, the radicalization of an establishment party is by no means an exclusively American phenomenon. Establishment parties in other liberal democracies have also been radicalized, but not to the same extent.[6]

It is not clear at this point whether or when the Republican Party will deradicalize and return to the political mainstream. These words are being written within days of the insurrection and at a time when feelings are still running high. Whatever the future of the Republican Party, the important point for present purposes is that democracy is fragile, and that extremism is a force to which even supposedly advanced liberal democracies can succumb. Many readers will be used to seeing extremism as foreign or alien, as an external threat to liberal democracy but not an internal threat. However, the extremism that was on view in the United States on 6 January 2021 was home-grown, an indigenous American extremism with deep roots in American political culture.

It goes without saying that the extremism of the GOP under Trump was different from other, perhaps more familiar varieties of extremism. Even if the storming of the Capitol was an act of 'domestic terrorism', as President Biden described it, it was not an act of terrorism in anything like the sense in which, say, 9/11 was an act of terrorism. Yet, despite being much less lethal, the storming of the Capitol was if anything a *greater* threat to American democracy than 9/11. American democracy survived 9/11 but might not have survived a successful attempt to overturn the result of the 2020 election and kill Members of Congress who stood in the way. Extremism has many different faces, and the fact that the person promoting extremist ideas and methods happens to reside in the White House does not make him, or his ideas and methods, any less extremist. What is new about the 'new' extremism is not its content but its source.

How did the radicalization of the GOP come about? This is more a question for political scientists rather than for philosophers but there are philosophical lessons to be drawn from the recent history of the Republican Party. The first concerns the role of narrative in radicalization while the second concerns the role of violence in mainstream political culture. It was noted in Chapter 8 that extremism is always underpinned by a narrative, and the radicalization of the GOP provides further support for this claim. The radicalization of the GOP did not begin with Trump. Before Trump, there was the Tea Party, which emerged in 2010. The Tea Party was a grassroots organization, not under the control of the GOP. However, the vast majority of Tea Party participants were conservative Republicans who did not see themselves as moderates and succeeded in pulling the GOP sharply to the right.[7] Tea Party members, predominantly middle-class, older white men, subscribed to a narrative that was taken up by Trump.

In the narrative shared by the Tea Party and President Trump, America is divided into workers and non-workers. The latter are the unproductive, undeserving poor. The Tea Parry was not opposed to government programmes as such, but it did oppose programmes that, in its view, benefited the undeserving. Since the latter category included illegal immigrants, hostility to immigration was a core element of the Tea Party narrative, and one that Trump recycled in his bid for the presidency with his promise to build a wall along America's border with Mexico. As has often been pointed out, the distinction between the deserving and undeserving poor was implicitly understood in Tea Party ideology in racial or ethnic terms: to be black or Latino was, almost by definition, to be undeserving. A study of racial resentment among Tea Partiers found that 'though many opponents of the social safety net tend to hold negative views about racial minorities, Tea Partiers espouse views more extreme than those offered by other conservative Republicans' (Williamson, Skocpol and Coggin 2011: 34). To put it another way, the Tea Party's narrative of racial grievance and resentment formed the basis of a political ideology that was on the extreme right of the left-right spectrum.

Seen in this light, Trump's narrative simply amplified a pre-existing narrative whose influence among GOP members had already shifted the party to the right prior to his election in 2016. The further radicalization of the GOP under Trump brought out the power of narratives and of politicians who are able to exploit narratives of grievance and racial resentment. If 'they' (blacks, Latinos, illegal immigrants) are ripping 'us' (white, hard-working Americans) off, then the only remedy is to keep them out or, failing that, to make sure that they receive no handouts from the federal government. What Trump practised was what Jason Stanley calls 'the politics of us and them'.[8] Stanley uses the label 'fascism' for 'ultranationalism of some variety (ethnic, religious cultural), with the nation represented in the person of an authoritarian leader who speaks on its behalf' (2018: xiv). Trump tried to be that leader. The fact that he succeeded to the extent that he did demonstrates the effectiveness of the politics of us and them, even in the context of a supposedly sophisticated liberal democratic state.

There remains the question why the Tea Party narrative that Trump exploited proved so effective. What makes citizens of a democracy so receptive to this narrative? It might be suggested that the Tea Party narrative is especially potent when addressed to the victims of globalization. Yet Tea Party supporters had higher incomes than typical Americans.[9] This is not to deny that socio-economic factors account, at least to an extent, for vulnerability to extremist messages, but that cannot be all there is to it. The ability of extremists to exploit feelings of resentment and grievance is especially worrying when they have no rational basis. The new extremism thrives on manufactured rage and resentment and can only be countered, if at all, by counter-narratives that display the virtues identified in Chapter 8.

The radicalization of establishment political parties extends beyond the exploitation of extremist narratives. There is also the issue of violence. Jay Griffiths was quoted in Chapter 2 as saying that fascism not only promotes violence but relishes it, viscerally so.[10] This is also true of extremism generally. Extremism doesn't have to be Pro-Violence but often is. Trump relished the violence he unleashed in 2021 but his attitude to violence was by no means unique in American politics. In a penetrating discussion, John Gray points out that the neo-conservative ideologues who were a pivotal force in the Republican administration of President George W. Bush in the early 2000s believed that 'the condition of humanity could be transformed by the use of force' (2007: xii). Their foreign policy, which led to the invasion of Iraq in 2003, was 'based on a utopian faith in creative destruction' (ibid.: xiii). This form of Pro-Violence is striking enough, but it is even more striking how much neo-conservative thinking on this issue had in common with extremist thinking.

Gray traces the extremist faith in the power of creative destruction to the nineteenth-century Russian anarchist, Mikhail Bakunin. In addition:

> The belief that human progress requires the destruction of existing institutions animated a long line of twentieth-century revolutionaries that includes Lenin, Trotsky and Mao. Its remoter origin is in the Jacobin faith in violence as a means of regenerating society, which produced the Great Terror in revolutionary France. Despite their position on the political spectrum, neo-conservatives belong in this Jacobin and Leninist tradition.
>
> (ibid.: xiv)

So does Al-Qaeda, and this is the basis of Gray's striking view that 'radical Islam is a uniquely modern pathology' (ibid.: xix). Al-Qaeda is often labelled 'medieval', but Gray argues that in medieval times nobody imagined that violence could be used to improve the human condition.

President Trump had little interest in improving the human condition, but he tried to retain power through the destruction of democratic institutions in the United States. At least in this sense, he had faith in the power of creative destruction. However, he went further than the neo-conservatives. The latter unleashed the power of creative destruction against a foreign power – Iraq. Trump targeted the democratic norms and institutions of the United States. On a lesser scale, a faith in the power of a non-violent form of creative destruction can be detected in the approach of some British politicians who argued for Britain's exit from the European Union.[11]

It is sobering that even democratic politics and parties can be radicalized from within. It is comforting to think that democracy is a bulwark against extremism, and maybe it is, up to a point. However, the protections offered by democratic norms and institutions are limited. This was a hard lesson that Europe learned in the 1930s and it is a lesson that needs to be relearned today. When democracy in America is so fragile as to be seriously threatened by homegrown extremism, we should all be worried. It is too early to say whether the events in Washington in the last days of the Trump Presidency were a lucky escape for American democracy or a sign of things to come. It could go either way, but a positive outcome is more likely if moderates rise to the challenge of developing an effective strategy to counter extremism. Chapter 8 provided some indications of what such a strategy might look like, but it cannot be denied that there is much more work to be done in this area.

Marx famously claimed that philosophers have so far only interpreted the world and that the point is to change it. It would be nice if philosophers even got as far as interpreting the world. Philosophers who have any interest in doing this cannot fail to notice that extremism in its different forms is not a peripheral phenomenon in the world today. Extremist thinking, attitudes and preoccupations are depressingly common, extreme methods continue to be used in many places as a substitute for politics, and extremist ideologies are gaining in popularity. The question is whether philosophy has anything to say about any of this. There are questions about extremism that philosophers are neither trained nor equipped to answer but there are also questions about extremism that are plainly philosophical. That is the case for a philosophy of extremism, and one can only hope that the reflections in this book will mark the beginning rather than the end of philosophical research in this field.

Notes

1 For example, by Ronald Brownstein in an article published in *The Atlantic* on 4 February 2021, 'How the GOP Surrendered to Extremism'. Available at: www.theatlantic.com/politics/archive/2021/02/republican-extremism-and-john-birch-society/617922/

2 A YouGov poll found that 45 per cent of Republicans supported the actions of those at the Capitol on 6 January 2021, 'Most Voters Say the Events at the US Capitol Are a Threat to Democracy'. Available at: https://today.yougov.com/topics/politics/articles-reports/2021/01/07/US-capitol-trump-poll

3 'Officers' Injuries, Including Concussions, Show Scope of Violence at Capitol Riot', *The New York Times*, 11 February 2021. Available at: www.nytimes.com

4 Em Steck and Andrew Kazcynski, 'Marjorie Taylor-Greene Indicated Support for Executing Prominent Democrats in 2018 and 2019 Before Running for Congress', *CNN Politics*, 27 January 2021.

5 'Who Is the Republican Extremist Marjorie Taylor-Greene?' *The Guardian*, 6 February 2021.

6 For example, it is arguable that the British Conservative Party underwent something like a radicalization process under the leadership of Boris Johnson, as did the Labour Party under the leadership of Jeremy Corbyn.

7 Williamson, Skocpol and Coggin (2011: 27).

8 Stanley (2018).

9 Williamson, Skocpol and Coggin (2011: 27).

10 Griffiths (2017).

11 Former British Prime Minister David Cameron once described one of his own pro-Brexit cabinet colleagues as 'basically a bit of a Maoist' who believes that 'the world makes progress through a process of creative destruction' (Laws 2017: 368). The colleague in question was Michael Gove, who is still a Cabinet member.

References

Aikin, S. F. and Talisse, R. B. (2020). *Political Argument in a Polarized Age*. Cambridge: Polity Press.

Alexander, M. (2019). *The New Jim Crow: Mass Incarceration in the Age of Color Blindness*. London: Penguin Books.

Almond, G. A., Sivan, E. and Scott Appleby, R. (2004). 'Fundamentalism: Genus and Species', in M. Marty and R. Scott Appleby (eds), *Fundamentalisms Comprehended* Chicago: University of Chicago Press: 399–424.

Arendt, H. (1969). *On Violence*. New York: Harcourt Inc.

Ashour, O. (2009). *The De-Radicalization of Jihadists: Transforming armed Islamist Movements*. Abingdon: Routledge.

Ashour, O. (2010). 'Online De-Radicalization? Countering Violent Extremist Narratives: Message, Messenger and Media Strategy', *Perspectives on Terrorism*, 4: 16–19.

Atran, S. (2010). *Talking to the Enemy: Violent Extremism, Sacred Values, and What it Means to Be Human*. London: Penguin Books.

Bail, C. et al. (2018). 'Exposure to Opposing Views on Social Media Can Increase Political Polarization', *Proceedings of the National Academy of Sciences* 115 (37): 9216–21.

Baron, J. (1985). *Rationality and Intelligence*. Cambridge: Cambridge University Press.

Beck, C. J. (2015). *Radicals, Revolutionaries, and Terrorists*. Cambridge: Polity Press.

Berger, J. M. (2018). *Extremism*. Cambridge, MA: The MIT Press.

Berlin, I. (2013a). *The Proper Study of Mankind: An Anthology of Essays*. London: Vintage Books.

Berlin, I. (2013b). *The Crooked Timber of Humanity: Chapters in the History of Ideas*, 2nd edn, ed. Henry Hardy. London: Pimlico.

Bhui, K. et al. (2020). 'Extremism and Common Mental Illness: Cross-Sectional Community Survey of White British and Pakistani Men and Women Living in England', *British Journal of Psychiatry*, 217: 547–54.

Borchgrevink, A. (2013). *A Norwegian Tragedy: Anders Behring Breivik and the Massacre of Utøya*. Cambridge: Polity Press.

Boucek, C. (2008). 'Counter-Terrorism from Within: Assessing Saudi Arabia's Religious Rehabilitation and Disengagement Programme', *The RUSI Journal*, 153: 60–5.

Braddock, K. and Horgan, J. (2016). 'Towards a Guide for Constructing and Disseminating Counternarratives to Reduce Support for Terrorism', *Studies in Conflict and Terrorism*, 39: 381–404.

Breton, A., Galeotti, G., Salmon, P. and Wintrobe, R. (eds) (2002). *Political Extremism and Rationality*. Cambridge: Cambridge University Press.

Breton, A. and Dalmazzone, S. (2002). 'Information Control, Loss of Autonomy, and the Emergence of Political Extremism', in A. Breton, G. Galeotti, P. Salmon and R. Wintrobe (eds), *Political Extremism and Rationality*. Cambridge: Cambridge University Press: 44–66.

Brons, L. (2015). 'Othering, an Analysis'. *Transcience*, 6: 69–90.

Brownstein, R. (2021). 'How the GOP Surrendered to Extremism, *The Atlantic*, 4 February.

Byford, J. (2011). *Conspiracy Theories: A Critical Introduction*. Basingstoke: Palgrave Macmillan.

CAG (2005). 'Genocide in Gujarat'. Available at: www.sabrang.com/MODI/CAGModiDossier.pdf

Cassam, Q. (2003). '*A Priori* Concepts', in H-J. Glock (ed.), *Strawson and Kant*. Oxford: Oxford University Press: 87–108.

Cassam, Q. (2018). 'The Epistemology of Terrorism and Radicalisation', *Royal Institute of Philosophy Supplement*, 84: 187–209.

Cassam, Q. (2019a). *Vices of the Mind: From the Intellectual to the Political*. Oxford: Oxford University Press.

Cassam, Q. (2019b). *Conspiracy Theories*. Cambridge: Polity Press.

Cassam, Q. (2021). 'The Polarization Toolkit', in A. Tanesini and M. Lynch (eds), *Polarisation, Arrogance, and Dogmatism*. London: Routledge: 212–28.

Chenoweth, E. and Stephan, M. (2011). *Why Civil Resistance Works: The Strategic Logic of Nonviolent Conflict*. New York: Columbia University Press.

Chouraqui, F. (2019). 'Fanaticism as a Worldview', *The Philosophical Journal of Conflict and Violence*, 3: 9–19.

Coady, C. A. J. (1986). 'The Idea of Violence', *Journal of Applied Philosophy*, 3: 3–19.

Coady, C. A. J. (2021). 'On Radicalisation and Violent Extremism', in M. Sardoč et al. 'Philosophy of Education in a New Key: On Radicalization and Violent Extremism', *Educational Philosophy and Theory*. https://doi.org/10.1080/00131857.2020.1861937

Craiutu, A. (2012). *A Virtue for Courageous Minds: Moderation in French Political Thought, 1748–1830*. Princeton, NJ: Princeton University Press.

Cronin, A. K. (2009). *How Terrorism Ends: Understanding the Decline and Demise of Terrorist Campaigns*. Princeton, NJ: Princeton University Press.

Davey, J. and Ebner, J. (2019). *"The Great Replacement": The Violent Consequences of Mainstreamed Extremism*. London: Institute for Strategic Dialogue.

Douglas, M. (2002). *Purity and Danger: An Analysis of Concepts of Pollution and Taboo*. London: Routledge Classics.

Dweck, C. S. (2012). *Mindset: Changing the Way You Think to Fulfil Your Potential*. London: Robinson.

Eatwell, R. (1996). 'On Defining the "Fascist Minimum": The Centrality of Ideology', *Journal of Political Ideologies*, 1: 303–19.

Eatwell, R. and Goodwin, M. (eds) (2010). *The New Extremism in 21st Century Britain*. London: Routledge.

Ebner, J. (2020). *Going Dark: The Secret Lives of Extremists*. London: Bloomsbury Publishing.

Edelman, S. (2006). *Change Your Thinking with CBT*. London: Vermilion.

El-Said, H. (2013). 'Introduction: Definitions and Conceptual Framework', in H. El-Said and J. Harrigan (eds), *Deradicalizing Violent Extremists: Counter-radicalization and Deradicalization Programmes and Their Impact in Muslim Majority States*. London: Routledge: 1–14.

El-Said, H. and Barrett, R. (2013). 'Saudi Arabia: The Master of Deradicalization', in H. El-Said and J. Harrigan (eds), *Deradicalizing Violent Extremists: Counter-radicalization and Deradicalization Programmes and Their Impact in Muslim Majority States*. London: Routledge: 194–226.

Emcke, C. (2019). *Against Hate*. Cambridge: Polity Press.

English, R. (2003). *Armed Struggle: The History of the IRA*. London: Macmillan.

English, R. (2009). *Terrorism: How to Respond*. Oxford: Oxford University Press.

English, R. (2016). *Does Terrorism Work? A History*. Oxford: Oxford University Press.

Evans, G. (1982). *The Varieties of Reference*, ed. John McDowell. Oxford: Clarendon Press.

Evans, R. (2008). *The Third Reich at War, 1939–1945*. London: Penguin Books.

Fanon, F. (2001). *The Wretched of the Earth*. London: Penguin Classics.

Finlay, C. J. (2015). *Terrorism and the Right to Resist: A Theory of Just Revolutionary War*. Cambridge: Cambridge University Press.

Fischer, W. R. (1987). *Human Communication as Narration: Towards a Philosophy of Reason, Value, and Action*. Columbia, SC: University of South Carolina Press.

Foot, P. (1978). *Virtues and Vices and Other Essays in Moral Philosophy*. Oxford: Blackwell.

Fraser, G. (2021). *Chosen: Lost and Found Between Christianity and Judaism*. London: Allen Lane.

Freedman, L. (2006). 'Networks, Cultures and Narratives', in *The Transformation of Strategic Affairs*. New York: Routledge: 11–26.

Galtung, J. (1969). 'Violence, Peace, and Peace Research', *The Journal of Peace Research*, 6: 167–91.

Garrett, S. A. (2004). 'Terror Bombing of German Cities in World War II', in I. Primoratz (ed.), *Terrorism: The Philosophical Issues*. Basingstoke: Palgrave Macmillan: 141–60.

Garrison, W. L. (1973). *The Letters of William Lloyd Garrison*, vol. III, ed. W. Merrill, Cambridge, MA: Harvard University Press.

Gelderloos, P. (2016). *The Failure of Nonviolence*. Seattle: Left Bank Books.

Gerges, F. (2016). *ISIS: A History*. Princeton, NJ: Princeton University Press.

Gerwarth, R. (2011). *Hitler's Hangman: The Life of Heydrich*. New Haven, CT: Yale University Press.

Gessen, M. (2016). *The Brothers: The Road to an American Tragedy*. New York: Riverhead Books.

Geuss, R. (1981). *The Idea of a Critical Theory: Habermas and the Frankfurt School*. Cambridge: Cambridge University Press.

Giddens, A. (1991). *Modernity and Self-Identity: Self and Society in the Late Modern Age*. Cambridge: Polity Press.

Githens-Mazer, J. and Lambert, R. (2010). 'Why the Conventional Wisdom on Radicalization Fails: The Persistence of a Failed Discourse', *International Affairs*, 86: 889–901.

Goertzel, T. (1994). 'Belief in Conspiracy Theories', *Political Psychology*, 15: 731–42.

Goodall, H. L. (2016). *Counter-Narrative: How Progressive Academics Can Challenge Extremists and Promote Social Justice*. New York: Routledge.

Gray, J. (2007). *Al Qaeda and What it Means to Be Modern*. London: Faber and Faber.

Green, M. (2008). *The Wizard of the Nile: The Search for Africa's Most Wanted*. London: Portobello Books.

Griffiths, J. (2017). 'Fire, Hatred and Speed!', *Aeon*. Available at: https://aeon.co/essays/the-macho-violent-culture-of-italian-fascism-was-prophetic.

Hacking, I. (1999). *The Social Construction of What?* Cambridge, MA: Harvard University Press.

Hardin, R. (2002). 'The Crippled Epistemology of Extremism', in A. Breton, G. Galeotti, P. Salmon and R. Wintrobe (eds), *Political Extremism and Rationality*. Cambridge: Cambridge University Press: 3–22.

Hare, R. M. (1963). *Freedom and Reason*. Oxford: Oxford University Press.

Hare, R. M. (1981). *Moral Thinking: Its Levels, Method and Point*. Oxford: Oxford University Press.

Haslanger, S. (2012). 'Social Construction: the "Debunking" Project', in S. Haslanger, *Resisting Reality: Social Construction and Social Critique*. Oxford: Oxford University Press: 113–38.

Heath-Kelly, C. (2017). 'The Geography of Pre-Criminal Space: Epidemiological Imaginations of Radicalisation Risk in the UK Prevent Strategy, 2007–2017', *Critical Studies on Terrorism*, 10: 297–319.

Hegel, G. W. F. (2001). *The Philosophy of History*, trans. J. Sibree. Kitchener: Batoche Books.

Heywood, A. (2017). *Political Ideologies: An Introduction*, 6th edn. London: Palgrave.

Hitchens, C. (2007). 'Defending Islamofascism. It's a Valid Term. Here's Why', *Slate*, 22 October.

Hitchens, C. (2012). *Arguably*. London: Atlantic Books.

HM Government (2011). *Prevent Strategy*. London: The Stationery Office.

HM Government (2015). *Individuals at Risk of Being Drawn into Serious and Organised Crime – a Prevent Guide*. London: The Stationery Office.

Hoffer, E. (1951). *The True Believer: Thoughts on the Nature of Mass Movements*. New York: Harper & Row Publishers Inc.

Hofstadter, R. (2008). *The Paranoid Style in American Politics*. New York: Vintage Books.

Holmes, R. (2017). *This Long Pursuit: Reflections of a Romantic Biographer*. London: HarperCollins.

Horgan, J. (2003). 'The Search for the Terrorist Personality', in A. Silke (ed.), *Terrorists, Victims, and Society*. Chichester: John Wiley & Sons Ltd: 3–27.

Hume, D. (1985). 'Of Superstition and Enthusiasm', in D. Hume, *Essays: Moral, Political, and Literary*, ed. E. Miller. Indianapolis, IN: Liberty Fund Inc.: 73–9.

Hume, D. (2007). *A Treatise of Human Nature*, eds D. Norton and M. Norton. Oxford: Clarendon Press.

Israel, J. (2009). *A Revolution of the Mind: Radical Enlightenment and the Intellectual Origins of Modern Democracy*. Princeton, NJ: Princeton University Press.

Jackson, R. (2011). 'In Defence of "Terrorism": Finding a Way through a Forest of Misconceptions', *Behavioral Sciences of Terrorism and Political Aggression*, 3: 116–30.

Jackson, R., Jarvis, L., Gunning, J. and Breen-Smyth, M. (2011). *Terrorism: A Critical Introduction*. Basingstoke: Palgrave Macmillan.

Jacobson, M. (2010). *Terrorist Dropouts: Learning from Those Who Have Left*. Washington DC: The Washington Institute for Near East Policy.

Kant, I. (1932). *Critique of Pure Reason*, trans. N. Kemp Smith. London: Macmillan.

Kant, I. (2007a). 'Observations on the Feeling of the Beautiful and Sublime', in *Immanuel Kant: Anthropology, History, and Education*, eds G. Zöller and R. Louden. Cambridge: Cambridge University Press: 23–62.

Kant, I. (2007b). 'Essay on the Maladies of the Head', in *Immanuel Kant: Anthropology, History, and Education*, eds G. Zöller and R. Louden. Cambridge: Cambridge University Press: 65–77.

Katsafanas, P. (2019). 'Fanaticism and Sacred Values', *Philosophers' Imprint*, 19: 1–20.

Kendall, E. (2016). 'Jihadist Propaganda and its Exploitation of the Arab Poetic Tradition', in E. Kendall and A. Khan (eds), *Reclaiming Islamic Tradition: Modern Interpretations of the Classical Heritage*. Edinburgh: Edinburgh University Press: 223–46.

Kiernan, B. (2008). *The Pol Pot Regime,* 3rd edn. New Haven, CT: Yale University Press.

Kimmel, M. (2017). *Angry White Men: American Masculinity at the End of an Era*. New York: Bold Type Books.

Kitcher, P. (1981). 'How Kant Almost Wrote "Two Dogmas of Empiricism"', *Philosophical Topics*, 12: 217–49.

Kraditor, A. (1989). *Means and Ends in American Abolitionism: Garrison and His Critics of Strategy and Tactics, 1834–1850*. Chicago: Elephant Paperback.

Kundnani, A. (2012). 'Radicalisation: The Journey of a Concept', *Race & Class*, 54: 3–25.

Laqueur, W. (1999). *The New Terrorism: Fanaticism and the Arms of Mass Destruction*. New York: Oxford University Press.

Lawrence, B. (ed.) (2005). *Messages to the World: The Statements of Osama bin Laden*. London: Verso.

Laws, D. (2017). *Coalition: The Inside Story of the Conservative-Liberal Coalition Government*. London: Biteback Publishing.

Lewis, B. (2003). *The Crisis of Islam: Holy War and Unholy Terror*. London: Weidenfeld & Nicolson.

Lind, M. (2020). *The New Class War: Saving Democracy from the Metropolitan Elite*. New York: Atlantic Books.

Linton, M. (2013). *Choosing Terror: Virtue, Friendship, and Authenticity in the French Revolution*. Oxford: Oxford University Press.

Luther King Jr, M. (2018). *Letter from Birmingham Jail*. London: Penguin.

Lyons, J. (2020). *The Philosophy of Isaiah Berlin*. London: Bloomsbury.

Macdonald, A. (1978). *The Turner Diaries*. Laurel Bloomery: The National Alliance.

MacIntyre, A. (1981). *After Virtue: A Study in Moral Theory*. London: Duckworth.

Maio, G. and Haddock, G. (2015). *The Psychology of Attitudes and Attitude Change*, 2nd edn. London: Sage.

Malik, S. (2007). 'My Brother the Bomber', *Prospect Magazine*, 30 June.

Mandela, N. (1994). *Long Walk to Freedom*. London: Little Brown and Company.

Mantel, H. (2010). *A Place of Greater Safety*. London: Fourth Estate.

Marantz, A. (2019). *Antisocial: How Online Extremists Broke America*. London: Picador.

Margalit, A. (2010). *On Compromise and Rotten Compromises*. Princeton, NJ: Princeton University Press.

McCants, W. (2015). *The ISIS Apocalypse: The History, Strategy, and Doomsday Vision of the Islamic State*. New York: Picador.

McDermott, T. and Meyer, J. (2012). *The Hunt for KSM: Inside the Pursuit and Takedown of the Real 9/11 Mastermind Khalid Sheikh Mohammed*. New York: Back Bay Books.

McMahan, J. (2009). *Killing in War*. Oxford: Oxford University Press.

Međedovic, J. and Knežević, G. (2019). 'Dark and Peculiar: The Key Features of Militant Extremist Thinking Pattern?', *Journal of Individual Differences*, 40: 92–103.

Meleagrou-Hitchens, A. (2020). *Incitement: Anwar Al-Awlaki's Western Jihad*. Cambridge, MA: Harvard University Press.

Michel, L. and Herbeck, D. (2001). *American Terrorist: Timothy McVeigh and the Oklahoma City Bombings*. New York: Regan Books.

Miller-Idriss, C. (2020). *Hate in the Homeland: The New Global Far Right*. Princeton, NJ: Princeton University Press.

Mishra, P. (2018). *Age of Anger: A History of the Present*. London: Penguin Books.

Mudde, C. (2019). *The Far Right Today*. Cambridge: Polity Press.

Nagel, T. (2016). 'By Any Means or None', *London Review of Books*, 38: 19–20.

Naji, A. (2006). *The Management of Savagery: The Most Critical Stage Through Which the Umma Will Pass*, trans. W. McCants. Cambridge, MA: John Olin Institute for Strategic Studies.

Neumann, P. (2011). *Preventing Violent Radicalization in America*. Washington, DC: Bipartisan Policy Center.

Neumann, P. (2013). 'The Trouble with Radicalization', *International Affairs*, 89: 873–93.

Nozick, R. (1997). 'The Characteristic Features of Extremism', in R. Nozick, *Socratic Puzzles*. Cambridge, MA: Harvard University Press: 296–9.

Nussbaum, M. (2007). *The Clash Within: Democracy, Religious Violence, and India's Future*. Cambridge, MA: Harvard University Press.

Nussbaum, M. (2008). 'The Clash Within: Democracy and the Hindu Right', in I. A. Karawan et al. (eds), *Values and Violence: Intangible Aspects of Terrorism*. Dordrecht: Springer.

Olson, J. (2007). 'The Freshness of Fanaticism: The Abolitionist Defence of Zealotry', *Perspectives on Politics*, 5: 685–701.

Oz, A. (2012). *How to Cure a Fanatic*. London: Vintage Books.

Papineau, D. (2009). 'The Poverty of Analysis', *The Aristotelian Society Supplementary Volume*, 83: 1–30.

Paul, L. A. (2014). *Transformative Experience*. Oxford: Oxford University Press.

Paxton, R. O. (2004). *The Anatomy of Fascism*. London: Penguin Books.

Pickard, H. (2015). 'Self-Harm and Violence: When Perpetrator and Victim Are One', in H. Marway and H. Widdows (eds), *Women and Violence: The Agency of Victims and Perpetrators*. Basingstoke: Palgrave Macmillan: 71–90.

Ramsey, F. P. (1931). 'Truth and Probability', in F. P. Ramsey, *The Foundations of Mathematics and Other Logical Essays*, ed. R. B. Braithwaite. London: Kegan Paul: 156–98.

Reeve, S. (1999). *The New Jackals: Ramzi Yousef, Osama bin Laden and the Future of Terrorism*. Boston: Northeastern University Press.

Reginster, B. (1997). 'Nietzsche on Ressentiment and Valuation', *Philosophy and Phenomenological Research*, 57: 281–305.

Robespierre, M. (2017). *Virtue and Terror*. London: Verso.

Rorty, R. (1998). *Achieving Our Country: Leftist Thought in Twentieth-Century America*. Cambridge, MA: Harvard University Press.

Roth, P. (1997). *American Pastoral*. London: Vintage Books.

Ruthven, M. (2007). *Fundamentalism: A Very Short Introduction*. Oxford: Oxford University Press.

Sageman, M. (2008). *Leaderless Jihad: Terror Networks in the Twenty-First Century*. Philadelphia, PA: University of Pennsylvania Press.

Sageman, M. (2017). *Misunderstanding Terrorism*. Philadelphia, PA: University of Pennsylvania Press.

Sageman, M. (2019). *The London Bombings: Counterterrorism Strategy After 7/7*. Philadelphia, PA: University of Pennsylvania Press.

Salmon, P. (2002). 'Extremism and Monomania', in A. Breton, G. Galeotti, P. Salmon and R. Wintrobe (eds), *Political Extremism and Rationality*. Cambridge: Cambridge University Press: 69–88.

Saucier, G. et al. (2009). 'Patterns of Thinking in Militant Extremism', *Perspectives on Psychological Science*, 4: 256–71.

Scales-Trent, J. (2001). 'Racial Purity Laws in the United States and Nazi Germany: The Targeting Process', *Human Rights Quarterly*, 23: 259–307.

Scruton, R. (2007). *The Palgrave Macmillan Dictionary of Political Thought*, 3rd edn. Basingstoke: Palgrave Macmillan.

Scurr, R. (2007). *Fatal Purity: Robespierre and the French Revolution*. London: Vintage.

Seierstad, A. (2015). *One of Us: The Story of a Massacre in Norway – and Its After-math*. New York: Farrar, Strauss and Giroux.

Short, P. (2004). *Pol Pot: The History of a Nightmare*. London: John Murray.

Shriver, L. (2020). *The Motion of the Body through Space*. London: The Borough Press.

Silke, A. (2003). 'Becoming a Terrorist', in A. Silke (ed.), *Terrorists, Victims, and Society*. Chichester: John Wiley & Sons Ltd: 29–53.

Sinha, M. (2016). *The Slave's Cause: A History of Abolition*. New Haven, CT: Yale University Press.

Sluka, J. (2011). 'Death from Above: UAVs and Losing Hearts and Minds', *Military Review*, 91: 70–6.

Smith, M. (1987). 'The Humean Theory of Motivation', *Mind*, 96: 36–61.

Stankov, L., Saucier, G. and Knežević, G. (2010). 'Militant Extremist Mind-Set: Prov-iolence, Vile World, and Divine Power', *Psychological Assessment*, 22: 70–86.

Stanley, J. (2018). *How Fascism Works: The Politics of Us and Them*. New York: Random House.

Stern, A. M. (2019). *Proud Boys and the White Ethnostate: How the Alt-Right Is Warping the American Imagination*. Boston: Beacon Press.

Strawson, P. F. (1992). *Analysis and Metaphysics: An Introduction to Philosophy*. Oxford: Oxford University Press.

Strawson, P. F. (2008a). 'Freedom and Resentment', in P. F. Strawson, *Freedom and Resentment and Other Essays*. London: Routledge: 1–28.

Strawson, P. F. (2008b). *Scepticism and Naturalism: Some Varieties*. London: Routledge.

Sunstein, C. R. (2009). *Going to Extremes: How Like Minds Unite and Divide*. New York: Oxford University Press.

Sunstein, C. (2014). *Conspiracy Theories and Other Dangerous Ideas*. New York: Simon & Schuster.

Taylor, A. J. P. (1977). 'Accident Prone, or What Happened Next', *The Journal of Modern History*, 49 (1): 1–18.

Thi Nguyen, C. (2018). 'Escape the Echo Chamber.' *Aeon Magazine*. Available at: https://aeon.co/essays/why-its-as-hard-to-escape-an-echo-chamber-as-it-is-to-flee-a-cult.

Thompson, R. L. (2011). 'Radicalization and the Use of Social Media', *Journal of Strategic Security*, 4: 167–90.

Toscano, A. (2017). *Fanaticism: On the Uses of an Idea*. London: Verso.

Uscinski, J. and Parent, J. (2014). *American Conspiracy Theories*. Oxford: Oxford University Press.

Velleman, D. (2003). 'Narrative Explanation', *The Philosophical Review*, 112: 1–25.

Von Behr, I., Reding, A., Edwards, C. and Gribbon, L. (2013). *Radicalisation in the Digital Era: The Use of the Internet in 15 Cases of Terrorism and Extremism*. Santa Barbara, CA: RAND Corporation. Available at: www.rand.org/pubs/research_reports/RR453.html

Walzer, M. (2004a). 'Emergency Ethics', in M. Walzer, *Arguing About War*. New Haven, CT: Yale University Press: 33–50.

Walzer, M. (2004b). 'Terrorism: A Critique of Excuses', in M. Walzer, *Arguing About War*. New Haven, CT: Yale University Press: 51–66.

Weick, K. (1995). *Sensemaking in Organizations*. Thousand Oaks, CA: Sage Publications.

Wilkinson, W. (2016). 'On the Saying "Extremism in Defense of Liberty Is No Vice"' Available at: www.niskanencenter.org/on-the-saying-that-extremism-in-defense-of-liberty-is-no-vice/

Williams, B. (1973). 'Morality and the Emotions', in B. Williams, *Problems of the Self*. Cambridge: Cambridge University Press: 207–29.

Williamson, T. (2020). *Philosophical Method: A Very Short Introduction*. Oxford: Oxford University Press.

Williamson, V., Skocpol, T. and Coggin, J. (2011). 'The Tea Party and the Remaking of Republican Conservatism', *Perspectives on Politics*, 9: 25–43.

Wittgenstein, L. (1978). *Philosophical Investigations*, trans. G. E. M. Anscombe. Oxford: Basil Blackwell.

Wolff, R. P. (1998). *In Defense of Anarchism*. Berkeley, CA: University of California Press.

Wood, G. (2015). 'What ISIS Really Wants', *The Atlantic*, 10 March.

Wood, G. (2018). *The Way of Strangers: Encounters with the Islamic State*. London: Penguin Books.

Žižek, S. (2009). *Violence*. London: Profile Books.

Index

Note: Page numbers followed by "n" denote endnotes.

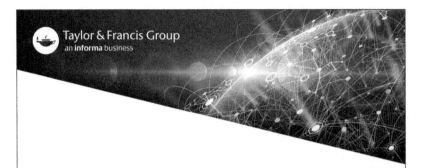

Printed in the United States
by Baker & Taylor Publisher Services